VOLUME 8

PART 6

CONTENTS

DORSET

ABBREVIATIONS FOR RECORD REPOSITORIES, LIBRARIES AND SOCIETIES

Researchers are advised to make a preliminary telephone enquiry about opening times and conditions of admission.

A.   **National**

AAB   Archives of the Archbishop of Birmingham
Cathedral House, St Chad's Ringway, Birmingham B4 6EX

AAW   Archives of the Archbishop of Westminster,
16a Abingdon Road, Kensington, London W8 6AF

AFCC   Armed Forces Chaplaincy Centre, Amport House, Amport, Andover, Hampshire SP11 8BG. Registers for RAF station chaplaincies, when completed, or when station closes.

BL   The British Library, Euston Road, London NW1 2DB
A reader's ticket is required.
Web-site, including on-line catalogue: *www.blpc.bl.uk*

Bod   Department of Western Manuscripts, Bodleian Library,
Broad Street, Oxford OX1 3BG.

BRS   British Record Society, c/o College of Arms, below.

C of A   College of Arms, Queen Victoria Street, London
EC4V 4BT. The Library is not open to the public.

GL   Guildhall Library, Aldermanbury, London EC2P 2EJ.

Harl Mss Harleian Manuscripts, in the Department of Manuscripts,
The British Library.

MoD   [Army registers] Ministry of Defence Chaplains (Army), Trenchard Lines, Upavon, Pewsey, Wiltshire SN9 6BE
[Naval registers] Central Services (Records Management) Room 1/07, 3-5 Great Scotland Yard, London SW1A 2HW. Registers will be moved to PRO, new class ADM 338, in due course.

Phil Mss Manuscript copies of parish registers, formerly in the possession of Phillimore and Co. Ltd, Shopwyke Manor Barn, Chichester.
Now transferred to the Society of Genealogists.

PRO   Public Record Office, Ruskin Avenue, Kew, Richmond TW9 4DU
Web-site with online catalogue: *www.pro.gov.uk*
Non-parochial registers in the PRO may be seen on microfilm at:
Family Records Centre, 1 Myddleton Street, London EC1R 1UW

RCRO   Roman Catholic Records Office, Bishopric of the Forces, AGPDO, Middle Hill, Aldershot, Hampshire GU11 1PP.
Registers of RC chaplaincies to the Royal Navy, Army and RAF, in Britain and abroad.

SG   Society of Genealogists, 14 Charterhouse Buildings,
Goswell Road, London EC1M 7BA.
The library is open to non-members on payment of hourly, half-daily and daily fees. Some publications listed in this volume can be obtained through the Society's on-line bookshop.
Web-site: *www.sog.org.uk*

SLC   The Genealogical Society of Utah, 35 North West Temple Street, Salt Lake City, Utah 84150 U.S.A.

B.   <u>Local repositories and libraries holding Dorset material</u>

DRO   Dorset Record Office, Bridport Road, Dorchester DT1 1RP
Tel: 01305 250550   Web-site: *www.dorset-cc.gov.uk/archives*

DCM   Dorset County Museum, High West Street, Dorchester DT1 1XA
Tel: 01305 262735   Library of Dorset Natural History and
Archaeological Society open free to members, and to other
researchers for a daily or half-daily fee.

Dorchester Reference Library, Colliton Park, Dorchester DT1 1XJ
Tel: 01305 244448 / 224501

Devon RO   Devon Record Office, Castle Street, Exeter EX4 3PU
Tel: 01392 384253   Web-site: *www.devon.gov.uk/dro*

HRO   Hampshire Record Office, Sussex Street, Winchester SO23 8TH
Tel: 01962 846154   Web-site: *www.hants.gov.uk/record-office*

PDA   Plymouth Diocesean Archives (RC), The Priest's House,
20 Newcomen Road, Dartmouth, Devon TQ6 9BN   Tel: 01803 832860

PLHC   Poole Local History Centre, Waterfront Museum, 4 High Street,
Poole BH15 1BW   Tel: 01202 262600

SRO   Somerset Record Office, Obridge Road, Taunton TA2 4BU
Tel: 01823 337600. Web-site (with online catalogue):
www.somerset.gov.uk/archives/mainpage.htm

W&SRO   Wiltshire and Swindon Record Office, County Hall East,
Bythesea Road, Trowbridge BA14 8BS   Tel: 01225 713709
Web-site via: *www.wiltshire.gov.uk*

WSL   Westcountry Studies Library, Exeter Central Library,
Castle Street, Exeter EX4 3PQ   Tel: 01392 384210

C.   <u>Other local abbreviations</u>

DFHS   Dorset Family History Society
Secretary: Mrs Debbie Winter, Dorset FHS Research Centre,
Unit 49 Mannings Heath Works, Mannings Heath Road, Poole, Dorset
BH12 4NJ   Web-site: *www.dorsetfhs.freeserve.co.uk*

S&DFHS   Somerset and Dorset Family History Society
The Secretary, S&DFHS, PO Box 4502, Sherborne, Dorset DT9 6YL
Web-site: *www.sdfhs.org*

GT   *The Greenwood Tree*: journal of S&DFHS

NQSD   *Notes and Queries for Somerset and Dorset* 1888+
Vols 1-6 1888-99 also available on CD from Archive CD Books.
see p.19

Pine   *see* Bishop's Transcripts, p.9

SBA   Current member of Southern Baptist Association.

they have been extracted onto the IGI (*see* p.10) where they provide the bulk of the entries for the county.

Terry Pine has transcribed entries from BTs of 37 parishes. The data is available on four CDs from 19 Osborne Court, Osborne Road, Windsor, Berkshire SL4 3EP. References are to be found in our parish lists in the form (Pine: CD 1). The data does not include marriages where these have been transcribed by Phillimore, or any included on the Vital Records Index.

PRINTED COPIES

Marriages from sixty parishes, in most cases to 1812, are printed in the seven volumes of *Phillimore's Dorset Marriages*, published between 1906 and 1914. These volumes are also available on microfilm at Salt Lake City, and on seven CD-ROMs from S & N Genealogy Supplies, Greenacres, Salisbury Road, Chilmark, Salisbury SP3 5AH.

The Parish Register Society printed pre-1812 registers of Almer, Beer Hackett, Lydlinch, Swanage and Tarrant Hinton. Charles Mayo edited the registers of Bishop Caundle, Long Burton and Holnest for publication in 1894-95. The registers of Ashmore, Sturminster Marshall and North Wootton have also appeared in print.

Copies of most printed transcripts are available in the library of the Society of Genealogists, and locally in Dorset libraries and the collections of the family history societies. They should otherwise be obtainable through inter-library loan.

OTHER COPIES

Collections of manuscript, typescript and microform copies of registers and of bishop's transcripts are held by Dorset Record Office, the Society of Genealogists, Dorset FHS, Somerset and Dorset FHS, the Genealogical Society of Utah, and other repositories. Details of these, and of those in other locations, are given in our parish lists.

THE INTERNATIONAL GENEALOGICAL INDEX

Baptisms and marriages in 323 parish churches and Nonconformist chapels in Dorset, for various periods, are to be found in the International Genealogical Index of the Genealogical Society of Utah, U.S.A., held on computer and published on microfiche. The Index may also be searched on the internet at *www.familysearch.org*. In the county, copies of the IGI on fiche are held at the Public Libraries at Bournemouth, Dorchester, Poole and Weymouth. Print-outs may also be obtained from the local family history societies. For the location of other copies see the latest edition of: J.Gibson and M.Walcot *Where to find the International Genealogical Index* (FFHS, 1985)

The Dorset IGI has considerable limitations, by comparison with that for other counties, in that the compilers did not in general have access to original registers of the Church of England, and had to rely largely on microfilms of Bishop's Transcripts and on such registers as were available in print. For this reason, the IGI is less useful in many respects than the various county indexes, and will be eclipsed by them when they are fully extended back to 1538. Almost all the older parishes are represented, but in many cases only from the 1730s. Among the absentees are Kinson, Melbury Sampford and Wimborne All Saints, with registers from the seventeenth century but no BTs of their own. The Index does include the baptisms and marriages from all the 39 Catholic and Nonconformist chapels with registers in the Public Record Office, with the exception of those of the Quakers, and that of the Baptists of Lyme Regis which contains only burials.

This useful but incomplete source of information should be used with caution, and original registers should always be checked. This is particularly the case with the 1992 and later editions of the IGI. A key to which parishes are represented, and the years covered, is to be found in the Parish and Vital Records List. Instructions for the 1992 IGI contain the note : *'Changes have been made in the way names are added to the International Genealogical Index. As a result, the Parish and Vital Records List does not coordinate with the current [1992] edition of the International Genealogical Index exactly as it did in the past, the relationship between the two sources will continue to evolve over the next few years... .You can no longer tell by using the Parish and Vital records List whether a name will be listed in the International Genealogical Index. You must look in the index....the Parish and Vital Records Index does not indicate gaps in the records.'*

For the purposes of this volume we have used a copy of the PVRL dated July 1998 and included those entries which are marked with a double asterisk, indicating that *'records in this batch and period are not in the 1988 edition of the IGI'*. It may therefore be safer to take the IGI dates given in this volume as indicating the availability in general of genealogical material from a variety of Mormon sources, rather than the certain presence of entries in the IGI itself. The PVRL lists dates of burials in 60 Dorset parishes, and it is not clear whether some or all these are in fact included in the IGI. In the present volume we have not included these burials, dates of which in almost all cases are identical with those for baptisms.

Material held at Salt Lake City is listed in the *Family History Library Catalog,* available on CD-Rom and on the LDS web-site *www.familysearch.org.* Microfilms and fiches of registers, as listed in our volume, may be ordered for a nominal fee through Latter Day Saints' Family History Centres, for consultation in the centres. Contact should be by telephone, not by mail. In Dorset itself there is a centre at 8 Mount Road, Parkstone. Telephone: 01202 730646. Others in England and world-wide may be located on the same LDS web-site.

MARRIAGE INDEXES

DMI   **Dorset Marriage Index**

Maintained by Somerset and Dorset FHS. Slip-index in process of being transferred to computer. Marriages from 274 parishes for various periods, taken from original registers, bishop's transcripts, and occasionally other secondary sources. Fee charged.

Contact: Ken and Val Andrew, 69 Sopwith Crescent, Merley, Wimborne, Dorset BH21 1SW.

Boyd   Boyd's Marriage Index

Typescript index of marriages in 79 Dorset parishes indexed in Boyd's
Miscellaneous Series. There is no separate Dorset section. Held at the
Society of Genealogists, with microfiche copies at Salt Lake City, where
catalogued as Second and Third Series. Being transferred to web-site
www.englishorigins.com where, for a fee, it will be available for searches.

Pallot   Pallot's Marriage Index

Slip-index of marriages in 66 Dorset parishes, mostly 1790-1837 or
1790-1812. Covering dates in our parish lists are taken from:
C.Humphery-Smith *The Phillimore Atlas and Index of Parish Registers* 1984
edition. Index held at Institute of Heraldic and Genealogical Studies,
Northgate, Canterbury, Kent CT1 1BA. A fee is charged. Also available
online at *www.ancestry.com* with links to images of original slips.

MARRIAGE LICENCES

Marriage licences for the Archdeaconry of Dorset, as with Bishops
Transcripts, do not survive before the 18th century. The earliest are from
1798 and are in Wiltshire and Swindon Record Office. They are not numerous.
Full abstracts have been made to 1823. Wiltshire FHS has transcribed over
75,000 Sarum licence bonds, and published them on microfiche. For the
peculiar jurisdiction of the Dean of Sarum there is a substantial series of
bonds and allegations 1638-45, 1762-86 published in *Wiltshire Notes and
Queries*, 6 and 7: 1908-13: *passim*. Bonds and allegations for the Peculiar
of Gillingham 1664-66, 1672, 1674, 1698-1729, 1745-1816 are also held.
Abstracts of licences for Corfe Castle peculiar are published in British
Record Society Index Series Vol.22 (1922).

There are microfilm copies at Salt Lake City of original records of Dorset
Archdeaconry bonds and allegations, for the peculiars of the Dean and
Chapter, and for Gillingham peculiar 1612-1818.

PROBATE RECORDS

Probate records for Dorset up to 1858 are located at Dorset Record Office.
The main court for the county was the Archdeaconry Court of Dorset, much
less Dorset business being done in the Consistory Court of Bristol (Dorset
Division), records of which are also at Dorchester. There are in addition
a number of peculiar jurisdictions (noted in our parish lists), for which
there are some records at Dorchester, but most belonged to the Dean and
Chapter of Sarum, and their records are at Wiltshire and Swindon Record
Office.

At Dorset Record Office there is a consolidated card-index to all Dorset
wills from 1383 to the 1940s, proved not only in the local and peculiar
courts, but also at the Prerogative Court of Canterbury up to 1858, and
later in the Probate Court, and from 1873 the Probate Division of the High
Court. DRO also has on microfiche the National Probate Calendars of wills
and administrations, covering 1858 to 1935.

The British Record Society published in volumes 22 (1900) and 53 (1922) of
its *Index Library* series lists and an index of the Dorset wills and
administrations in the Archdeaconry Court 1568-1799 and the Bristol

Consistory Court (Dorsetshire Division) 1681-1799, together with those of the peculiars, 1660-1799. In 1911 George Fry published a *Calendar of Dorset Wills proved in the Prerogative Court of Canterbury 1385-1700*. He listed PCC Administrations 1559-1725 in a number of articles in *Notes and Queries for Somerset and Dorset*, vols 2 to 6 (1891-99).

see also Miriam Scott *Dorset PCC Wills and Adminstrations 1821-58*: S&DFHS: *c.*1999, now available in a second edition, in print or on microfiche.

A number of other books and articles relating to Dorset probates are listed by Stuart Raymond in *Dorset - A Genealogical Bibliography* (1991) pp.54-62.

Dorset FHS offers a surname search facility in its index of wills and administrations in the courts of the Diocese of Bristol, the Archdeaconry of Dorset, and the peculiars, *c.*1566-1799. A fee is charged. Enquiries to Dorset FHS Research Centre, Unit 40, Mannings Heath Works, 18 Mannings Heath Road, Poole BH12 4NJ.

Somerset and Dorset FHS has a database of some 7500 wills, from 1363 to 1994, submitted by members and others, from a variety of sources. Details of their enquiry service are obtainable on the Society's web-site at *www.sdfhs.org* and from the Society.

see A.Camp   *Wills and their whereabouts:* 1974
     J. Gibson   *Simplified Guide to Probate Jurisdiction*: 4th ed.:
                 FFHS: 1994

MONUMENTAL INSCRIPTIONS

Somerset and Dorset FHS has transcripts of the monumental inscriptions of over 250 burial grounds. It offers members and non-members a search service for which a charge is made. Contact: Mrs Olive Damon, 37 Beaucroft Lane, Colehill, Wimborne, Dorset BH21 2PD.

Dorset FHS has transcripts of the inscriptions from 243 graveyards, and offers a similar service. Contact: Dorset FHS Research Centre, Unit 40, Mannings Heath Works, 18 Mannings Heath Road, Poole BH12 4NJ.

Dorset Record Office has transcriptions from 205 Dorset graveyards, and the Society of Genealogists from 140. The Society also has a manuscript *Index to Miscellaneous MI* by A.Pratt (1983), with extracts from eight Dorset parishes. Many inscriptions from churches, and some from churchyards, are printed in the four volumes of Hutchins.

M. Monk's *10,000 Fallen Remembered on Dorset War Memorials* (SDFHS: 2000) has a list of 300 parishes and the names found on their war-memorials or in books of remembrance.

OTHER DENOMINATIONS

For the purposes of this volume we have identified 508 churches. chapels and meetings in Dorset, other than those of the Church of England, existing at various dates. These included 36 Baptist chapels, and 282 Methodist chapels of which 164 were identifiably Wesleyan in origin, 82 Primitive Methodist, and 5 Bible Christian. Presbyterians, Congregationalists, Independents, and Unitarians together totalled 80, with 39 Roman Catholic parishes or missions, 20 Meetings of the Society of Friends, and 15 of (Plymouth) Brethren. A return to Parliament in 1882 recorded 236 buildings registered for use by various denominations.

A very useful introduction to nonconformity in the county is provided by G.J.Davies in an article 'Early Dorset Nonconformity', published in the *Proceedings of the Dorset Natural History and Archaeological Society* 97: 1978: 24-30. The article contains details of licences granted to Baptists, Presbyterians and Congregationalists in 1672. In the present volume we have included this data as an indication of early nonconformist activity in the various parishes.

Roman Catholics

From 1688 the Catholics of Dorset came under the authority of the Vicars Apostolic of the Western District, which included the south-western counties and Wales. From 1850, together with Cornwall and Devon, it formed part of the new Diocese of Plymouth, in the Province of Westminster. From 1911 the diocese was incorporated into the Province of Birmingham.

In the reigns of Elizabeth I and Charles I a total of three priests and four laymen were hanged at Dorchester as martyrs for their faith. In the seventeenth century Jesuit priests of the district of St Thomas of Canterbury maintained a travelling mission from Dorset to Sussex, mainly among the poorer Catholics. The most substantial Catholic family in the county at this period was that of the Welds of Lulworth Castle, where a Mass-centre was maintained. Among the other early post-Reformation missions were those founded in the seventeenth century at Canford, Stapehill, Marnhull and Chideock. Towards the end of the eighteenth century came Weymouth, Spetisbury and Poole. The earliest surviving registers are those for the missions at Canford and Stapehill from 1711, Chideock from 1788, Marnhull from 1772, Weymouth from 1819 and Spetisbury from 1837. The Public Record Office has registers for Lulworth Castle from 1755, of which Dorset Record Office has contemporary duplicates.

The Catholic Record Society has published the registers of the missions at Stapehill, Lulworth and Marnhull, and Charles Crisp that of Canford Magna.

see also:
G.Oliver *Collections illustrating the history of the Catholic Religion in the counties of Cornwall, Devon, Dorset, Somerset, Wiltshire and Gloucestershire*: 1857

M.Gandy   *Catholic Missions of England and Wales*: Vol.3 *Wales and the West of England*: 1993
          Catholic Family History: A Bibliography of Local Sources: 1996
          Catholic Family History: A Bibliography of General Sources: 1996

M.Walcot 'Catholic Dorset': *Catholic Ancestor* Vol.8 No.6: Nov 2001

South-Western Catholic History: 1983+: miscellaneous articles.

Baptists

The *Baptist Handbook* for 1861 lists nine chapels in the county. The oldest in date was that at Lyme Regis (1655). Only Gillingham belonged at that date to the Baptist Union. Those at Dorchester, Lyme and Wimborne belonged to the Western Association; Poole to the Southern Association; and Bourton to Bristol Association. Those at Bridport and Iwerne were unattached. Eleven chapels were listed in the 1882 Return.

There are 13 Baptist churches in historic Dorset currently in membership of the Southern Baptist Association. The oldest claimed foundation dates are those of Dorchester 1648, Poole 1804, and Weymouth 1813.

The Public Record Office has surrendered Baptist registers for Wimborne Minster from 1778, Poole from 1797, Melcombe Regis from 1810, Lyme Regis from 1823, Wareham from 1823 and Langton Matravers from 1833. Dorset Record Office has registers for Melcombe Regis (Weymouth) 1824-91 and for Venn, Broadwindsor for 1843-1925.

see also: G.Breed *My ancestors were Baptists*: 3rd edit.: 1995

Independents, Congregationalists, Presbyterians, Unitarians

The *Congregational Yearbook* of 1871 lists twenty-nine chapels in the county, all but four of which were members of the Dorsetshire Association of Congregational Churches, founded in 1795. Of these, thirteen had seventeenth century foundation dates. There were also twenty-five out-stations and three village chapels.

Recorded in the 1882 Return there were in Dorset thirty Independent or Congregational churches, and two Unitarian. There are currently twenty-three churches of the United Reformed Church, in the Wessex Synod, Dorset District, within the historic county boundaries. Oldest in claimed foundation date are Blandford Forum, Bridport, Dorchester, Poole (Skinner Street), Shaftesbury, Sherborne and Wimborne, all from 1662; Wareham 1670, Swanage 1705 and Lytchett Minster 1770. There are two members of the Congregational Federation, at Buckland Newton and Corfe Castle, both of the 1830s.

The Public Record Office has registers from twenty chapels described as Independent or Congregational. The earliest is for Weymouth from 1734, followed by Wareham 1740, Poole 1741, Bridport 1750, Blandford 1760, Wimborne 1768, Lyme Regis 1775, Charmouth 1779, Sherborne 1785, Dorchester 1788, Swanage 1794, Beaminster 1796, Shaftesbury 1799, Corfe Castle 1810, Stalbridge 1810, Sydling St Nicholas 1811, Portland 1829, Whitchurch Canonicorum 1831, Maiden Newton 1833 and Sturminster Marshall 1833. It also has Presbyterian registers from Bridport 1720, Dorchester 1750, Poole 1750, and Wareham 1788. Dorset Record Office has overlapping or duplicate pre-1837 Independent registers for Poole from 1704, Wareham from 1740, and Beaminster from 1777, as well as for Wareham Presbyterians from 1828, and Bridport Unitarians from 1720, as well as later registers from other churches.

see also:
W.Densham & J.Ogle *The Story of the Congregational Churches of Dorset*: 1899
L.Brown   *The Story of the Dorset Congregational Association*: 1971
D.Clifford *My Ancestors were Congregationalists in England and Wales*: 1997
A.Ruston *My Ancestors were English Presbyterians/Unitarians*: 2nd ed.: 2001

15

Methodist

In his booklet *The Wesleys and the Early Dorset Methodists* (1987) B.J.Biggs provides a useful survey of early progress, and in an appendix, 'The Location of Methodists in 18th century Dorset', gives registration dates and owners or occupiers of Wesleyan chapels and houses in 45 towns and villages, 1746-99. We have incorporated this data into our parish lists. Biggs also lists the names of persons associated with the locations at the date of registration.

The 1882 Return lists 97 Wesleyan chapels, 57 Primitive Methodist, 3 Bible Christian and 2 United Methodist Free Church.

The Public Record Office has early Wesleyan registers from Gillingham, Portland, Shaftesbury and Weymouth, all from 1796, and from Swanage and Wimborne 1805, Poole 1809, Sherborne 1819, Dorchester 1831 and Bridport 1834. It has none for Primitive Methodists.

Dorset Record Office has pre-1837 overlapping or duplicate Wesleyan registers for Poole, Sherborne and Weymouth, as well as un-surrendered registers for Portland Wesleyan Circuit from 1796, Swanage Wesleyan Circuit from 1805, and Poole and Motcombe Primitive Methodist Circuits from 1827. It also has a substantial collection of later Methodist registers.

B.J.Biggs *The Wesleys and the Early Dorset Methodists*: 1987
J.S.Simon *History of Methodism in Dorset*: 1870

see also: W.Leary *My Ancestors were Methodists*: 3rd edit.: 1999

Society of Friends

Dorset Quarterly Meeting was formed in 1668. Its constituent Monthly Meetings were Bridport and Dorchester. Around 1690 additional Monthly Meetings were formed at Sherborne and Poole. Shaftesbury MM was formed in 1743 from Sherborne MM. Dorchester MM was dissolved in 1753. In 1783 Bridport and Sherborne amalgamated as one MM, which was joined in 1804 by Shaftesbury, forming Shaftesbury, Bridport and Sherborne MM, later known as Shaftesbury and Sherborne MM.

In 1804 Dorset QM was united with Hampshire QM as Dorset and Hampshire QM, at which date there were four constituent Monthly Meetings: Poole; Shaftesbury, Bridport and Sherborne; Ringwood; and Alton. Poole MM and Ringwood MM were united as Poole and Ringwood, later Poole and Southampton MM. The QM was dissolved in 1855. Poole and Southampton MM joined Sussex, Surrey and Hampshire QM. Shaftesbury and Sherborne MM joined Bristol and Somerset QM.

Records covering Dorset are therefore divided among a number of archives. Dorset Record Office has those of Dorset QM 1668-1804 and of Shaftesbury and Sherborne MM. Hampshire Record Office at Winchester has those of Dorset and Hampshire QM from 1804, and of Poole MM 1690-1804 and those which succeeded it. Somerset Record Office at Taunton holds those of Bristol and Somerset QM, and East Sussex Record Office at Lewes those of Sussex, Surrey and Hampshire QM 1855-1929. The Public Record Office has registers for Dorset and Hampshire QM 1673-1837, and for Poole MM 1659-1837, and Shaftesbury and Sherborne MM 1742-1837.

see also E.Milligan & M.Thomas *My Ancestors were Quakers*: 2nd edit.: 1999

CENSUSES

Dorset Record Office has a number of pre-1841 census returns providing varying amounts of information about the inhabitants. An early return for Poole in 1574 was printed in *Poole Borough Archives Transcripts Series* No.1 (1992). Returns for Puddletown 1724-29 and 1769 were published by Dorset Record Society in 1988. A return for Corfe Castle, *c.*1790, which has inhabitants' ages, was printed by Hutchins, and an index appears in the *Journal of Dorset FHS* 3 (Dec.1989). One for Oborne in 1801 appears in *Somerset and Dorset Notes and Queries* 16 (1916-17), and also on the website *www.melcombe.freeserve.co.uk/dorset/lookups.htm.* Other early returns in DRO include those for Lyme Regis in 1577 (7 householders), 1696, 1697, 1701, 1702 and 1703; Beaminster 1775; Tolpuddle 1776, 1791, 1796, 1804; Melbury Osmond 1800 (and 1839-53); Sturminster Newton and Winterborne St Martin 1801; Rowbarrow Hundred 1803; Corfe Castle 1803, 1811, 1821, 1831; Poole 1803; Buckland Newton 1808; Whitchurch Canonicorum 1811; West Parley 1815; Thornford, Horton, Woodlands, Compton Abbas, Litton Cheney, Marnhull, Shaftesbury St James and Winterborme Whitechurch in 1821; Wimborne St Giles in 1822; Allington Fontmell, Litton Cheney and Ryme Intrinseca in 1831, and Pentridge in 1836. Full details of these, and of other post-1841 local returns, are given in:

J.Gibson & M.Medlycott *Local Census Listings 1522-1930*: 3rd.ed: FFHS: 1997

Census returns for the entire county, 1841-91, filmed by parish, are available at Salt Lake City, as are those of Whitchurch Canonicorum (1811), and Corfe Castle, Fontmell and Litton Cheney 1831. The Society of Genealogists has films of censuses for 1841 to 1861, and 1881 on CD-ROM.

Dorchester Reference Library has census returns on microfilm, for the whole county, 1841-91. Poole Central Library has them for the county in 1841, 1881 and 1891, and for the Poole area 1851-71. Weymouth Reference Library has them for the Weymouth area 1841-91. The 1881 census for Great Britain is available for purchase on CD-ROM, and on microfiche at Poole and Bournemouth Libraries.

For further details *see*:
J Gibson & E.Hampson *Census Returns 1841-1891 in Microform*: FFHS: 1997

Somerset and Dorset FHS has issued the 1851 Census on CD-ROM, with surname, forenames, age, occupation, birthplace, census parish and PRO piece and folio number. It is also available on 15 floppy disks, A surname index giving parish is available on fiche and in a printed version in 15 volumes with a master index. The Society also publishes the 1891 Census on CD-ROM, in print and on fiche, and census indexes for 1841, 1861 and 1871 for Swanage, Langton Matravers, Worth Matravers, Studland, Wareham and Arne, Corfe Castle (including 1790 census) and Church Knowle. It can provide print-outs from the 1881 Census. The Society web-site *www.sdfhs.org* has full details.

Dorset FHS offers a search service into the censuses for the whole of England in 1881, and for Corfe Castle 1790-91, Swanage 1841, Turnerspuddle 1841-91 and Affpuddle 1841-91. Contact: Dorset FHS Research Centre, Unit 40, Mannings Heath Works, 18 Mannings Heath Road, Poole BH12 4NJ

OTHER INDEXES

VRI   Vital Records Index

Includes, with material from other counties, baptisms and marriages, for various periods, extracted from Bishop's Transcripts of 183 Dorset parishes, and from the nonconformist records at Dr Williams Library, London (C 1766-1837 M 1723-74). Available on CD-ROM from LDS Distribution Centre, 399 Garretts Green Lane, Birmingham B33 0UH.

NBI   National Burial Index

First edition (2001) contains only two Dorset parishes, Chilfrome (1678-1995) and Frome Vauchurch (1813-1998), contributed by Maiden Newton Museum Trust. Available on CD-ROM from the FFHS bookshop via their web-site at *www.familyhistorybooks.co.uk/shop/pages/nbi.htm*, or by post from Unit 15, Chesham Industrial Centre, Oram Street, Bury, Lancashire BL9 6EN.

DBI   Dorset Burial Index

An ongoing project by Somerset and Dorset FHS, with a database currently containing over 264,000 entries for Dorset (and over 675,000 for Somerset), intended to cover the full range of dates from 1538 to 1837, and extending in some cases into the 20th century. Dates given are as at 14 October 2001. An up-to-date list of parishes and dates is available. An enquiry service is provided. Further information is on the Society's web-site *www.sdfhs.org* Contact: S&DFHS (Burials), 18 Bincleaves Road, Weymouth, Dorset DT4 8RL.

PRI   Parish Register Index

An ongoing project by Dorset FHS, currently (November 2001) covering 265 Dorset parish churches and Poole Independent church, for various dates, mainly within the period 1790-1837, but in some cases earlier or later. A master index on 9 microfiche is available. A search service is provided. Contact: Dorset FHS Research Centre, Unit 40, Mannings Heath Works, 18 Mannings Heath Road, Poole BH12 4NJ.

Strays Indexes

Computer database of over 69,000 Dorset strays maintained for Somerset and Dorset FHS by: Debby Rose, 4 Chafeys Avenue, Weymouth DT4 0EQ. Further details on the Society's web-site *www.sdfhs.org*.

Dorset FHS: Dorset Strays Master Index on microfiche, with additional information on names selected from index fiche available for a fee. Enquiries and contributions to Michael Blakeston, 4 Halsford Park Road, East Grinstead, West Sussex RN19 1PN.

Pedigree Service

Somerset and Devon FHS has a collection of over 1200 pedigrees, family trees and other documents. A list of principal names in the collection is available (the Millennium List). Searches of the collection can be made and copies provided. Further information is on the Society's web-site at *www.sdfhs.org*   Contact: Mr Philip Nash, 37 Lower Golf Links Road, Broadstone, Dorset BH18 5BQ.

NEWSPAPERS

The earliest long-lasting newspaper circulating in Dorset was the Sherborne and Yeovil Mercury or Western Flying Post, 1737-1867, containing news from all the south-western counties. Copies are available to 1826 at Dorchester Library; to 1867 at the libraries in Exeter (Devon) and Redruth (Cornwall); and from 1749 to 1867 at the British Library Newspaper Library at Colindale, London. The latter also has the Sherborne Mercury or Weekly Advertiser 1737-49; the Sherborne Journal and Western Advertiser 1780-86; and the Dorchester and Sherborne Journal and Weekly Advertiser 1791-1816, which continued as the Sherborne, Dorchester and Taunton Journal, with copies to 1886 both at Colindale and at Somerset Record Office.

The *Dorset County Chronicle*, printed at Dorchester, started in 1823. Dorchester Library has a run that year (2 issues only) to 1857 and Colindale from 1824 to 1957. The *Poole and Dorset Herald* ran from 1846 to 1983. There is a good run at Poole Library, and Colindale has it to 1937. The *Southern Times* (1851-1954) was printed at Weymouth with various sub-titles. Copies are at Weymouth and Dorchester Libraries, and at Colindale.

The Colindale web-site *www.bl.uk/collections/newspapers.html* lists its holdings of over 250 newspapers and magazines of all kinds, published in Dorset.

Dorset FHS provides a search service for births, marriages and deaths reported in the *Christchurch and Bournemouth Chronicle* 1872-75, *Dorset Free Press* 1874-75, *Parkstone Reminder* 1880-81, *Poole and S.W.Herald* 1865, and *Poole and Dorset Herald* 1881-87 and 1891.
Contact: Dorset FHS Research Centre, Unit 40, Mannings Heath Works,
    18 Mannings Heath Road, Poole BH12 4NJ

DIRECTORIES

Post Office or Kelly's Directories for the county were issued for various years between 1848 and 1939. Early editions were bound with neighbouring counties. A good selection may be found at libraries in the county, at the Westcountry Studies Library in Exeter, the Society of Genealogists, the British Library and elsewhere.

The Society of Genealogists has published on microfiche Pigot's 1830 Directory of Dorsetshire. S & N Genealogy has produced on CD-ROM Pigot's directories for 1823 and 1844. Pigot's Commercial Dirsctory 1823/23 is available on microfiche from MM Publications, The White Cottage, The Street, Lidgate, Newmarket, Suffolk CB8 9PP. Post Office and Trade Directories for Dorset, 1880, may be purchased on CD-ROM from Stepping Stones PO Box 295 York YO31 1YS. Pigot for 1830 and 1842/44, Harrod's Dorset and Wiltshire Directory for 1865, and Kelly's Post Office Directory for Dorset 1903 are sold on CD-ROM by Archive CD Books Ltd, 51 St Whites Road, Cinderford, Gloucestershire GL14 3DF. Tel: 01594 829359. Web-site: *www.archivecdbooks.com.*

POLL BOOKS AND ELECTORAL REGISTERS

Dorset Record Office and Weymouth Library hold poll books for the county for various years from 1726/27. The Record Office has them for Wareham from 1689, Dorchester from 1705, Weymouth from 1727, and Bridport from 1795. Poole Library has a number for Poole, starting in 1698. The Society of Genealogists has them for 1807, 1831 and 1857, and has published the first on microfiche.

For further details *see* Jeremy Gibson and Colin Rogers *Poll Books c.1696-1872: a Directory of Holdings*: FFHS: 3rd edit: 1994

The Record Office has electoral registers for the county from 1833 to the present day, and for Bridport from 1832 and Dorchester from 1843, as well as burgess rolls for Corfe Castle 1780, Lyme Regis 1835-91, Dorchester 1835-1900 and Blandford Forum 1887. More recent electoral registers are held at local libraries in the county. The Society of Genealogists has one for the county in 1838, and the Public Record Office has one for 1874, as well as copies for Poole 1871 and Sheftesbury and Wareham 1873.

For further details *see* Jeremy Gibson and Colin Rogers *Electoral Registers since 1832, and Burgess Rolls*: FFHS: 1989.

MILITARY HISTORY

The Public Record Office has muster rolls for the county for 1539, 1542 and 1569. These were edited by T.L.Stoate and published in *Dorset Tudor Muster Rolls*: 1978. There are also later partial rolls for 1597-1601, 1624 and 1626-27. Dorset Record Office has muster rolls for Bridport in 1319 and 1457.
see J.Gibson & A.Dell *Tudor and Stuart Muster Rolls*: FFHS: 1991

Surviving militia records are more substantial. Dorset Record Office has ballot lists for various places from 1757 to 1799, liable books 1758-59, enrolments 1761-81 and other material including *levée en masse* lists for Corfe Castle Borough and Rowbarrow Hundred 1803. Dorset Military Museum has militia enrolments for the county 1821-31 and succession books for officers and NCOs 1799-1881. The Public Record Office holds county regimental returns of militia 1781-1876, supplementary militia 1798-1814 and local militia 1808-16.

Somerset and Dorset FHS has published Militia Ballot Lists for 1759-99, in print and on fiche, in two volumes, for East and West Dorset.

see J.Gibson and M.Medlycott *Militia Lists and Musters 1757-1876:* FFHS: 4th ed. 2000.
M.Medlycott *'Dorset militia lists and the levées en masse 1757-1803'*: GT 13, 3: July 1988: 92-93

The Dorset Regiment had two separate strands in its early history. In 1702 Colonel Richard Coote raised in Ireland a Regiment of Foot which saw service in Spain and in Gibraltar before going in 1754 to India where it fought in the battle of Plassey, returning to defend Gibraltar against Spain. In 1751 it became the 39th Regiment of Foot and in 1807 the 39th (Dorsetshire) Regiment. Only in 1879 was a depot was established in the county, at Dorchester. In 1755 Colonel John Campbell raised a regiment in Salisbury which became the 54th (West Norfolk Regiment) in 1782. It served in the War of American Independence and spent some time in Canada. In 1881 the 39th merged with the 54th as the Dorsetshire Regiment, the 39th becoming the First Battalion and the 54th the Second. In the First World War six battalions of the Regiment saw service in France, Palestine, India, Turkey and Mesopotamia, gaining forty-eight battle honours. In the Second World War the Dorsets took part in the defence of Malta, served in India against Japan, and at the invasion of Sicily, before landing in France on D-Day and taking part in the battle of Arnhem. The Dorsetshire was renamed the Dorset Regiment in 1951. In 1959 it amalgamated with the Devonshire Regiment to form what is now the Devonshire and Dorset Regiment. The Military Museum of Devon and Dorset is at The Keep, Bridport Road, Dorchester DT1 1RN.

see H.Popham *The Dorset Regiment*: 1970

Soldiers died in the Great War 1914-1919: *Part 43 The Dorsetshire Regiment.* Facsimile edition published 1988. Information also available on CD-ROM and on the Commonwealth War Graves Commission website *www.cwgc.org.*

Kelly's directories (*see* p.19) give details of military units based in the county, with the names of officers. Thus for example in 1903, at the depot of the Dorsetshire Regiment at Dorchester were the 1st and 2nd Battalions (39th and 54th) and the 3rd Battalion (Dorsetshire Militia). There was also a Royal Artillery Barracks at Poundbury Road. The Dorset (Queen's Own) Imperial Yeomanry had its headquarters at Sherborne and squadrons at Sherborne, Dorchester, Gillingham, Blandford and Weymouth. There were Volunteers of the 1st Dorsetshire Royal Garrison Artillery, with headquarters at Weymouth and companies at Weymouth, Bournemouth, Lyme Regis, Bridport, Swanage, Portland, Poole and Parkstone. Of the Wiltshire and Dorset Volunteer Infantry Brigade the 1st Battalion Dorsetshire Regiment had its headquarters at Princes Street, Dorchester, and there were companies at Dorcheter, Bridport, Wareham, Longfleet, Weymouth, Wimborne, Sherborne, Blandford, Shaftesbury and Gillingham.

In the Second World war there were military airfields at Hamworthy, Henstridge, Tarrant Rushton and Warmwell.
G.Smith *Dorset airfields in the Second World War*: 1999

Various accounts have been published of wartime activity in the county:

G.Forty *Frontline Dorset: a county at war, 1939-45*: 1994
R.Legg *Dorset at war: diary of WW 2*: 1986; expanded 1990
        D-Day Dorset: 1994
        Battle of Britain Dorset: 1995
J.Murphy *Dorset at war*: 1979

SELECTIVE BIBLIOGRAPHY

S.Raymond *Dorset: a genealogical bibliography*: 1991

K.Carter & E Pitman *Dorset, a catalogue of the books and other printed material on the history, topography* [etc] *of Dorset in Dorset County Library:* 1974

The catalogue of Dorset County Libraries, including a great deal of local material, may be accessed online via *www.dorset-cc.gov.uk.*

Records

Compiled by Hugh Jaques, Dorset Archives Service:
A Guide to the Location of the Parish Registers of Dorset: 2000
A guide to the Location of Dorset Nonconformist and Roman Catholic Registers: 2000
A Guide to the Transcripts held in the Dorset Record Office: 2000
Who's Afeard of Family History: A guide to sources for family history in Dorset Record Office: 1999

N.Taylor ed. *County Sources - Dorset and Somerset*: Society of Genealogists: 2002. A guide to material in the Society's collections.

History and Topography

C.Cullingford *A History of Dorset*: 3rd edit.: 1999
J.Bettey   *Dorset:* City and County Histories: 1974
F.Heath   *Dorset*: Methuen's Little Guides: 1907. Revised E.Long: 1949
P.Stanier   *Dorset*: Shire County Guides: 1986
T.Goodwin   *Dorset in the Civil War*: 1996
J.Marlow   *The Tolpuddle Martyrs*: 1985
H.Lea   *Thomas Hardy's Wessex*: 1913
A.Fagersten   *The place-names of Dorset*: 1933
J.Newman & N.Pevsner *Dorset*: The Buildings of England: 1972

Towns and Villages

J.Brocklebank *Affpuddle in the County of Dorset 1787-1953*: 1968
M.Eedle   *A History of Beaminster*: 1984
F.Pitfield   *The Book of Bere Regis*: 1978
B.Cox   *The Book of Blandford Forum*: 1983
A Harfield   *Blandford and the Military*: 1984
T.Almack   *A Village Heritage: the story of Blandford St Mary*: 1962
R,Legg   *Bridport and Lyme Regis*: 1999
M.Jones   *Cerne Abbas: the Story of a Dorset Village*: 1952
L.Coffin   *Cerne Abbas and Villages*: 1987
J.Draper   *Dorchester - an illustrated history*: 1992
C.Howe   *Gylla's Home Town* [Gillingham]: 1983
J.Berkeley   *Lulworth and the Welds*: 1971
H.Chessell   *A portrait of Lyme*: 1974
J.Fowles   *A short history of Lyme Regis*: 1982
S.Percival   *Lytchett Matravers: a Dorset village*: 1982
C.Cullingford *History of Poole*: 1988
J.Bettey   *The Island and Royal Manor of Portland*: 1970
J.Edwards & R.Legg *Old Portland*: 1983
R.Legg   *Purbeck Island*: 1972
L.Sydenham   *Sheftesbury and its Abbey*: 1959
B.Innes   *Shaftesbury - an illustrated history*: 1992
R.Legg   *The Book of Swanage*: 2001
I,Bond   *Tyneham, a lost heritage*: 1984
T,Davis   *Wareham, Gateway to Purbeck*: 1984
J.Ash   *West Stour in Dorset*: 1980
M.Boddy & J.West *Weymouth, an illustrated history*: 1983
J.James   *Wimborne Minster*: 1982
N.Hayward   *Yetminster and Beyond*: 1997

Parishes appear in these lists in alphabetical order. Modern parishes are grouped with the ancient parish from which they are descended, except where a former chapelry had early registers of its own. The figure in square brackets at the head of each parish is its population in 1831. Where there has been historic or local variation in the spelling of parish names, the present usage of the Ordnance Survey has in general been adopted.

ABBEY MILTON   *see* MILTON ABBAS

ABBOTSBURY St Nicholas [Uggscombe Hundred; Weymouth Union] [874]
Now with PORTESHAM, LANGTON HERRING.
OR   C 1574-1950 M 1567-1976 B 1567-1576, 1584-1919 (DRO)
BT   CMB 1731-1811, 1813-79 (W&SRO)
Cop C 1574-1665, 1790-1837 M 1567-1837 B 1567-1638, 1813-37 (DRO);
    C 1574-1704 M 1567-1837 (SG); C 1790-1837 MB 1813-37 (PRI); M 1565-1771
    (Phil Ms at SG); M 1567-1812 (Boyd); M 1567-1837 from OR (DMI);
    B 1567-1919 (DBI); CMB 1731-1879 from BT (Pine: CD 2)
Cop (Mf) CB 1731-1879 M 1731-1836 (Mf of BT, DRO, SLC); M 1565-1771 (Mf of
        Phil Ms, SLC); Extr C 1731-1879 M 1731-1836 from BT (IGI)

ABBOTSBURY St Catherine's Chapel. 14th cent. In care of English Heritage.

ABBOTSBURY (Cong) Licence for house of Humphrey Miller, 1672

ABBOTSBURY (Ind/Cong) f 1795. Out-station of WEYMOUTH [*Cong. Yearbook* 1871]
[Kelly 1939]
OR   C 1877-1970 (DRO)

ABBOTSBURY (Prim Meth) Weymouth Circuit [Kelly 1939]
OR   C 1868-72 (DRO)

ADMISTON   *see* ATHELHAMPTON

AFFPUDDLE or **AFFPIDDLE**   St Laurence [Hundredsbarrow Hundred; Wareham and
Purbeck Union] [442] Included tithing of Bryantspuddle. United 1970 with
TURNERSPUDDLE. Now also with BERE REGIS.
OR   C 1728-1872 M 1731-1753, 1776-1837 B 1722-1832 Banns 1824-1900 (DRO)
    Noted in 1831: CB 1722+ M 1776+ 'It is supposed that the earlier
    Registers have been destroyed by fire'.
BT   CMB 1734-1879 (W&SRO)
Cop C 1728-1850 M 1731-1850 B 1722-1850 (DRO, SG); CMB 1722-1850 from BT
    (W&SRO); C 1728-1837 MB 1813-37 (PRI); M 1734-76 from BT (DRO);
    M 1731-1837 (SG); M 1731-1837 from OR, 1734-76 from BT (DMI);
    B 1722-1837 (DBI); CMB 1734-1879 from BT (Pine: CD 3)

23

AFFPUDDLE cont.
Cop (Mf) CB 1734-1879 M 1734-1849 (Mf of BT, DRO, SLC); Extr C 1734-1879
M 1734-1849 from BT (IGI)
MI (S&DFHS); (DFHS); (DRO); Ch, cy 1971 (SG)

AFFPUDDLE (Wes) Bryantspuddle [Kelly 1903]

ALCESTER Liberty within parish of SHAFTESBURY St James. Civil parish
created 1894 [Shaftesbury Union 1894-1921]

ALDERHOLT *see* CRANBORNE

ALLINGTON St Swithun [Gooderthorne Hundred; Bridport Union] [1300] Rebuilt
1826-27. Now with BRIDPORT benefice.
OR C 1570-1970 M 1570-1662, 1682-1993 B 1673-1783, 1827-1934 Banns
1753-1809, 1824-1998 (DRO) Noted in 1831 CMB 1570-1747 'imperfect and
partly illegible'. 'Burials' [apparently post-1747] 'entered in the
Registers of Bridport.'
BT CMB 1732-1811, 1813-79 (W&SRO)
Cop M 1570-1812 (Ptd Phil 2: 1907; & on CD-ROM); C 1648-1747, 1790-1836
M 1570-1837 B 1673-1747, 1827-37 (DRO); C 1570-1751 M 1570-1812
B 1672-1757 (SG); C 1790-1837 MB 1813-37 (PRI); M 1570-1812 (Boyd);
M 1790-1812 (Pallot); M 1570-1837 from OR (DMI); B 1673-1837 (DBI);
CMB 1732-1879 from BT (Pine: CD 2)
Cop (Mf) M 1570-1812 (Mf of Phil, SLC); CB 1732-1879 M 1732-1837 (Mf of BT,
DRO, SLC); Extr C 1732-1879 from BT, M 1570-1731 from OR,
1732-1837 from BT (IGI)
MI (S&DFHS); (DFHS); (DRO); (SG)

ALMER St Mary [Loosebarrow Hundred; Blandford Union 1835-94; Wimborne
and Cranborne Union 1894-1930] [176 with Mapperton] United 1972 with
CHARBOROUGH. Now with RED POST benefice.
OR C 1539-41, 1548-1641, 1663-97, 1731-1990 M 1538-1640, 1654, 1663-79,
1688, 1695-98, 1731-1836 B 1538-1640, 1669-70, 1677-78, 1694-97,
1731-1993 Banns 1825-1975 (DRO) Noted in 1831 of first register to
1695: 'irregularly entered and very imperfect'. Gap to 1731 also
noted.
BT CMB 1731-1879 (W&SRO)
Cop CMB 1538-1812 (Ptd PRS, 1907); C 1539-1702, 1731-1837 M 1538-1688,
1695-1702, 1731-1811, 1814-36 B 1538-1702, 1731-1837 (DRO);
C 1791-1837 M 1814-36 B 1813-37 (PRI); M 1731-55 from BT (DRO);
M 1541-1698, 1731-1811, 1814-36 (SG); M 1790-1811 (Pallot); M 1541-1836
from OR, 1731-55 from BT (DMI); B 1536-1837 (DBI); CMB 1731-1879 from
BT (Pine: CD 3)
Cop (Mf) CMB 1538-1812 (Mf of PRS, SLC); CB 1731-1879 M 1731-1836 (Mf of
BT, DRO, SLC); C 1538-1812 M 1538-1811 (Printout, Mf, SLC);
Extr C 1538-1812 M 1538-1811 from OR, C 1731-1879 M 1731-1836 from
BT (IGI)
MI (S&DFHS); (DFHS); (DRO); (SG)

ALTON PANCRAS St Pancras [Alton Pancras Liberty; Cerne Union] [210]
Peculiar of Dean of Sarum, until 1847. Rebuilt 1874-75. Now with
PIDDLETRENTHIDE, PLUSH, PIDDLEHINTON.
OR C 1673-1961 M 1674-1988 B 1674-1997 (DRO)
BT CMB 1586-88, 1594-1600, 1607-39, 1642, 1664-1830, 1834-40, 1845-79
(W&SRO)

ALTON PANCRAS cont.
Cop M 1674-1812 (Ptd Phil 6: 1912; & on CD-ROM); C 1673-1812 M 1674-1836
     B 1674-1837 (DRO); C 1790-1837 M 1674-1836 B 1813-37 (PRI); M 1674-1756
     from BT (DRO); M 1673-1812 (Boyd); M 1790-1812 (Pallot); M 1674-1836
     from OR, 1586-1756, 1836-38 from BT (DMI); B 1731-1837 (DBI);
     CMB 1586-1879 from BT (Pine: CD 3)
Cop (Mf) M 1674-1812 (Mf of Phil, SLC); CB 1586-1879 M 1586-1847 (Mf of
         BT, DRO, SLC); Extr C 1586-1879 M 1576-1847 from BT (IGI)
MI   (S&DFHS); (DFHS); (DRO)

ALWESTON hamlet of FOLKE

ANDERSON *see* WINTERBORNE ANDERSON

ANSTY   *see* HILTON

ARNE St Nicholas [Hasilor Hundred; Wareham and Purbeck Union] [171]
Chapelry in WAREHAM Holy Trinity. Now with WAREHAM benefice.
OR   C 1762-1816 M 1763-1994 B 1763-1819 Banns 1845-1942 (DRO) *and see*
     WAREHAM. Noted in 1831: 'The earlier Registers were destroyed by
     fire at Wareham A.D. 1762'.
BT   CMB 1731-32, 1736-1810, 1814-46 C 1847-80 (W&SRO)
Cop M 1763-72, 1782-1840 (DRO, SG); C 1731-1837 M 1731-1840 B 1732-1824
     from BT (DRO); C 1731-1837 M 1813-40 B 1813-19 (PRI); M 1763-72,
     1782-1840 from OR, 1731-63, 1772-82 from BT (DMI); B 1763-1819 (DBI)
Cop (Mf) C 1731-1880 MB 1731-1846 (Mf of BT, DRO, SLC); Extr C 1731-1880
         M 1731-1848 (IGI)
MI   (DFHS)

ASHINGTON *see* CANFORD MAGNA

ASHMORE St Nicholas [Cranborne Hundred; Shaftesbury Incorporation/Union]
[191] Now with TOLLARD ROYAL, FARNHAM, GUSSAGE ST MICHAEL, GUSSAGE ALL
SAINTS, CHETTLE.
OR   C 1651-1845 M 1667-81, 1688-1742, 1754-1994 B 1654-82, 1687-1847
     Banns 1824-1903 (DRO)
BT   CMB 1732-38, 1741-42, 1745-1879 (W&SRO)
Cop Index CMB 1651-1820 (Ptd E.Watson *Ashmore, Dorset: A History of the
     Parish*: 1890); C 1651-1900 M 1667-1900 B 1654-1923 (DRO); M 1742-54,
     1810-14, 1838-46 from BT (DRO); C 1813-99 M 1667-81, 1687-1742,
     1754-1838 B 1813-1923 (SG); C 1790-1837 M 1667-1838 B 1813-37 (PRI);
     M 1790-1820 (Pallot); M 1667-1742, 1754-1838 from OR, 1731-54, 1810-14,
     1838-42 from BT (DMI); B 1654-1847 (DBI); CMB 1732-1879 from BT
     (Pine: CD 3)
Cop (Mf) CB 1732-1879 M 1732-1842 (Mf of BT, DRO, SLC); Index CMB 1651-1820
         (Mf of Watson, SLC); C 1653-1820 (Printout, Mf, SLC);
         Extr C 1653-1829 M 1732-1842 from BT (IGI)
MI   (S&DFHS); (DFHS); (DRO)

ASHMORE (Wes) Erected 1855 [1882 Return]; Meth [Kelly 1939]

ASKERSWELL St Michael [Eggerton Hundred; Bridport Union] [228] Now with
LODERS, POWERSTOCK, WEST MILTON, WITHERSTONE, NORTH POORTON
OR   C 1560-1665, 1673-1997 M 1560-72, 1586, 1593-1663, 1676-90 1700-13,
     1718-1991 B 1560-1667, 1673-93, 1698-1999 Banns 1754-1804, 1824-1999
     (DRO) Noted in 1831: CMB 1558+. 'The Registers of Chilcombe were kept
     in this Parish until 1748'.
BT   CMB 1731-97, 1800-36, 1841-79 (W&SRO)

ASKERSWELL cont
<u>Cop</u> M 1560-1812 (Ptd Phil 6: 1912; & on CD-ROM); M 1560-1837 B 1722-1986
(DRO); C 1790-1812 (I, DRO); CB 1559-1772 M 1560-72, 1586, 1593-1610,
1616-65, 1676-90, 1700-13, 1718-1837 (SG); C 1790-1837 M 1560-1837
(PRI); M 1560-1812 (Boyd); M 1790-1812 (Pallot); M 1560-1837 from OR,
1590 from Hutchins (DMI); B 1813-1986 (SG); B 1682-1996 (DBI);
CMB 1731-1879 from BT (Pine: CD 1)
<u>Cop (Mf)</u> M 1560-1812 (Mf of Phil, SLC); CB 1731-1879 M 1731-1835 (Mf of BT,
DRO, SLC); Extr C 1731-1879 M 1741-1835 from BT (IGI)

ATHELHAMPTON or **ADMISTON** St John [Puddletown Hundred; Dorchester Union]
[67] Rebuilt on new site 1861-62. United 1967 with PUDDLETOWN and
BURLESTON. Redundant 1976. Privately purchased 1984. Now St Edward King and
Martyr, used by Greek Orthodox community.
<u>OR</u> C 1692-1973 M 1694-1966 B 1692-1976 Banns 1867-1966 (DRO) Noted in
1831: 'no Bur.Register 1757-1807 can be found'. Now at DRO.
<u>BT</u> CMB 1732, 1737-57, 1760-66, 1769-1813 (mainly BURLESTON), 1814-79
(W&SRO)
<u>Cop</u> C 1790-1837 M 1755-1848 B 1814-37 (PRI); M 1694-1848 (DRO);
M 1755-1851 (SG); M 1755-1848 from OR, 1732-55 from BT (DMI);
B 1692-1837 (DBI); CMB 1732-1879 from BT (Pine: CD 4)
<u>Cop (Mf)</u> CB 1732-1879 M 1732-1845 (Mf of BT, DRO, SLC); Extr C 1732-1879
M 1732-1845 from BT (IGI)
<u>MI</u> (S&DFHS)

AXMINSTER [Part Axminster Hundred (Devon), part Whitchurch Canonicorum
Hundred. Transferred to Devon 1844]
<u>OR</u> *see* NIPR Vol.8 Part 5 Devon

AXMINSTER (Wes) Axminster Circuit. Included BEAMINSTER, BURTON BRADSTOCK,
LYME REGIS, NETTLECOMBE, SALWAY ASH, SHIPTON GORGE, all later in BRIDPORT
CIRCUIT *q.v.*
<u>OR</u> C 1809-37 (WSL)

BATCOMBE St Mary Magdalene [Yetminster Hundred; Cerne Union] [178]
Now with YETMINSTER WITH RYME INTRINSECA AND HIGH STOY benefice.
<u>OR</u> C 1800-08 M 1767-1803, 1814-1938 B 1799-1808, 1814-1991 Banns
1825-1943 (DRO) Noted in 1831: C 1783+ B 1784+; 'No marriage
register prior to 1813'.
<u>BT</u> CMB 1731-77, 1781-1844, 1847-79 (W&SRO)
<u>Cop</u> C 1800-08 M 1731-1837 B 1799-1837 (DRO); M 1732-1814 from BT (DRO);
M 1813-37 B 1814-37 (PRI); M 1767-1837 from OR, 1731-1814 from BT
(DMI); B 1799-1837 (DBI); CMB 1731-1879 from BT (Pine: CD 1);
Extr CMB 1767-1808 (SG)
<u>Cop (Mf)</u> CB 1731-1879 M 1731-1867 (Mf of BT, DRO, SLC); Extr C 1731-1879
M 1731-1867 (IGI)
<u>MI</u> (S&DFHS); (DFHS); (DRO); Ch, cy 1971 (SG)

BAUNTON *see* BOTHENHAMPTON

BEAMINSTER AREA Modern benefice including BEAMINSTER, BROADWINDSOR with
BURSTOCK, BLACKDOWN, DRIMPTON, HOOKE, MELPLASH with MAPPERTON, MOSTERTON,
NETHERBURY, SALWAY ASH, SEABOROUGH, SOUTH PERROTT and CHEDINGTON, STOKE
ABBOTT, TOLLER PORCORUM

BEAMINSTER St Mary of the Annunciation [Beaminster Forum and Redhone Hundred; Beaminster Union] [2968 including 50 labourers 'excavating a tunnel'] Chapelry in NETHERBURY; Peculiar of the Prebend of Netherbury and Beaminster, Sarum Cathedral until 1847. separate parish 1849. Now with Beaminster Area benefice.

OR C 1585-1940 M 1585-1993 B 1585-1899, 1916-54 Banns 1835-1988 (DRO)
  Noted in 1831: CMB 1659+
BT CMB 1585-88, 1591-94, 1600-27, 1633-38, 1669-75, 1678-1707, 1710-28, 1734-1837, 1847-79 (W&SRO)
Cop M 1585-1636, 1669-88, 1720-28, 1735 (Ptd Phil 3 1908; 1: 1906;
  & on CD-ROM); C 1632-1837 M 1585-1837 B 1677-1768, 1813-37 (DRO);
  M 1685-1718, 1731-33, 1736-53 from BT (DRO); C 1585-1730 M 1558-1837
  M 1558-1636, 1669-1837 B 1585-1735 (SG); C 1790-1837 MB 1813-37 (PRI);
  M 1555-1812 (Boyd); M 1790-1812 (Pallot); M 1585-1837 from OR,
  1685-1754 from BT (DMI); B 1677-1845 (DBI)
Cop (Mf) M 1585-1812 (Mf of Phil, SLC); CMB 1585-1638, 1669-1837 CB 1847-79
    (Mf of BT, DRO, SLC); Extr C 1585-1837, 1847-79 M 1585-1837 from
    BT (IGI)
MI (S&DFHS); (DFHS); (DRO); (Mf, SLC); (SG)

BEAMINSTER Holy Trinity. Chapel-of-ease erected 1849-51. Redundant 1978. Sold 1987 for residential use.
OR C 1857-1943 B 1851-1916 (DRO)
BT CMB 1857-79 (W&SRO) *and see* St Mary
Cop C 1857-79 from BT (VRI); B 1851-1916 (DBI)
Cop (Mf) CMB 1857-79 (Mf of BT, DRO, SLC); Extr C 1857-79 (IGI)
MI (S&DFHS); (SG)

BEAMINSTER (RC) St John, Shortmoor. Erected 1966-67

BEAMINSTER (Ind/Cong) East Street. f 1662. Erected 1749 [Pevsner]
[*Cong. Yearbook* 1871]
OR ZC 1796-1836 (RG 4/2403, PRO); C 1777-89, 1796-1837, 1868-1966
  M 1837-55 (DRO)
Cop ZC 1796-1836 (DRO, S&DFHS, SG)
Cop (Mf) ZC 1796-1836 (Mf of OR, SLC); C 1796-1836 (Printout, Mf SLC);
    Extr C 1796-1836 (IGI)

BEAMINSTER (Presb) General preaching licences to Ambrose Clare, John Willis and William Craine of Beaminster; licences for houses of Lancelot Cox and John Locke; and for a room under the Market House, 1672

BEAMINSTER (Wes) [Harrod 1865] [1882 Return]; Fleet Street n.d.
[Kelly 1903, 1939]
OR *see* AXMINSTER [Devon] and BRIDPORT Circuits

BEAMINSTER (Latter Day Saints)
OR Records of membership 1851-96 (SLC)
Cop (Mf) Records of membership 1851-96 (Mf of OR, SLC)

BEAMINSTER Poor Law Union Workhouse. Erected 1626 at POWERSTOCK. New building 1838 at Stoke Water, Beaminster. Chapel erected 1907. Later Stoke Water House. Converted into flats 1974.

BEDCHESTER *see* FONTMELL MAGNA

BEER HACKETT St Michael [Sherborne Hundred; Sherborne Union] [110] Rebuilt 1882 ? Peculiar of the Dean of Sarum until 1847. Now with BRADFORD ABBAS, THORNFORD.
OR   C 1549-1630, 1640-46, 1659-71, 1696-1745, 1773-1993 M 1549-1630, 1641, 1662-71, 1696-1745, 1757-1992 B 1549-1630, 1640-46, 1659-71, 1686, 1696-1745, 1773-1812, 1814-1993 (DRO) Noted in 1831: CB 1773+ M 1757+
BT   CMB 1580-82, 1591-96, 1600-10, 1613-38, 1670-1751, 1753-83, 1796-1831, 1847-79 (W&SRO)
Cop CMB 1548-1812 (Ptd PRS: 1896); C 1549-1837 M 1549-1837 B 1549-1835 (DRO); M 1552-1628, 1640-41, 1662-71, 1695-1704, 1726-42, 1757-1836 (SG); M 1580-1744 from BT (DRO); C 1790-1837 M 1814-36 B 1813-37 (PRI); M 1790-1812 (Pallot); M 1552-1836 from OR, 1580-1814 from BT (DMI); B 1549-1837 (DBI)
Cop (Mf) CMB 1548-1812 (Mf of PRS, SLC); CMB 1549-1812 (Mf of Ms, SLC); CB 1580-1879 M 1580-1831 (Mf of BT, DRO, SLC); CM 1549-1812 (Printout, Mf SLC); Extr C 1549-1879 M 1549-1831 (IGI)
MI   (S&DFHS); (DFHS); (DRO); Ch cy 1975 (SG)

BELCHALWELL St Aldhelm [Cranborne Hundred; Sturminster Union 1835-84] [205] Now with HAZLEBURY BRYAN AND THE HILLSIDE PARISHES benefice.
OR   C 1842-1998 M 1760-1971 B 1821-1998 Banns 1754-67, 1843-83 (DRO) *see also* FIFEHEAD NEVILLE. Noted in 1831: CMB 1660-69, 1695-1740 CB 1744-1812 M 1754-1812
BT   CMB 1733, 1737-1879 (W&SRO)
Cop C 1813-37 M 1733-1837 B 1730-47, 1821-41 (DRO); CM 1813-37 B 1821-40 (PRI); M 1733-1838; entries from FIFEHEAD NEVILLE registers CB 1703, 1713-22, 1730-1800 (S&DFHS, SG); M 1733-60 from BT (DRO); M 1754-1838 from OR, 1733-60, 1810-13 from BT (DMI); B 1821-39 (DBI)
Cop (Mf) CB 1735?-1879 M 1735?-1839 (Mf of BT, DRO, SLC); Extr C 1735-1879 M 1735-1839 from BT (IGI)

BELCHALWELL (Wes) [1882 Return]; (Meth) n.d. [Kelly 1939]

BERE REGIS St John the Baptist [Bere Regis Hundred; Wareham and Purbeck Union] [1483] Peculiar of the Dean of Sarum until 1847. Included hamlet of MILBORNE STILEHAM until 1890 (when latter joined MILBORNE ST ANDREW); and chapelry of WINTERBORNE KINGSTON until 1972; and tithing of Shitterton. Now with AFFPUDDLE, TURNERSPUDDLE.
OR   C 1788-1981 M 1788-1989 B 1788-1927 Banns 1835-1971; M 1732-50 in incumbent's memoranda (DRO) Noted in 1831: 'the earlier Registers were destroyed by fire (with the Vicarage House) in 1788'. *see also* MILBORNE STILEHAM
BT   CMB 1585-94, 1603-08, 1613-26, 1627-35, 1638-40, 1665-95, 1698-1812, 1814-79 (W&SRO)
Cop CB 1585-1786, 1790-1837 M 1585-1837 (DRO); C 1790-1837 MB 1813-37 (PRI); M 1788-1837 (SG); M 1585-1788 from BT (DRO); M 1585-94 (Boyd); M 1788-1837 from OR, 1585-1786 from BT, 1608 from Hutchins, 1732-50 from incumbent memoranda (DMI); B 1777-1837 (DBI); Extr CMB 1585-1713 (SG)
Cop (Mf) CB 1585-1879 M 1585-1836 (Mf of BT, DRO, SLC); Extr C 1585-1879 M 1585-1836 from BT (IGI)
MI   (S&DFHS); (DFHS); (DRO)

BERE REGIS (Cong) f 1662 [*Cong. Yearbook* 1871] [Kelly 1939]

BERE REGIS (Wes) [Harrod 1865] [1882 Return]; Meth [Kelly 1939]

BERE REGIS (Wes) Bere Heath [1882 Return]; (Meth) [Kelly 1939] Dorchester Circuit

BERE REGIS (S of F) Constituent meeting of POOLE MM *q.v.* Closed before 1804.

BETTISCOMBE St Stephen [Frampton Liberty; Beaminster Union] [65] Included in Peculiar of Manor and Liberty of Frampton. Rebuilt 1862. Joined 1953 by chapelries of Marshwood and Fishpond from WHITCHURCH CANONICORUM. Now with GOLDEN CAP Team Benefice.
OR C 1746-1963 M 1746-1808, 1814-1963 B 1746-1991 Banns 1824-1976 (DRO)
    No earlier register noted in 1831, under 'Batiscombe'.
BT CMB 1732-41, 1748, 1751-81, 1785-1879 (W&SRO)
Cop C 1790-1837 M 1746-1836 (DRO, PRI); M 1747-63, 1805-13 from BT (DRO);
    M 1746-71, 1778-1804, 1813-36 (SG); M 1824-36 (Phil Ms at SG);
    M 1824-36 (Boyd); M 1746-1836 from OR, 1732-63, 1812-14 from BT (DMI);
    B 1813-1993 (DBI)
Cop (Mf) CB 1732-1879 M 1732-1836 (Mf of BT, DRO, SLC); M 1824-36 (Mf of
         Phil Ms, SLC); Extr C 1732-1879 M 1732-1836 from BT (IGI)

BETTISCOMBE (Presb) Licence to John Pinney, for his house, 1672

BEXINGTON Ancient parish united 1451 to PUNCKNOWLE.

BINCOMBE Holy Trinity [Frampton Liberty; Weymouth Union] [177] Included in Peculiar of Manor and Liberty of Frampton. United 1970 with BROADWAY. Now also with UPWEY, BUCKLAND RIPERS.
OR C 1658-1991 M 1658-1753, 1759-1948 B 1658-1991 Banns 1824-1992 (DRO)
    Noted in 1831: 'Bap. 1657-1668, and 1795; Bur. 1657-1670 and 1799;
    Marr. 1657-1688 and 1731, some leaves appear to have been cut out '
    see also BROADWEY
BT CMB 1731-1879 (W&SRO)
Cop C 1786-1837 M 1658-1837 B 1658-1812 (DRO); C 1658-1812 M 1658-1853
    B 1658-1813 (SG); C 1786-1837 M 1658-1838 B 1813-37 (PRI); M 1731-59,
    1813-15 from BT (DRO); M 1658-1753, 1759-1837 from OR, 1754-58, 1813-15
    from BT (DMI); B 1658-1991 (DBI)
Cop (Mf) CB 1731-1879 M 1731-1848 (Mf of BT, DRO, SLC); Extr C 1731-1879
         M 1731-1848 from BT (IGI)
MI (S&DFHS); (DFHS); (DRO)

BINDON ABBEY   *see* WOOL

BINNEGAR   *see* EAST STOKE

BISHOP'S CAUNDLE *see* CAUNDLE, BISHOP'S

BLACKDOWN   *see* BROADWINDSOR

BLAGDON   tithing of CRANBORNE

BLANDFORD FORUM St Peter and St Paul [Coombs Ditch Hundred; Blandford Union] [3109] Rebuilt after fire, 1733-39. Now with LANGTON LONG BLANDFORD.
OR C 1732-1899 M 1731-1927 B 1732-1921 Banns 1823-1918, 1964-84 (DRO)
BT CMB 1738-1812, 1814-79 (W&SRO)
Cop CB 1731-1883 M 1731-1883 (DRO); CB 1732-1883 M 1731-1859 (SG);
    C 1732-1851 M 1731-1859 B 1732-1842 (I, SG); C 1732-1851 M 1731-1859
    B 1732-1859 (DCM); C 1790-1837 M 1813-37 B 1813-42 (PRI); M 1731-1837
    from OR (DMI); B 1743-1843 (DBI)
Cop (Mf) CMB 1738-1879 (Mf of BT, DRO, SLC); Extr C 1738-1879 M 1738-1848
         from BT (IGI)
MI (S&DFHS); (DFHS); (DRO); Cy 1931 (SG); Blandford School Close (S&DFHS)

BLANDFORD FORUM Blandford School of Signals Church.

BLANDFORD FORUM St Leonard's Chapel Now part of a range of barns.

BLANDFORD FORUM (RC) Mission 1813-30 served jointly with Sion House, Spetisbury. Succeeded by Our Lady of Lourdes and St Cecilia, White Cliff Mill Street f 1926.

BLANDFORD FORUM (RC) Army camp chaplaincy, served from BLANDFORD.

BLANDFORD FORUM (Anabaptist) Licence to John Persons, for his house, 1672.

BLANDFORD FORUM (Ind/Cong now URC) Salisbury Street f 1662. Rebuilt 1867 [*Cong. Yearbook* 1871] [1882 Return] [Kelly 1939]
OR ZC 1760-1816 C 1818-36 B 1803-17, 1819-37 (RG 4/2404, 531, 2405, PRO)
Cop C 1760-1836 B 1803-08, 1817-37 (DRO, S&DFHS, SG); B 1803-37 (DBI)
Cop (Mf) CB 1780-1808; ZCB 1803-37 (Mf of OR, SLC); C 1760-1836 (Printout, MF SLC); Extr C 1760-1836 (IGI)

BLANDFORD FORUM (Cong) Licences for houses of Richard Spicer and John Paige, 1672.

BLANDFORD FORUM (Wes) House of John Twentyman in the Doctors Close registered 1789 [Biggs] Blandford and Sturminster Circuit, later Stour Valley Meth Circuit. 'In the Plocks' [1882 Return]; The Close erected 1850 [1882 Return] [Kelly 1939] Wimborne Circuit
OR C 1864-82, 1905-71 (DRO)

BLANDFORD FORUM (Prim Meth) Blandford Circuit. Later Stour Valley Meth Circuit
OR C 1875-1970 (DRO)

BLANDFORD FORUM (Prim Meth) Albert Street. Erected 1877 [1882 Return] [Kelly 1939]
OR M 1912-71 (DRO)

BLANDFORD FORUM (S of F) Constituent meeting of POOLE MM *q.v.* Closed before 1804.

BLANDFORD FORUM ('Who object to be designated') Ragged School, Bryanston Street [1882 Return]

BLANDFORD FORUM ('Who object to be designated') East Streeet Hall, East Street [1882 Return]; (Open Brethren) East Street. Erected 1882 [Kelly 1903, 1939]

BLANDFORD FORUM (Brethren) Assembly Rooms, and Iron Room, Alexandra Street [Harrod 1865]

BLANDFORD FORUM Blandford Cemetery, Salisbury Road. (Blandford Forum Town Council)

BLANDFORD FORUM Blandford Poor Law Union Workhouse, East Street. New building Salisbury Road erected 1856-57. Demolished in 1970s.

BLANDFORD ST MARY St Mary [Coombs Ditch Hundred; Blandford Union] [363] Included LITTLETON ancient parish from 1430. Now with SPETISBURY, CHARLTON MARSHALL.
OR C 1581-1889 M 1594-1953 B 1586-1942 Banns 1823-50, 1882-91 (DRO)
BT CMB 1732-92, 1796-1823, 1826-79 (W&SRO)
Cop M 1700-1918 (Ptd NQSD 28: 1961-67: 65, 98, 100); C 1581-1837
M 1594-1837 B 1586-1837 (DRO); CMB 1581-1812 Banns 1804-12 (S&DFHS,
SG); C 1790-1837 MB 1813-37 (PRI); M 1594-1841 from OR (DMI);
B 1586-1837 (DBI)
Cop (Mf) M 1700-1918 (Mf of Cop, SLC); CB 1732-1879 M 1732-1848 (Mf of BT,
DRO, SLC); Extr C 1732-1879 M 1708-18, 1732-1849 from BT (IGI)
MI (S&DFHS); (DFHS); (DRO); Cy, cemetery (SG); (Ptd T.Almack *A village
heritage: the story of Blandford St Mary*: 1962)

BLOXWORTH or **BLOCKSWORTH** St Andrew [Coombs Ditch Hundred; Wareham and Purbeck Union] [251] Peculiar of the Dean of Sarum, until 1847. Now with RED POST benefice.
OR C 1579-1970 M 1581-1648, 1654-57, 1662-1837 B 1579-1992 Banns 1823-25,
1919-84 (DRO)
BT CMB 1591-94, 1600-40, 1666, 1669-95, 1701-1830, 1847-79 (W&SRO)
Cop C 1579-1716, 1813-37 M 1581-1837 B 1579-1716, 1813-37 (DRO);
C 1579-1870 M 1581-1869 B 1579-1869 (SG); C 1790-1837 MB 1813-37 (PRI);
M 1591-1754 from BT (DRO); M 1790-1837 (Pallot); M 1581-1837 from OR,
1591-1754 from BT (DMI); B 1813-37 (DBI)
Cop (Mf) CB 1591-1879 M 1591-1830 (Mf of BT, DRO, SLC); Extr C 1591-1879
M 1591-1830 from BT (IGI)
MI 1638-1939 (S&DFHS); (DFHS); (DRO); Ch cy 1971 (SG)

BLOXWORTH (Prim Meth) 'close to the Heath' [Kelly 1903]

BOROUGH, NEW, AND LEIGH *see* WIMBORNE MINSTER

BOTHENHAMPTON or **BAUNTON** Holy Trinity [Loders and Bothenhampton Liberty; Bridport Union] [424] Old church disused; redundant 1971: Churches Conservation Trust. New church of Holy Trinity erected 1887-89. Now with BRIDPORT benefice.
OR C 1726-1977 M 1734-1992 B 1725/6-1915 Banns 1754-1809; M 1636-1714 in
LODERS register (DRO) No earlier registers noted in 1831.
BT CMB 1731-1879 (W&SRO)
Cop M 1636-1812 (Ptd Phil 1: 1906; & on CD-ROM); C 1813-37 M 1734-1837
B 1813-37 (DRO); C 1790-1837 M 1734-1837 B 1813-37 (PRI); M 1731-34
from BT (DRO); M 1636-41, 1734-1837 (SG); M 1636-75, 1700-1812 (Boyd);
M 1790-1812 (Pallot); M 1734-1837 from OR, 1731-54, 1813-37, 1846 from
BT, 1636-1733 from Phil (DMI); B 1725-1915 (DBI)
Cop (Mf) M 1636-1812 (Mf of Phil, SLC); CB 1731-1879 (Mf of BT, DRO, SLC);
Extr C 1731-1879 M 1731-1837 from BT (IGI)
MI (DRO) Cy 1901 (*Ye Olde Mortality* 3: Ms, SG)

BOTHENHAMPTON ((Presb) Licence for house of William Sampson, 1672

BOURNEMOUTH [Hampshire] Transferred to Dorset 1974. Became a unitary authority in 1997.
OR *see* NIPR Vol.8 Part 6 Hampshire

BOURTON *see* GILLINGHAM

BOVERIDGE *see* CRANBORNE

BOVINGTON CAMP *see* WOOL

BRADFORD ABBAS St Mary [Sherborne Hundred; Sherborne Union] [595] United 1824 with CLIFTON MAYBANK. Now also with THORNFORD, BEER HACKETT.
OR   C 1579-83, 1588-1982 M 1580-83, 1588-1728, 1754-1989 B 1579-83, 1588-1992 Banns 1654/5-1658, 1754-1812, 1860-1926, 1930-85 (DRO)
BT   CMB 1729, 1732, 1737, 1739-1811, 1813-34, 1836-75 (W&SRO)
Cop CMB 1572-76, 1579-81 (Ptd NQSD 17: 1923: 259-62; and on web-site *www.melcombe.freeserve.co.uk/dorset/lookups.htm*); C 1572-1652, 1790-1812 M 1572-1836 B 1572-1651, 1750-1837 (DRO); C 1572-81 M 1580-1733, 1754-1836 (SG); C 1813-37 (I, DRO); M 1729-54 from BT (DRO); C 1729-1875 M 1729-47 from BT, VRI); C 1790-1837 M 1572-1836 B 1813-37 (PRI); M 1580-1836 from OR, 1729-54 from BT (DMI); B 1813-37 (DBI);
Cop (Mf) CB 1729-1875 M 1729-1847 (Mf of BT, DRO, SLC); Extr C 1729-1875 M 1729-1847 from BT (IGI)
MI   (S&DFHS); (DFHS); (DRO); Ch cy 1974 (SG)

BRADFORD ABBAS (Presb) Licences to Jeremiah French and Benjamin Walters for their houses, 1672

BRADFORD ABBAS (Meth) n.d. [Kelly 1939]

BRADFORD PEVERELL St Mary, now Church of the Assumption [George Hundred; Dorchester Union] [330 including Muckleford] Rebuilt 1849-51. Now with STRATTON, FRAMPTON, SYDLING ST NICHOLAS.
OR   C 1653-1883 M 1653-1712, 1721-26, 1732-1810, 1815-1982 B 1654-80, 1696-1992 Banns 1852-1969 (DRO) Noted in 1831: CMB 1653+.
     see NQSD copy below for MB 1572-82 from an early fragment.
BT   CMB 1732-1879 (W&SRO)
Cop MB 1572-82 (Ptd NQSD 17: 1923: 262-67; and on web-site *www.melcombe. freeserve.co.uk/dorset/lookups.htm*); CMB 1572-1800 (SG, SLC); C 1572-82 M 1578-81, 1653-1836 (SG); CB 1572-82, 1813-37 M 1578-1837 (DRO); C 1796-1879 M 1796-1837 from BT (VRI); C 1790-1837 M 1578-1838 B 1813-37 (PRI); M 1732-54, 1810-15 from BT (DRO); M 1578-81, 1653-1838 from OR, 1732-54, 1810-15 from BT, 1572-1653 from NQSD and SG copies (DMI); B 1572-1837 (DBI);
Cop (Mf) CMB 1572-1800 (Mf of Cop, SLC); CB 1732-1879 M 1732-1837 (Mf of BT, DRO, SLC); CM 1572-96 (Printout, Mf SLC); Extr C 1572-1879 M 1572-1837 (IGI)

BRADFORD PEVERELL Mission Room, Muckleford [Kelly 1903]

BRADLE tithing of CHURCH KNOWLE [97]

BRADPOLE Holy Trinity [Beaminster Forum and Redhone Hundred; Bridport Union] [1018] Rebuilt 1845-46. Now with BRIDPORT benefice.
OR   C 1695-1996 M 1695-1990 B 1695-1993 Banns 1754-1808, 1823-1982 (DRO)
BT   CMB 1731-1836, 1841, 1844-78 (W&SRO)
Cop M 1695-1812 (Ptd Phil 1: 1906; & on CD-ROM); C 1695-1835 B 1695-1849 (Ms 2702, GL); C 1790-1837 M 1695-1837 B 1813-37 (DRO); C 1731-1878 1731-1836 from BT (VRI); C 1790-1837 MB 1813-37 (PRI); M 1595-1837 (SG); M 1731-58 from BT (DRO); M 1695-1812 (Boyd); M 1790-1812 (Pallot); M 1695-1837 from OR, 1731-58 from BT (DMI); B 1813-37 (DBI);
Cop (Mf) C 1695-1835 B 1695-1849 (Mf of Ms, SLC); M 1693-1812 (Mf of Phil, SLC); CB 1731-1878 M 1731-1836 (Mf of BT, DRO, SLC); Extr C 1731-1878 M 1731-1836 from BT (IGI)
MI   Cy 1901 (*Ye Olde Mortality* 3: Ms, SG)

BRADPOLE (Wes) House occupied by George Bartley registered 1797 [Biggs]

BRANKSEA *see* STUDLAND

BRANKSOME Civil parish created 1894 from KINSON. Joined POOLE civil parish 1905.[Poole Union 1894-1905] For ecclesistical parish, see CANFORD MAGNA.

BREDY, LITTLE *see* LITTLEBREDY

BREDY, LONG or LONGBREDY St Peter [Eggerton Hundred; Dorchester Union] [333] Included chapelry of LITTLEBREDY and hamlet of KINGSTON RUSSELL. Now with BRIDE VALLEY benefice.
OR C 1628-35, 1649-1999 M 1628-38, 1649/50-1995 B 1628-35, 1649-1998 Banns 1778-98, 1824-83 (DRO) Noted in 1831: CMB 1649+. 'The register dates regularly from the year 1649 but retains a few leaves from 1628' [Kelly 1903]
BT CMB 1732-1812, 1814-80 (W&SRO)
Cop C 1628-36, 1649-1837 M 1630-1839 B 1628-1812 (DRO); C 1732-1880 M 1732-1838 from BT (VRI); C 1813-37 M 1630-1839 (PRI); C 1627-1796 (S&DFHS); M 1630, 1635-37, 1649, 1652-1839 (SG); M 1630-1839 from OR, 1732-54 from BT (DMI); B 1627-1998 (DBI)
Cop (Mf) CB 1732-1880 M 1732-1838 (Mf of BT, DRO, SLC); Extr C 1732-1880 M 1732-1838 from BT (IGI)
MI Ch (Ptd *Miscellanea Genealogica et Heraldica*. series 5: 8: 1932: 336-37)

BREDY, LONG (Prim Meth) Weymouth Circuit [Kelly 1903]
OR C 1937-66 (DRO)

BRIANTSPUDDLE or BRYANTSPUDDLE, tithing of AFFPUDDLE

BRIDE VALLEY Modern benefice including BURTON BRADSTOCK and CHILCOMBE, LITTLE BREDY, LITTON CHENEY, LONG BREDY, PUNCKNOWLE, SHIPTON GORGE, SWYRE

BRIDETON *see* BURTON BRADSTOCK

BRIDPORT Modern benefice including BRIDPORT, WEST BAY, ALLINGTON, BOTHENHAMPTON, BRADPOLE, WALDITCH.

BRIDPORT St Mary [Whitchurch Canonicorum Hundred; Bridport Union] [4242] Now with BRIDPORT Benefice.
OR C 1600-1976 M 1600-1991 B 1600-1898, 1956-66 Banns 1934-87 (DRO)
BT CMB 1731-1879 (W&SRO)
Cop CB 1600-38 M 1600-1837 (DRO); CB 1600-38 M 1600-80 (SG); C 1790-1837 B 1813-37 (I, DRO); C 1731-1879 M 1731-1836 from BT (VRI); C 1790-1837 MB 1813-37 (PRI); M 1600-1837 from OR (DMI); B 1600-1837 (DBI)
Cop (Mf) CB 1731-1879 M 1731-1836 (Mf of BT, DRO, SLC); Extr C 1731-1879 M 1731-1836 from BT (IGI)
MI (S&DFHS); (DFHS); (DRO); (SG); (Ts and Mf SLC)

BRIDPORT St Andrew, St Andrew's Road. Chapel-of-ease erected 1860. Redundant 1978. Sold for use as organ repair workshop.

BRIDPORT St Andrew, West Bay. Mission church served from BURTON BRADSTOCK [Kelly 1903]

BRIDPORT St John, West Bay. Erected 1939; served from BRIDPORT [Kelly 1939]. Now with BRIDPORT benefice.
OR 1939+ (Inc)

BRIDPORT Christ Church, East Road. *see* WALDITCH

BRIDPORT St Saviour, Dottery. *see* LODERS

BRIDPORT (RC) St William? and St Catherine, Victoria Grove. Erected 1846. New church 1978.
OR   C 1858+ M 1864+ DB 1857+ Confirmations 1865+ (Inc) For earlier entries *see* CHIDEOCK. Confirmations 1865, 1869, 1874, 1880, 1890, 1802-1935 (PDA)

BRIDPORT (Bapt) f 1830 [*Bapt. Handbook* 1861] Chardsmead, Victoria Grove. Erected 1841 [Kelly 1939]

BRIDPORT (Ind/Cong now URC) East Street. f 1662. Rebuilt 1859 [*Cong. Yearbook* 1871] [1882 Return] [Kelly 1939] Became Bridport United Church URC/Meth 1971

BRIDPORT (Cong) Licence to Richard Downe for house of John Golding; licences for houses of Elizabeth Hallett and John Coutines (Cousens ?), 1672

BRIDPORT (Ind) New Meeting, Barrack Street.
OR   C 1750-86 1786-1838 D 1750-86 (RG 4/71, 343, 457, 583, PRO)
Cop   C 1751-1836 B 1750-86 (DRO, S&DFHS, SG); B 1750-86 (DBI)
Cop (Mf)   C 1750-1836 D 1750-86 (Mf of OR, SLC); C 1750-1836 (Printout, Mf SLC)   Extr C 1750-1836 (IGI)

BRIDPORT (Presb)
OR   C 1720-64, 1769-87 ZC 1820-37 B 1820-35 (RG 4/2406, 2407, 344, 2160, PRO)
Cop   C 1720-1837 (DRO, S&DFHS)
Cop (Mf)   C 1720-64, 1769-87 ZC 1820-37 B 1820-35 (Mf of OR, SLC); C 1720-64 (Printout, Mf SLC); Extr C 1720-1837 (IGI)

BRIDPORT (Unit) East Street. f 1672. Erected 1690 ? Demolished 1791. Rebuilt 1794 [Kelly 1939]
OR   C 1720-1968, 1971 M 1865-1967 B 1820, 1825-35, 1843-84, 1927-69 (DRO)

BRIDPORT (Wes) Bridport Circuit. Including BEAMINSTER, BRIDPORT, BURTON BRADSTOCK, LYME REGIS, SALWAY ASH, NETTLECOMBE, SHIPTON GORGE, formerly in AXMINSTER CIRCUIT *q.v.*
OR   C 1837-49, 1885-1970 (DRO)

BRIDPORT (Wes) f *c.*1791 [Biggs] South Street erected 1838/39 [1882 Return] [Kelly 1939]
OR   ZC 1834-37 (RG 4/1227, PRO); C 1834-37 M 1891, 1907-70 (Devon RO)
Cop   C 1834-37 (DRO, S&DFHS)
Cop (Mf)   ZC 1834-37 (Mf of OR, SLC); C 1834-37 (Printout, Mf SLC); Extr C 1834-37 (IGI)

BRIDPORT (Wes) Bridport Harbour [Harrod 1865] [1882 Return]

BRIDPORT (Wes) West Bay. Erected 1849 [Kelly 1939]

BRIDPORT (S of F) Bridport Monthly Meeting
OR   C 1776-82 M 1782-83 B 1780-83 (DRO)

BRIDPORT (S of F) f 1697. Erected 1700. Meeting House, South Street [Harrod 1865] [1882 Return] [Kelly 1939] Part of Shaftesbury, Bridport and Sherborne Monthly Meeting *q.v.* under SHAFTESBURY
OR   Z 1778-99 M 1797-1803 B 1777-99 (RG 6/432-33, 1577, PRO)
Cop (Mf) Z 1778-99 M 1797-1803 B 1777-99 (Mf of OR, SLC)

BRIDPORT (Latter Day Saints)
OR   Records of members 1847-86 (SLC); records of members, Bristol Conference *c.*1896-47 (SLC)
Cop (Mf) Records of members 1847-86 (Mf of OR, SLC); records of members, Bristol Conference *c.*1896-47 (Mf of OR, SLC)

BRIDPORT (Plymouth Brethren) [Harrod 1865] A Building belonging to Mr Roper [1882 Return]; Rope Walks [Kelly 1903]

BRIDPORT (Christian Mission) Templars' Hall, Barrack Street [1882 Return]

BRIDPORT (Salvation Army) The Grove Rooms, Rope Walks [1882 Return]

BRIDPORT Poor Law Union Workhouse, Barracks Street and Bedford Place. Became Port Bredy Hospital 1948. Closed 1996 and converted into residences 1999.

BROADMAYNE formerly MAYNE MARTELL St Martin [George Hundred; Dorchester Union] [362] Now with WEST KNIGHTON, OWERMOIGNE, WARMWELL.
OR   C 1663-1962 M 1667-1744, 1754-1980 B 1663-1927 Banns 1877-1981 (DRO)
BT   CMB 1731-1811, 1813-33, 1840-80 (W&SRO)
Cop C 1663-1749, 1813-37 M 1667-1837 B 1663-1749, 1813-37 (DRO);
     C 1731-1880 M 1731-1833 from BT (VRI); C 1790-1837 M 1667-1837
     B 1813-37 (PRI); M 1667-1722, 1725-44, 1754-1837 (SG); M 1731-54 from
     BT (DRO); M 1667-1837 from OR, 1731-54 from BT (DMI); B 1802-39 (DBI)
Cop (Mf) CB 1731-1880 M 1731-1833 (Mf of BT, DRO, SLC); Extr C 1731-1880
          M 1731-1833 from BT (IGI)
MI   (S&DFHS); (DFHS); (DRO); (SG)

BROADMAYNE (Wes) [1882 Return]; (Meth) erected 1865 [Kelly 1939] Dorchester Circuit

BROADOAK   *see* SYMONDSBURY

BROADSTONE   *see* CANFORD MAGNA

BROADWEY or BROADWAY St Nicholas [Culliford Tree Hundred; Weymouth Union] [385] Rebuilt 1874. United 1970 with BINCOMBE. Now also with UPWEY, BUCKLAND RIPERS.
OR   C 1661-1977 M 1673-1966 B 1674-1956 Banns 1756-1937 (DRO) *and see* BINCOMBE
BT   CMB 1713-1879 (W&SRO)
Cop C 1731-1879 M 1731-1855 from BT (VRI); CB 1806-13 M 1673, 1695-1709,
     1720, 1730-1837 (SG); C 1797-1837 M 1673-1837 B 1813-37 (PRI);
     M 1731-56 from BT (DRO); M 1673-1837 from OR, 1731-56 from BT (DMI);
     B 1813-37 (I, DRO); B 1674-1837 (DBI)
Cop (Mf) CB 1731-1879 M 1731-1855 (Mf of BT, DRO, SLC); Extr C 1731-1879
          M 1731-1855 from BT (IGI)
MI   (S&DFHS); (DFHS); (DRO); Ch, cy, old and new graveyards, war memorial
     (SG)

BROADWEY (Wes) Erected 1839 [1882 Return] [Kelly 1903]; (Meth) erected 1928 [Kelly 1939] Weymouth Circuit

BROADWINDSOR St John the Baptist [Broadwindsor Liberty; Beaminster Union] [1570] Included hamlets of Blackdown and Netherhay and tithings of Childhay, Deberford and Drimpton; and Little Winsor [Redhone Hundred] United 1971 with BURSTOCK. Now with Beaminster Area benefice.
OR   C ?1562-73, 1582-86, 1592-1999 M 1563-1753, 1761-1984 B 1562-1611, 1625-39, 1648-1999 Banns 1762-83 1824-1922 (DRO) Noted in 1831: CMB 1563-1668 'much mutilated'. CB 1761-94 M 1753-61 'lost'. Register 1558+ 'but there are some previous entries which are much decayed. The registers have been rebound and carefully restored at the Record Office, London' [Kelly 1903]
BT   CMB 1731-1844, 1847-79 (W&SRO)
Cop M 1563-1812 (Ptd Phil 3: 1908; & on CD-ROM); C 1790-1837 B 1813-37 (DRO); C 1731-1879 M 1731-1838 from BT (VRI); C 1563-1669 (S&DFHS); C 1790-1837 MB 1813-37 (PRI); M 1750-61 from BT (DRO); M 1563-1775 (Boyd); M 1790-1812 (Pallot); M 1563-1837 from OR, 1750-61 from BT (DMI); B 1562-1880 (DBI)
Cop (Mf) M 1563-1812 (Mf of Phil, SLC); CB 1731-1879 M 1731-1838 (Mf of BT, DRO, SLC); Extr C 1731-1879 M 1731-1838 from BT (IGI)
MI   (S&DFHS); (DFHS); (DRO); (SG); (SLC)

BROADWINDSOR Holy Trinity, Blackdown. Erected 1839-40. Parish created from BROADWINDSOR. Now with Beaminster Area benefice.
Cop B 1841-44 (DBI)
MI   (S&DFHS); (DFHS); (DRO); (SG); (SLC)

BROADWINDSOR St Mary, Drimpton. Chapel-of-ease erected 1867. Now with Beaminster Area benefice.
MI   (S&DFHS); (DFHS); (DRO); (SG); (SLC)

BROADWINDSOR (Part Bapt) At Venn until 1860 when ejected members built own chapel, Ebenezer, at Stony Knapps, continuing to use old register. [1882 Return]
OR   C 1843-97, 1925 B 1851-91 (DRO)
Cop C 1843-97, 1925 (DRO); Venn C 1843-57 D 1852-94 B 1851-61; Stony Knapps C c.1864-97 D 1878-95 B 1862-91 (SG)

BROADWINDSOR (Part Bapt) Blackdown n.d. [Kelly 1903, 1939]

BROADWINDSOR (Presb) Licence for house of Edward Marks, 1672

BROADWINDSOR (Cong) Blackdown. Erected 1821 [*Cong. Yearbook* 1871] [Kelly 1939]

BROADWINDSOR (Ind/Cong) Venn. Out-station of BROADWINDSOR [*Cong. Yearbook* 1871]
OR   C 1891-1901, 1912 M 1906-29 B 1900-41 (DRO)

BROADWINDSOR (Ind/Cong) Little Winsor. Out-station of BROADWINDSOR [*Cong. Yearbook* 1871]

BROADWINDSOR (Wes) Netherhay Chapel. Erected 1838 [1882 Return] [Kelly 1939]

BROCKHAMPTON AND KNOWLE tithing of BUCKLAND NEWTON [162]

BROWNSEA ISLAND   *see* STUDLAND St Mary, Branksea

BRYANSTON St Martin [Pimperne Hundred; Blandford Union] [155] Old church, or Portman Chapel, erected 1745, redundant 1976; leased for use as private chapel. St Martin erected 1895-98; redundant 1973; now used by Bryanston School. Parish now with PIMPERNE, STOURPAINE, DURWESTON.
OR C 1598-1643, 1649-99, 1763-1973 M 1599-1637, 1756-1975 B 1598-1643, 1661-97, 1764-91, 1813-88, 1967 Banns 1903-75 (DRO)
BT CMB 1732-40, 1746-56, 1762-66, 1772-78, 1780-1837, 1847-78 (W&SRO)
Cop CB 1598-1899 M 1599-1637, 1756-1899 (DRO, SG); C 1598-1899 M 1599-1899 B 1598-1888 (Ts, DCM); CMB 1598-1837 (PRI); C 1732-1878 M 1732-1837 from BT (VRI); M 1731-56 from BT (DRO); M 1599-1637, 1756-1837 from OR, 1732-56, 1812 from BT (DMI); B 1598-1837 (DBI)
Cop (Mf) CB 1732-1878 M 1732-1837 (Mf of BT, DRO, SLC); Extr C 1732-1878 M 1732-1837 from BT (IGI)
MI Portman chapel (SG)

BRYANSTON Bryanston School. Using former St Martin's church.

BRYANTSPUDDLE or BRIANTSPUDDLE, tithing of AFFPUDDLE

BUCKHORN WESTON St John the Baptist [Redland Hundred; Wincanton Union 1835-94; Shaftesbury Union 1894-1930] [403] Now with GILLINGHAM benefice.
OR C 1677-1702, 1725-1952 M 1679-1702, 1725-1836, 1839-1992 B 1677-1702, 1726-1929 Banns 1823-80 (DRO)
BT CMB 1731-1879 (W&SRO)
Cop CB 1677-1702, 1725-65 M 1679-1837 (DRO); C 1731-1879 M 1731-1841 from BT (VRI); C 1766-1837 M 1679-1837 B 1813-37 (PRI); CB 1813-37 (I, DRO); M 1731-55 from BT (DRO); M 1679-1702, 1725-1836 (SG); M 1679-1836 from OR, 1731-55 from BT (DMI); B 1813-37 (DBI)
Cop (Mf) CB 1731-1879 M 1731-1841 (Mf of BT, DRO, SLC); Extr C 1731-1979 M 1731-1841 from BT (IGI)

BUCKHORN WESTON (Prim Meth) [1882 Return] [Kelly 1903]

BUCKLAND NEWTON or BUCKLAND ABBAS   Holy Rood [Buckland Newton Hundred; Cerne Union] [786] Included chapelry and tithing of PLUSH until 1937, and tithings of Brockhampton and Knowle, Buckland Newton, Duntish, Minterne Parva. Now with DUNGEON HILL benefice.
OR C 1568-1628, 1653-1981 M 1568-1625, 1654-1995 B 1568-1625, 1653-1974 Banns 1849-98 (DRO)
BT CMB 1731-1879 (W&SRO)
Cop CB 1568/9-1581 C 1790-1837 M 1568-1839 B 1813-37 (I, DRO); C 1790-1837 MB 1813-37 (PRI); C 1731-1879 M 1731-1855 from BT (VRI); M 1568-1625, 1654-1839 (SG); M 1731-53 from BT (DRO); M 1568-1839 from OR, 1731-53 from BT (DMI); B 1568-1974 (DBI)
Cop (Mf) CB 1731-1879 M 1731-1855 (Mf of BT, DRO, SLC); Extr C 1731-1879 M 1731-1855 from BT (IGI)
MI (S&DFHS); (DFHS); (DRO); Ch cy 1977 (SG)

BUCKLAND NEWTON St John the Baptist, Plush [154] Rebuilt 1848. Chapelry of BUCKLAND NEWTON until 1937 when divided between PIDDLETRENTHIDE and MAPPOWDER. Now with PIDDLETRENTHIDE, ALTON PANCRAS, PIDDLEHINTON. Redundant 1988. Sold for cultural and community purposes.
OR C 1850-1986 M 1851-1982 B 1850-1997 Banns 1851-1959 (DRO)
BT *see* BUCKLAND NEWTON
Cop C 1850-1966 M 1925-60 B 1850-1967 (DRO)
MI (S&DFHS); (DFHS); Cy (SG)

BUCKLAND NEWTON (Bapt) Henley f 1862 [Kelly 1939]
MI (S&DFHS); Burial ground 1977 (SG)

BUCKLAND NEWTON (Cong, now Cong Fed) Duntish f 1839 [Kelly 1939]

BUCKLAND NEWTON (Prim Meth) [1882 Return] [Kelly 1903]

BUCKLAND NEWTON (Prim Meth) House in the occupation of William Beck [1882 Return]

BUCKLAND RIPERS St Nicholas [Culliford Tree Hundred; Weymouth Union 1836-94] [115] Now with BINCOMBE, BROADWEY, UPWEY.
OR   C 1695-1708,   1724-30,   1736-1982 M 1695-1711, 1719,   1725-1810,
     1816-1949 B 1696-1706, 1719, 1724, 1730, 1751-1976 (DRO)
BT   CMB 1739-68, 1774-1840, 1847-79 (W&SRO)
Cop C 1695-1810 M 1695-1840 B 1695-1812 (DRO); CB 1695-1812 M 1695-1753
     (I, SG); CB 1813-36/7 (I, DRO); C 1739-1879 M 1739-1840 from BT (VRI);
     C 1813-37 M 1695-1840 B 1814-36 (PRI); M 1695-1710, 1719, 1724,
     1731-64, 1778-85, 1790, 1795-1810, 1816-40 (SG); M 1739-55, 1810-16
     from BT (DRO); M 1695-1840 from OR, 1739-55, 1810-16 from BT (DMI);
     B 1695-1836 (DBI)
Cop (Mf) CB 1739-1879 M 1739-1840 (Mf of BT, DRO, SLC); Extr C 1739-1879
        M 1739-1840 from BT (IGI)
MI   (S&DFHS); (DFHS); (DRO); Cy (SG)

BURLESTON [Puddletown Hundred; Dorchester Union] [67] 'Church taken down 1861 and rebuilt at Athelhampton, about 500 yards distant' [Harrod 1865] 'Inhabitants attend Athelhampton' [Kelly 1939] 'Demolished, except chancel' [Kelly 1903] United 1967 with PUDDLETOWN, ATHELHAMPTON. Remains redundant 1971; sold for use as monument.
OR M 1839-56 (DRO) *and see* ATHELHAMPTON. Noted in 1831: 'Burleston and
    Athelhampton', with Athelhampton dates.
BT   *see* ATHELHAMPTON
MI   (S&DFHS); (DFHS); (DRO); Extr: Pratt (Ms, SG); Ch cy 1972; cy 1975
    (SG)

BURSTOCK St Andrew [Whitchurch Canonicorum Hundred; Beaminster Union] [261] United 1971 with BROADWINDSOR. Now with Beaminster Area benefice.
OR C 1587-1653, 1688-1981 M 1560-1636, 1695-1979 B 1603-43, 1695-1981
    Banns 1754-83, 1870-91 (DRO) Noted in 1831: C 1688+ MB 1695+
BT   CMB 1731-78, 1781-1845, 1847-78 (W&SRO)
Cop M 1563-1636, 1699-1811 Phil 4: 1909; & on CD-ROM); CB 1813-37
    M 1560-1837 (I, DRO); C 1790-1837 MB 1813-37 (PRI); C 1731-1878
    M 1731-1842 from BT (VRI); M 1560-1636, 1695-1723, 1728-1837 (SG);
    M 1563-1636, 1699-1812 (Boyd); M 1790-1812 (Pallot); M 1560-1837 from
    OR (DMI); B 1758-1837 (DBI)
Cop (Mf) M 1563-1812 (Mf of Phil, SLC); CB 1731-1878 M 1731-1842 (Mf of BT,
       DRO, SLC); Extr.C 1731-1878 M 1731-1842 from BT (IGI)
MI   (S&DFHS); (DRO); (SG); (SLC)

BURSTOCK (Presb) Licence for house of Matthew Bragg, 1672

BURTON Parish formed from Christchurch [Hampshire]. Transferred to Dorset 1974.
OR *see* NIPR Vol.8 Part 6 Hampshire

BURTON BRADSTOCK formerly BRIDETON St Mary [Frampton Liberty; Bridport Union] [1068] Included chapelry of SHIPTON GORGE, United 1954 with CHILCOMBE. Now with BRIDE VALLEY benefice.
OR C 1614-40, 1658-1907 M 1614-39, 1660-1966, 1976-90 B 1614-40, 1660-82,
    1740-1982 Banns 1754-1812, 1823-1920 (DRO) Noted in 1831: Nos. V, VI
    Marr. (for Burton and Shipton) 1755-1812.

BURTON BRADSTOCK cont.
BT   CMB 1731-32, 1740-1843, 1847-79; including SHIPTON GORGE 1732, 1744,
        1748, 1750-79, 1781-1811 (W&SRO)
Cop M 1614-1812 (Ptd Phil 5: 1910; & on CD-ROM); C 1610-40, 1658-1782,
        1790-1837 M 1614-1837 B 1614-40, 1660-77, 1740-82, 1813-37 (DRO);
        C 1614-39, 1659-69 M 1614-39, 1660-63 B 1614-39, 1660-68 (SG);
        C 1731-1879 M 1731-1836 from BT (VRI); C 1790-1837 MB 1813-37 (PRI);
        M 1731-54 from BT (DRO); M 1614-1837 (SG); M 1614-1812 (Boyd);
        M 1790-1812 (Pallot); M 1614-1837 from OR, 1731-54 from BT (DMI);
        B 1758-1837 (DBI)
Cop (Mf) M 1614-1812 (Mf of Phil, SLC); CB 1731-1879 M 1731-1836 (Mf of BT,
        DRO, SLC); Extr C 1731-1879 M 1731-1836 from BT (IGI)

BURTON BRADSTOCK St Martin, Shipton Gorge [Gooderthorne Hundred; Bridport
Union] [316] Chapelry in BURTON BRADSTOCK. Rebuilt 1861-62. Now with BRIDE
VALLEY benefice.
OR   C 1813-73 M 1814-1967 (DRO) M 1755-1812 *see* BURTON BRADSTOCK.
        Noted in 1831: 'Entered in the Registers of Burton Bradstock'.
BT   CMB 1745-46, 1749-50, 1790-92, 1813-14, 1817-79; for 1732, 1744, 1748,
        1750-79, 1781-1811 *see* BURTON BRADSTOCK (W&SRO)
Cop M 1614-1812 with Burton Bradstock (Ptd Phil 5: 1910; & on CD-ROM);
        C 1659-77, 1706-31, 1740-82 M 1626-1836 B 1676-77 (DRO); C 1813-37
        M 1814-37 (PRI); C 1813-38 (I, DRO); M 1626-39, 1646-1837 (SG);
        M 1790-1812 (Pallot); M 1626-1837 from OR (DMI); B 1848-1950 (DBI);
        CMB 1745-1879 from BT (Pine: CD 1); *and see* BURTON BRADSTOCK.
Cop (Mf) M 1614-1812 (Mf of Phil, SLC); C 1745-49, 1766, 1792, 1813-79
        M 1749, 1768, 1790, 1813-79 B 1749, 1768, 1792, 1813-79 (Mf of BT,
        DRO, SLC); Extr C 1745-49, 1768, 1792, 1813-79 M 1749, 1768, 1790,
        1813-79 from BT (IGI)

BURTON BRADSTOCK (Cong) Shipton. Out-station of BRIDPORT
[*Cong. Yearbook* 1871]

BURTON BRADSTOCK (Wes) Erected 1825 [1882 Return]; (Meth) [Kelly 1939]
OR   *see* AXMINSTER [Devon] and BRIDPORT Circuits

BURTON BRADSTOCK (Wes) Shipton Gorge. Erected 1849 [1882 Return]
[Kelly 1903]; Meth [Kelly 1939]
OR   *see* AXMINSTER [Devon] and BRIDPORT Circuits

BURTON, EAST   *see* WINFRITH NEWBURGH

BURTON, LONG   *see* LONGBURTON

BUSHEY   *see* CORFE CASTLE

CAME   *see* WINTERBORNE CAME

CANFORD MAGNA or GREAT CANFORD   dedication unknown [Cogdean Hundred; Poole
Union] [3100] Royal Peculiar until 1847. Included chapelry of POOLE St
James until 1538, tithing of PARKSTONE (separate parish 1834), tithing of
LONGFLEET (separate parish 1837); and tithing of KINSON or Kingston
(separate parish 1865)
OR   C 1563-1927 M 1563-1641, 1652-67, 1675-1969 B 1567/8-1646, 1652-1906
        Banns 1757-74, 1870-1969 (DRO) Included note of RC baptisms at Canford
        House 1810-18. Noted in 1831: CB 1656+ M 1661+:'no other Registers can
        be found.'
BT   CMB 1813-79 including KINSON (W&SRO)

CANFORD MAGNA cont.

Cop C 1563-1866 M 1563-1837 (DRO); C 1813-79 M 1813-42 from BT (VRI);
C 1790-1837 MB 1813-37 (PRI); M 1656-69, 1673-83, 1686-1837 (SG);
M 1656-1837 from OR, 1637 from Hutchins (DMI); B 1813-37 (I, DRO);
B 1750-1837 (DBI)

Cop (Mf) C 1656-1979 M 1656-69, 1674-1900, 1922-92 B 1656-68, 1674-84,
1709-1960 Banns 1754-1812, 1900-71, 1978-91 Confirmations 1910-90
(Mf, OKHC); CB 1813-79 M 1813-42 (Mf of BT, DRO, SLC);
Extr C 1813-79 M 1813-42 from BT (IGI)

MI (S&DFHS); (DFHS); (DRO); Canford burial ground (S&DFHS)

CANFORD MAGNA St John the Baptist, Macauley Road, Broadstone Erected 1888
as chapel-of-ease to CANFORD MAGNA. Parish created 1906 from CANFORD MAGNA,
LONGFLEET.

OR C 1887-1993 M 1903-89 B 1914-91 Banns 1988-97 (DRO)

Cop C 1887-1955 (DRO, PRI); C 1887-1939 M 1903-22 (surname indexes,
S&DFHS)

CANFORD MAGNA Ashington Mission Church. Erected 1900 [Kelly 1939]

CANFORD MAGNA The Lantern, Sopwith Crescent, Merley, Wimborne. Erected
c.1975 in parish of CANFORD MAGNA.

OR *see* CANFORD MAGNA

CANFORD MAGNA Bearwood Church, King John Avenue, Bearwood. Erected 1982 in
parish of CANFORD MAGNA.

OR *see* CANFORD MAGNA

> Churches in the area of the ancient parish of Canford Magna are
> here grouped for convenience under its three 19th century daughter
> parishes from which they were formed.

PARKSTONE

CANFORD MAGNA St Peter, Parkstone [Cogdean Hundred from 1866; Poole Union
1835-1905] [609] Tithing of Parkstone in CANFORD MAGNA. Parish created
1834. United 1971 with BRANKSEA. Now also with PARKSTONE St Osmund.

OR C 1833-1992 M 1839-1988 B 1833-1992 Banns 1839-1987 (DRO)

BT CMB 1847-79 (W&SRO)

Cop C 1833-37 (I, DRO, PRI); C 1847-79 from BT (VRI); B 1833-55 (DBI)

Cop (Mf) C 1833-1990 M 1839-1980 B 1833-1992 Banns 1943-57, 1984-87
Confirmations 1933-63 (Mf, PLHC); CB 1847-79 (Mf of BT, DRO, SLC);
Extr C 1847-79 from BT (IGI)

MI (S&DFHS); (DFHS); (DRO); Extr (Ptd *Records of the Church of St Peter,
Parkstone*: 1926)

CANFORD MAGNA Russell Coates Nautical School Chapel (Dr Barnardo's Home)
(Boys from all over the country)

OR C 1930-64 (DRO with records of St Peter)

Cop (Mf) C 1930-64 (Mf, PLHC)

CANFORD MAGNA Parkstone Sea Training School

OR C 1951-64 (DRO with records of St Peter)

Cop (Mf) C 1951-64 (Mf, PLHC)

CANFORD MAGNA All Saints, Western Road, Branksome Park. Erected 1877.
Parish created 1878 from PARKSTONE St Peter, KINSON

OR C 1878-1955 M 1878-1987 B 1878-1976 Banns 1878-1908, 1919-72 (DRO)

Cop CMB 1895-97 on web-site *www.melcombe.freeserve.co.uk/dorset/lookups.htm*

CANFORD MAGNA St Aldhelm, St Aldhelm's Road, Branksome Park. Erected 1892-94. Parish created 1930 from BRANKSOME PARK, PARKSTONE St Osmund.
OR   C 1876-1989 M 1918-90 Banns 1918-88 (DRO)
Cop CMB 1895-97 on web-site *www.melcombe.freeserve.co.uk/dorset/lookups.htm*

CANFORD MAGNA The Holy Angels, Lilliput Road, Sandbanks. Erected 1874. Parish created 1962 from PARKSTONE St Peter.
OR   C 1928-65 M 1908-71 Banns 1908-81 (DRO)

CANFORD MAGNA St Luke, Sandecotes Road / Wellington Road, Parkstone. Chapel-of-ease. Iron church erected 1900. Parish created 1903 from PARKSTONE St Peter
OR   C 1904-50 M 1908-73 Banns 1908-74 (DRO)

CANFORD MAGNA St Osmund, St Osmund's Road / Bournemouth Road, Parkstone Parish created 1911 from PARKSTONE St Peter. Erected 1913-16. Redundant 2001. *see also* BRANKSOME St Aldhelm. Now with PARKSTONE St Peter, BRANKSEA.
OR   C 1911-69 M 1911-79 B 1911-29 Banns 1911-69 (DRO)
Cop (Mf) Banns 1938-69 (Mf, PLHC)

CANFORD MAGNA Church of the Transfiguration, Chaddesley Glen, Canford Cliffs and Sandbanks. Parish created 1956 from PARKSTONE St Peter. Wooden building erected 1911. Conventional district 1945. New building 1962-65.
OR   M 1924-64 (DRO)

CANFORD MAGNA St Nicholas Chapel, Panorama Road, Sandbanks. Wooden building erected 1930. New building 1982. In parish of Canford Cliffs and Sandbanks.

LONGFLEET

CANFORD MAGNA St Mary, Longfleet Road, Longfleet [840] Hamlet and tithing of Longfleet in Canford Magna. Erected 1833; separate parish 1837. Rebuilt 1913-15. *see also* BROADSTONE, OAKDALE
OR   C 1833-1968 M 1838-1985 B 1833-1935 Banns 1908-18, 1913-80 (DRO)
BT   CMB 1847-80 (W&SRO)
Cop CB 1833-37 (I, DRO, PRI); B 1833-1904 (DBI)
Cop (Mf) C 1833-1968 M 1838-1969 B 1833-1935 Banns 1960-80 (Mf, PLHC);
         CB 1847-80 (Mf of BT, DRO, SLC); Extr C 1847-80 from BT (IGI)
MI   (DRO); (S&DFHS); (DFHS)

CANFORD MAGNA St George, Darbys Lane, Oakdale. Parish created 1946 from LONGFLEET. Part of OAKDALE ST GEORGE benefice.
OR   C 1938-73 M 1945-77 Banns 1945-80 (DRO)

CANFORD MAGNA St Paul, Culliford Crescent, Canford Heath. Erected 1981 (now church hall). New building 1989. Part of OAKDALE ST GEORGE benefice.
OR   CM 1981+ (Inc) No burial ground.

CANFORD MAGNA Christ Church, Northmead Road, Creekmoor.
(C of E/URC/Bapt/Meth) Part of OAKDALE ST GEORGE benefice

KINSON

CANFORD MAGNA St Andrew, Millhams Road, Kinson (or Kingston) [775] Tithing in CANFORD MAGNA; separate parish 1865. *see also* BRANKSOME PARK, HEATHERLANDS, BRANKSOME St Clement, TALBOT VILLAGE, ENSBURY; and BOURNEMOUTH [Hampshire] St John the Evangelist in NIPR Vol.8 Part 6 Hampshire.

CANFORD MAGNA St Andrew, Kinson cont.
OR C 1680-1891, 1915-75 M 1680-1981, 1985-92 B 1686-1956 Banns 1756-1812,
1908-56, 1982-92 (DRO)
BT *see* CANFORD MAGNA
Cop C 1680-1837 M 1680-1837 B 1686-1790 (DRO); C 1697-1711, 1715-17
B 1707-21 (S&DFHS); CMB 1813-37 (PRI); CB 1813-37 (I, DRO); M 1680-85,
1691-1837 (SG); M 1680-1837 from OR (DMI); B 1813-37 (DBI);
Extr M 1683-1720 (S&DFHS)
MI (S&DFHS); (DFHS); (DRO); Ch cy index *c.*1963 (SG)

CANFORD MAGNA Emmanuel, Kinson Road, Kinson. In parish of KINSON St Andrew.
Meeting in East Howe URC.
OR None. *see* KINSON St Andrew

CANFORD MAGNA St Philip, Moore Avenue, West Howe. Temporary church 1952/53.
New building 1986. In parish of KINSON St Andrew
OR C 1953-74 (DRO); CM 1987+ (Inc) No burial ground. For earlier period
see KINSON St Andrew.

CANFORD MAGNA St John the Evangelist, Ashley Road, Heatherlands, Upper
Parkstone. Parish created 1886 from KINSON. Erected 1902-03
OR C 1881-1947 M 1882-1964 B 1949-71 (DRO)

CANFORD MAGNA Good Shepherd, Herbert Avenue, Heatherlands. In parish of
HEATHERLANDS St John
OR 1931+ (Inc)

CANFORD MAGNA St Clement, Branksome (name of benefice; *alias* St Clement,
Parkstone) St Clement's Road, Newtown, Parkstone. Erected 1889 as chapel-
of-ease to KINSON St Andrew. Parish created 1904 from KINSON and LONGFLEET.
OR C 1891-1981 M 1894-1995 B 1896-1992 Banns 1894-1952, 1966-93 (DRO)
MI (S&DFHS)

CANFORD MAGNA St Barnabas, Ringwood Road, Branksome. In parish of BRANKSOME
St Clement
OR C 1958-90 (DRO)

CANFORD MAGNA St Mark, Talbot Village. Chapel-of-ease to parish church
[Kelly 1903]; parish created 1919 from KINSON. *see also* ENSBURY PARK
OR C 1870-1991, 1994-98 M 1905-98 B 1870-93 Banns 1906-93 (DRO)

CANFORD MAGNA St Saviour, Talbot Village. In parish of St Mark

CANFORD MAGNA St Thomas, Ensbury Park. Parish created 1967 from KINSON,
TALBOT VILLAGE
OR C 1942-78 M 1954-99 Banns 1954-92 (DRO)

CANFORD MAGNA (RC) Domestic chapel of Webb family from 17th cent. Mission
served by Jesuit priests. Convent of Carmelite nuns 1794-1825. Mission
subsequently merged with STAPEHILL (*see under* HAMPRESTON).
OR C 1711-18 (AAB). Catalogued as Worcester. Original registers, bound
with Stapehill, now missing. C 1810-18 ('baptised in the Catholic
Chapel of Canford House': Canford Magna parish register, above).
Entries after 1826 at Stapehill.
Cop C 1711-18 (Ptd Crisp *Catholic Registers of Worcester*: 1887);
CB 1799-1826 (Ptd CRS 43: 1949)
Cop (Mf) Canford Magna and Stapehill ZC 1772-1856 (Printout, Mf SLC);
Extr C 1772-1856 (IGI)

CANFORD MAGNA (RC) Upton House. Domestic chapel of Doughty-Tichborne family 1829-50
OR see POOLE registers

CANFORD MAGNA (RC) St Joseph and St Walburga, Bournemouth Road, Parkstone. f 1895. Rebuilt 1962.

CANFORD MAGNA (RC) Our Lady of Victories and St Bernadette, Ensbury Park f 1926

CANFORD MAGNA (RC) St Teresa of the Child Jesus, Kinson f 1940 [Cath Dir. 1965]; Christ the King, Durdells Avenue, Kinson, 1966 [Cath Dir.1967]

CANFORD MAGNA (RC) Our Lady of Fatima, Brixey Road, Upper Parkstone f 1950

CANFORD MAGNA (RC) St Anthony of Padua, York Road, Broadstone f 1959

CANFORD MAGNA (Bapt) Loch Road, Parkstone f 1891. SBA

CANFORD MAGNA (Bapt) Branksome. Erected 1896 [Kelly 1903, 1939]; =? Herbert Road fl 1961

CANFORD MAGNA (Bapt/FIEC) York Road, Branksome. Erected 1899 [Kelly 1903, 1939]; [FIEC} Broadstone Baptist Church, York Road.

CANFORD MAGNA (Bapt) Buckland Road, Parkstone f 1897. SBA

CANFORD MAGNA (Bapt) Ashley Road, Parkstone. Erected 1907-08

CANFORD MAGNA (Bapt) Alder Road, Parkstone f 1927. SBA

CANFORD MAGNA (Bapt) Wimborne Road, Longfleet f 1930. SBA

CANFORD MAGNA (FIEC) Parkstone Evengelical Free Church, Ringwood Road

CANFORD MAGNA (Presb) Licence for house of John Thorne of Newton, 1672

CANFORD MAGNA (Cong, now URC) Commercial Road, Parkstone. f 1804. Rebuilt 1892-93. [Kelly 1903]

CANFORD MAGNA (Cong, now URC) Higher Blandford Road, Broadstone f 1847; new chapel 1928 [Kelly 1939]

CANFORD MAGNA (Cong) Parkstone f 1830 [Cong. Yearbook 1871] = ? Buckland Chapel, Parkstone [1882 Return]

CANFORD MAGNA (Cong, now URC) Longfleet Road, Longfleet f 1892 [Kelly 1903]

CANFORD MAGNA (Cong) Corfe Hills. Out-station of POOLE [Cong. Yearbook 1871] = ? (Prot Diss) Corfe Hills, Broadstone [1882 Return]

CANFORD MAGNA (Ind/Cong now URC) East Howe f 1834 [Harrod 1865] [Kelly 1903] East Howe Lane/Kinson Road

CANFORD MAGNA (URC) Mitchell Road, Canford Heath f 1968

CANFORD MAGNA (Wes) Broadstone. Erected 1840 [Kelly 1903]
=? Meth: Broadstone, The Broadway. Poole and Swanage Circuit

CANFORD MAGNA (Wes) Parkstone [1882 Return]

CANFORD MAGNA (Wes) Newtown, Parkstone [1882 Return];
= ? Meth, Ringwood Road, Newtown: Poole and Swanage Circuit

CANFORD MAGNA (Wes) West Howe, Kinson [1882 Return]

CANFORD MAGNA (Wes) Waterloo. Poole Circuit [1882 Return]
OR   M 1935-57 (DRO)

CANFORD MAGNA (Wes) 3 chapels at Branksome [Kelly 1903]

CANFORD MAGNA (Wes) Kinson [Harrod 1865] [Kelly 1903]

CANFORD MAGNA (Wes) Creekmoor
OR   C 1957-79 (DRO)

CANFORD MAGNA (Prim Meth) Branksome. Bournemouth Circuit [Kelly 1903]
OR   M 1947-86 (DRO)

CANFORD MAGNA (Meth) Ashley Road, Parkstone. Poole and Swanage Circuit.

CANFORD MAGNA (Meth) Salterns Road, Lower Parkstone. Poole and Swanage
Circuit

CANFORD MAGNA (Meth) Ringwood Road, Parkstone. Poole and Swanage Circuit

CANFORD MAGNA (Meth) Dorchester Road, Upton. Poole and Swanage Circuit

CANFORD MAGNA (Meth) Oakdale, Brampton Road. Poole and Swanage Circuit

CANFORD MAGNA (Plymouth Brethren) Branksome [Kelly 1903]

CANFORD MAGNA (Latter Day Saints) 8 Mount Road, Parkstone

CANFORD MAGNA Parkstone Cemetery, Pottery Road, Poole (1894) (Poole Borough
Council)

CANFORD MAGNA Branksome Cemetery (1904) (Poole Borough Council)

CANFORD MAGNA Broadstone Cemetery, Dunyeats Road, Broadstone (1904)
(Poole Borough Council)

CANFORD, LITTLE hamlet of HAMPRESTON

CANN   see SHAFTESBURY St Rumbold

CASTLETON St Mary Magdalene [Sherborne Hundred; Sherborne Union] [186]
Chapelry in OBORNE. Consecrated 1715. Separate parish 1716. United 1970
with SHERBORNE.
OR   C 1715-1992 M 1716-1970 B 1715-1992 Banns 1754-1812, 1826-1959 (DRO)
      No earlier register noted in 1831.
BT   CMB 1600-03, 1617 [-27], 1634, 1638, 1669, 1672, 1684-1712, 1716-1836,
      1847-79; for 1606-35 see OBORNE (W&SRO)
Cop   M 1716-1836 (DRO, SG); CB 1813-37 (I, DRO); C 1600-03, 1634-38,
      1669-1836, 1847-79 M 1600-01, 1634-38, 1669-1834 from BT (VRI);
      C 1790-1837 M 1716-1836 B 1813-37 (PRI); M 1600-1756 from BT (DRO);
      M 1716-1836 from OR, 1600-1756 from BT (DMI); B 1750-1837 (DBI)

CASTLETON cont.
Cop (Mf) C 1600-03, 1634-38, 1669-1836, 1847-79 M 1600-01, 1634-36, 1669-1834 B 1688-1836, 1847-79 (Mf of BT, DRO, SLC); Extr C 1600-03, 1634-38, 1669-1836, 1847-79 M 1600-01, 1634-38, 1669-1834 from BT (IGI)
MI (S&DFHS); (DFHS); (DRO); Ch cy 1975 (SG); Cy (*Ye Olde Mortality* 9: Ms, SG)

CASTLETOWN *see* PORTLAND

CATHERSTON LEWESTON St Mary [Whitchurch Canonicorum Hundred; Bridport Union] [27] Rebuilt 1858. Now with GOLDEN CAP Team Benefice.
OR C 1837-1943 M 1839-1979 (DRO) Noted in 1831: 'Catherston Leweston is included in the Charmouth Registry'. *see also* WOOTTON FITZPAINE: 'The register appears to have been kept with that of Wootton Fitzpaine until December 1837' [Kelly 1903]
BT C 1837-78 (W&SRO) *and see* CHARMOUTH
Cop C 1837-1991 (DRO); C 1837-78 from BT (VRI)
Cop (Mf) C 1817-49 M 1817-37 with WOOTTON FITZPAINE (Mf of OR, SG); C 1837-78 (Mf of BT, DRO, SLC); Extr C 1837-78 from BT (IGI)

CATTISTOCK St Peter and St Paul [Cerne, Totbury and Modbury Hundred; Cerne Union] [427] Now with MELBURY benefice.
OR C 1558-1674, 1683-1869 M 1558-1644, 1652, 1658-1837 B 1558-1674, 1683-1703, 1799-1907 Banns 1764-65, 1783-1838, 1928-77 (DRO)
BT CMB 1731-1844, 1846-79 (W&SRO)
Cop M 1558-1812 (Ptd Phil 1: 1906; & on CD-ROM); CMB 1558-1838 (DRO); CMB 1558-1711 (I, SG); CMB 1558-1711 (Ts, SLC); CB 1700-1838 M 1811-38 (DCM); CB 1700-1838 M 1812-36 (SG); C 1731-1839, 1863-79 M 1731-1839 from BT (VRI); C 1790-1837 M 1558-1837 B 1700-1838 (PRI); M 1558-71, 1577-1644, 1652, 1658-74, 1684-88, 1693-1837 (SG); M 1731-54 from BT (DRO); M 1558-1812 (Boyd); M 1790-1812 (Pallot); M 1558-1837 from OR, 1731-54 from BT (DMI); B 1700-1838 (DBI)
Cop (Mf) M 1558-1812 (Mf of Phil, SLC); CB 1731-1879 M 1731-1863 (Mf of BT, DRO, SLC); C 1558-1882 M 1558-1876 (Printout, Mf SLC); Extr C 1558-1711, 1731-1879 M 1558-1711, 1731-1876 from OR and BT (IGI)

CATTISTOCK (Prim Meth) Erected 1870 [1882 Return] [Kelly 1903]
OR C 1871-72 (DRO)

CAUNDLE HADDON *see* CAUNDLE, STOURTON

CAUNDLE MARSH St Peter and St Paul [Sherborne Hundred; Sherborne Union] [70] Peculiar of the Dean of Sarum until 1847. Rebuilt 1857. Now with THE CAUNDLES WITH FOLKE AND HOLWELL benefice.
OR C ?1704-45, 1761-1991 M ?1704-41, 1764-1812, 1817-31, 1840-1988 B 1706-1992 Banns 1760-69 (DRO) No earlier register noted in 1831.
BT CMB 1579-81, 1585-87, 1592-97, 1600-06, 1609-27, 1630-40, 1670-1879 (W&SRO)
Cop C 1813-37 B 1707-1992 (I, DRO); C 1579-1879 M 1579-1849 from BT (VRI); C 1704-1837 M 1704-1831 B 1813-37 (PRI); M 1704-18, 1724-41, 1760-70, 1776, 1784-1812, 1817-31 (DRO, SG); M 1579-1764, 1812-17, 1831-46 from BT (DRO); M 1704-41, 1756-1831 from OR, 1580-1845 from BT (DMI); B 1706-1992 (I, SG); B 1707-1992 (DBI)
Cop (Mf) CB 1579-1879 M 1579-1849 (Mf of BT, DRO, SLC); Extr C 1579-1879 M 1579-1849 from BT (IGI)
MI (S&DFHS); (DFHS); (DRO); Ch cy 1975 (SG)

CAUNDLE WAKE *see* BISHOP'S CAUNDLE

CAUNDLE, BISHOP'S Decication unknown [Sherborne Hundred; Sherborne Union]
[376 including Caundle Wake] Now with THE CAUNDLES WITH FOLKE AND HOLWELL
benefice.
OR C 1570-99, 1618-41, 1648-1921 M 1570-1610, 1640, 1655-83, 1700-38,
    1754-1993 B 1570-99, 1618-40, 1651-1983 Banns 1754-1812, 1823-1921
    (DRO)
BT CMB 1732-1879 (W&SRO)
Cop CB 1570-1814 M 1570-1812 Banns of M not in parish 1761-81 (Ptd C.Mayo
    ed.: 1895); CMB 1570-1837 (DRO); C 1732-1879 M 1732-1846 from BT
    (VRI); C 1790-1837 MB 1813-37 (PRI); M 1738-52 from BT (DRO);
    M 1570-1640, 1655-1837 (SG); M 1790-1812 (Pallot); M 1570-1837 from OR,
    1738-53 from BT (DMI); B 1570-1837 (DBI)
Cop (Mf) CB 1570-1814 M 1570-1812 Banns of M not in parish 1761-81 (Mf, of
    Mayo, SG, SLC); CB 1732-1879 M 1732-1846 (Mf of BT, DRO, SLC);
    C 1570-1814 M 1570-1812 (Printout, Mf SLC); M 1570-1812 (I, Mf SG);
    Extr C 1570-1879 M 1570-1848 (IGI)
MI (S&DFHS); (DFHS); (DRO); Ch cy 1975 (SG)

CAUNDLE, BISHOP'S (Prim Meth) [1882 Return]; (Meth) erected 1908 [Kelly
1939]

CAUNDLE, PURSE St Peter [Sherborne Hundred; Sherborne Union] [180] Now with
THE CAUNDLES WITH FOLKE AND HOLWELL benefice.
OR C 1730-1992 M 1731-1988 B 1731-1991 Banns 1754-1812, 1824-1972 (DRO)
    No earlier register noted in 1831.
BT CMB 1732-78, 1781-1878 (W&SRO)
Cop M 1731-1841 (DRO, SG); CB 1813-37 (I, DRO); C 1732-1878 M 1732-1849
    from BT (VRI); M 1731-1841 from OR (DMI); B 1813-37 (DBI)
Cop (Mf) CB 1732-1878 M 1732-1849 (Mf of BT, DRO, SLC); Extr C 1731-1878
    M 1731-1849 from BT (IGI)
MI (S&DFHS); (DFHS); (DRO); (SG)

CAUNDLE, PURSE (Ind) Building occupied by Ann Clark [1882 Return]

CAUNDLE, STOURTON formerly CAUNDLE HADDON St Peter [Brownshall Hundred;
Sturminster Union] [349] Now with THE CAUNDLES WITH FOLKE AND HOLWELL
benefice.
OR C 1670-1881 M 1670-1993 B 1670-82, 1725-1957 Banns 1760-63, 1770-1811
    (DRO)
BT CMB 1731-1879 (W&SRO)
Cop C 1731-1879 M 1731-1837 from BT (VRI); CB 1813-37 M 1670-1836 (PRI);
    CB 1813-37 (I, DRO); C 1670-1721 (SG); M 1670-1836 (DRO, SG);
    M 1670-1763 (SG); M 1670-1763 (Boyd); M 1670-1836 from OR (DMI);
    B 1813-37 (DBI)
Cop (Mf) CB 1731-1879 M 1731-1837 (Mf of BT, DRO, SLC); Extr C 1731-1879
    M 1731-1837 from BT (IGI)
MI (Ptd G.Fernandes & A.Blades *Staunton Caundle formerly Caundle Haddon:
    a history of a Dorset village*: 1974)

CAUNDLE, STOURTON (Ind/Cong) Erected 1847 [1882 Return] [Kelly 1939]

CAUNDLE, STOURTON (Prim Meth) A building [1882 Return]

CAUNDLES WITH FOLKE AND HOLWELL   Modern benefice including BISHOP'S
CAUNDLE, CAUNDLE MARSH, PURSE CAUNDLE, STOURTON CAUNDLE, FOLKE, HOLWELL.

CERNE ABBAS St Mary [Cerne, Totbury and Modbury Hundred; Cerne Union] [1209] Included UP CERNE, NETHER CERNE, from 1971. Now with GODMANSTONE, MINTERNE MAGNA

OR C 1653-1958 M 1654-87, 1695, 1697, 1710-25, 1730, 1735, 1737, 1754-1983 B 1653-1985 Banns 1754-1802, 1823-1920 (DRO)

BT CMB 1731-1879 (W&SRO)

Cop M 1654-1812 (Ptd Phil 3: 1908; & on CD-ROM); C 1790-1837 B 1653-1837 (I, DRO); C 1731-1846, 1847-79 M 1731-1846 from BT (VRI); C 1790-1837 M 1654-1841 B 1813-37 (PRI); M 1654-58, 1662-70, 1675-97, 1710-37, 1745-1841 (DRO, SG); M 1735-54 from BT (DRO); M 1654-1775 (Boyd); M 1790-1812 (Pallot); M 1654-1841 from OR, 1735-54 from BT (DMI); B 1653-1837 (DBI)

Cop (Mf) M 1654-1812 (Mf of Phil, SLC); CMB 1731-1846 CB 1847-79 (Mf of BT, DRO, SLC); Extr C 1731-1879 M 1731-1846 from BT (IGI)

MI (S&DFHS); (DFHS); Extr: Pratt (Ms, SG)

CERNE ABBAS (Presb) Licence to James Hallet for house of John Dammer, Cerne, 1672

CERNE ABBAS (Grace Baptist)

CERNE ABBAS (Cong) Abbey Street f 1672. 'Cerne Abbas and Castle Hill' [*Cong. Yearbook* 1871] Rebuilt 1888 [Kelly 1939]

OR C 1863-74, 1893-1980 M 1864-73, 1894-1970 B 1898-1970 (DRO)

CERNE ABBAS (Wes) n.d. [Kelly 1903]

CERNE, NETHER All Saints [Cerne, Totbury and Modbury Hundred; Cerne Union] [83] United 1971 with CERNE ABBAS. Redundant 1971. Churches Conservation Trust.

OR C 1694-1704, 1718-1972 M 1716-44, 1813-1949 B 1693-1869 (DRO)

BT CMB 1731-47, 1752-1829, 1847-80 (W&SRO)

Cop M 1716-1812 (Ptd Phil 6: 1912; & on CD-ROM); C 1694-1704, 1718-1837 B 1693-1852 (I, DRO); C 1733-1829, 1847-80 M 1739-1827 from BT (VRI); CB 1813-37 M 1716-1838 (PRI); M 1716-1837 (DRO); M 1715-44, 1813-38 (SG); M 1716-50 (Boyd); M 1716-44, 1813-38 from OR, 1744-1813 from BT (DMI); B 1813-37 (DBI)

Cop (Mf) M 1716-1812 (Mf of Phil, SLC); CB 1731-1829, 1847-80 M 1731-1827 (Mf of BT, DRO, SLC); Extr C 1731-1829, 1847-80 M 1739-1827 from BT (IGI)

CERNE, UP or **UPCERNE** or **UPPER CERNE** Dedication unknown   [Sherborne Hundred; Cerne Union] [88] United 1971 with CERNE ABBAS. Redundant 1971. Given for use as private chapel.

OR C 1650-54, 1664-67, 1675-1967 M 1682-1961 B 1664-1968 Banns 1756-1811, 1860-1961 (DRO)

BT CMB 1731-77, 1780-1880 (W&SRO)

Cop M 1682-1811 (Ptd Phil 3: 1908; & on CD-ROM); C 1731-1880 M 1731-1853 from BT (VRI); CB 1813-37 M 1682-1837 (PRI); C 1813-37 (I, DRO); M 1682-1837 (DRO, SG); M 1735-1814 from BT (DRO); M 1682-1767 (Boyd); M 1790-1811 (Pallot); M 1682-1837 from OR, 1752-1814 from BT (DMI); B 1813-37 (DBI)

Cop (Mf) M 1682-1811 (Mf of Phil, SLC); CB 1731-1880 M 1731-1853 (Mf of BT, DRO, SLC); Extr C 1731-1880 M 1731-1853 from BT (IGI)

CHALBURY All Saints [Badbury Hundred; Wimborne and Cranborne Union] [157] Now with HINTON MARTELL, HORTON, HOLT.

OR C 1629-97, 1716-1992 M 1629-64, 1676-91, 1716-1993 B 1629-98, 1716-1992 Banns 1760-1830, 1840-1982 (DRO) Noted in 1831: CMB 1716+

CHALBURY cont.

BT CMB 1734-36, 1740-78, 1780-1879 (W&SRO)

Cop C 1629-97 M 1629-91 B 1629-98 (SG, SLC); CMB 1629-1700 (SG); C 1813-37
B 1813-36 (I, DRO); C 1734-1879 M 1734-1851 from BT (VRI); C 1782-1837
M 1813-37 B 1813-36 (PRI); M 1629-45, 1653, 1659-64, 1676-84, 1716-
1837 (DRO, SG); M 1734-55, 1810-13 from BT (DRO); M 1629-1837 from OR,
1734-55, 1810-13 from BT (DMI); B 1750-1836 (DBI)

Cop (Mf) CB 1734-1879 M 1734-1849 (Mf of BT, DRO, SLC); C 1629-97
(Printout, Mf SLC); Extr C 1629-97, 1734-1879 M 1629-91, 1734-1851
from OR and BT (IGI)

MI (S&DFHS); (DFHS); (DRO)

CHALDON BOYS or WEST CHALDON Ancient parish united 1446 to CHALDON HERRING.
'Church desecrated' [Kelly 1903]

CHALDON HERRING or EAST CHALDON St Nicholas [Bindon Liberty; Wareham and
Purbeck Union] [270] Now with EAST LULWORTH, WEST LULWORTH, WINFRITH
NEWBURGH.

OR C 1621-1895 M 1621-58, 1668/9-1776, 1782-1964 B 1621-1993 Banns
1754-1812 (DRO)

BT CMB 1731-1879 (W&SRO)

Cop C 1621-1781, 1813-37 M 1621-1837 B 1621-1780, 1813-37 (DRO);
C 1731-1879 M 1738-1838 from BT (VRI); C 1790-1837 M 1621-1837
B 1813-37 (PRI); M 1621-58, 1665-75, 1691, 1712-23, 1738-39, 1745-1837
(SG); M 1775-1814 from BT (DRO); M 1621-1837 from OR, 1775-82, 1814
from BT (DMI); B 1750-1837 (DBI)

Cop (Mf) CB 1731-1879 M 1738-1838 (Mf of BT, DRO, SLC); Extr C 1731-1879
M 1738-1838 from BT (IGI)

MI (S&DFHS); (DFHS); (DRO); (SG)

CHALDON HERRING (Cong) Licence for house of William Toope of Chaldon
parish, 1672

CHALDON, EAST *see* CHALDON HERRING

CHALDON, WEST *see* CHALDON BOYS

CHARBOROUGH *see* MORDEN

CHARDSTOCK St Andrew [Beaminster Forum and Redhone Hundred; Axminster
Union; transferred to Devon 1896 [1357] Peculiar of the Prebend of
Chardstock and Wambrook, Sarum Cathedral, until 1847. Now with Axminster
benefice, Devon; Diocese of Exeter.

OR C 1597-1947 M 1597-1987 B 1597-1964 (Devon RO)

BT CMB 1579-82, 1585-88, 1600-41, 1643-45, 1661-62, 1668-1700, 1719-23,
1743-46, 1755-1820, 1823-25, 1827-32, 1847-79 (W&SRO)

Cop CMB 1597-1850 (DRO, SG); M 1597-1837 (Phil Ms at SG); C 1579-1879
M 1579-1832 from BT (VRI); C 1813-37 M 1597-1840 B 1813-40 (PRI);
M 1597-1837 (Boyd); M 1597-1850 from Devon RO copy (DMI); B 1812-42
(DBI)

Cop (Mf) M 1597-1837 (Mf of Phil Ms, SLC); CB 1579-1879 M 1579-1832 (Mf of
BT, DRO, SLC); C 1579-1879 M 1579-1832 from BT (IGI); M 1597-1748
(IGI, Devon)

MI 1971-72 (WSL)

CHARDSTOCK All Saints. Parish created 1841 from CHARDSTOCK, AXMINSTER (Devon). Transferred to Devon 1896. Now with Axminster benefice. Diocese of Exeter.
OR   C 1840-1994 B 1841-1983 (Devon RO)
BT   CMB 1847-79; for earlier transcripts *see* CHARDSTOCK St Andrew (W&SRO)
Cop C 1847-79 from BT (VRI)
Cop (Mf) CB 1847-79 (Mf of BT, DRO, SLC); Extr C 1847-79 from BT (IGI)

CHARDSTOCK (Bible Christian) Ebenezer, Churchill [1882 Return]

CHARLESTOWN *see* CHICKERELL

CHARLTON MARSHALL St Mary the Virgin [Cogdean Hundred; Blandford Union] [324] Chapelry in SPETISBURY. Now with SPETISBURY, BLANDFORD ST MARY.
OR   C 1575/6-1669/70, 1705/6-1941 M 1575/6-1687, 1700/1-1978
     B 1575/6-1648, 1705-1919 Banns 1755-1966 (DRO) Noted in 1831: a gap
     CMB 1649-1704
BT   CMB 1731-78, 1780-1844, 1847-80 (W&SRO)
Cop CMB 1575/6-1900 (DRO); C 1575-1669, 1705-1899 M 1575-1898 B 1575-1648,
     1661, 1705-1899 (DCM, SG); C 1731-1880 M 1731-1865 from BT (VRI);
     C 1790-1837 M 1814-41 B 1813-38 (PRI); M 1575-1767, 1773-1837 (SG);
     M 1731-81, 1784-88, 1813 from BT (DRO); M 1575-1754, 1767-1837 from OR,
     1713-81, 1784-88, 1813 from BT (DMI); B 1813-38 (I, DRO); B 1705-1838
     (DBI)
Cop (Mf) CB 1731-1880 M 1731-1860 (Mf of BT, DRO, SLC); Extr C 1731-1880
         M 1731-1865 from BT (IGI)
MI   (S&DFHS); (DFHS); (DRO) Ch, cemeteries (SG)

CHARLTON MARSHALL (Ind/Cong) n.d. [Harrod 1865] [Kelly 1903]

CHARLTON MARSHALL (Wes) House occupied by Joseph Compton registered 1799 [Biggs]

CHARLTON MARSHALL (Prim Meth) Building belonging to William Hunt [1882 Return]

CHARLTON MARSHALL ('No religious appelation') The Chapel [1882 Return]

CHARMINSTER Bournemouth. *see* NIPR Vol. 8 Part 6 Hampshire

CHARMINSTER St Mary the Virgin [George Hundred; Dorchester Union] [596] Peculiar of the Dean of Sarum until 1847. Included chapelry of STRATTON; separate parish 1742. Now with STINSFORD
OR   C 1561-1953 M 1561-1749, 1756-1928, 1977-90 B 1561-1961 Banns 1756-89,
     1823-2000 (DRO)
BT   CMB 1591-97, 1600-22, 1625-39, 1668-1712, 1716-18, 1722-1832, 1847-79
     (W&SRO)
Cop M 1561-1812 (Ptd Phil 2: 1907; & on CD-ROM); C 1790-1837 B 1813-37
     (I, DRO); C 1591-1879 M 1591-1832, 1849-70 from BT (VRI); C 1790-1837
     M 1561-1837 B 1813-37 (PRI); M 1561-1840, 1647-1837 (DRO, SG);
     M 1591-1756 from BT (DRO); M 1561-1812 (Boyd); M 1790-1812 (Pallot);
     M 1561-1837 from OR, 1591-1756 from BT (DMI); B 1813-37 (DBI)
Cop (Mf) M 1561-1812 (Mf of Phil, SLC); CB 1591-1879 M 1591-1832, 1849-70
         (Mf of BT, DRO, SLC); Extr C 1591-1879 M 1591-1832, 1849-70 from
         BT (IGI)

CHARMINSTER Herrison Hospital. County Lunatic Asylum. Erected 1859-63. Chapel 1895-9
MI   (S&DFHS); (DFHS); (DRO); (SG)

CHARMINSTER (Cong) n.d. [Kelly 1939]
OR   C 1917-38 (DRO)

CHARMINSTER (Wes) n.d. [Kelly 1903]

CHARMINSTER (UMFC) [1882 Return]; (Meth) [Kelly 1939]

CHARMOUTH St Andrew [Whitchurch Canonicorum Hundred; Axminster Union
1836-94; Bridport Union 1894-1930] [724] Rebuilt 1836-38. Now with GOLDEN
CAP Team Benefice.
OR   C 1653-1874 M 1654-1837 B 1653-91, 1696-1932 Banns 1754-1816 (DRO)
     Noted in 1831: 'Catherston Leweston in included in the Charmouth
     Registry'
BT   CMB 1731-78, 1780-1844, 1847-78 (W&SRO)
Cop M 1654-1812 (Ptd Phil 4: 1909; & on CD-ROM); C 1653-1965 M 1654-1965
     B 1654-1966 (DRO); C 1731-80, 1794-1807, 1837-78 M 1731-1844 from BT,
     erroneously as 'Charmouth Independent' (VRI); C 1653-1837 M 1654-1837
     B 1813-40 (PRI); M 1654-1837 (SG); M 1731-54, 1795 from BT (DRO);
     M 1654-1812 (Boyd); M 1790-1812 (Pallot); M 1654-1806, 1812-37 from OR,
     1731-54 from BT (DMI); B 1813-40 (I, DRO); cemetery B 1887-1967 (DRO);
     B 1725-1840 (DBI)
Cop (Mf) Z 1653-61 C 1663-1871 M 1654-57, 1664-91, 1700-1837 B 1653-91,
          1696-1932, 1937 Banns 1754-1816 (Mf, SG); M 1654-1812 (Mf of Phil,
          SLC); CB 1731-80, 1794-1807, 1837-78 M 1731-1844 (Mf of BT, DRO,
          SLC); Extr C 1731-80, 1794-1807, 1837-78 M 1731-1844 from BT, as
          'Charmouth Independent' (IGI)

CHARMOUTH (Ind/Cong) f 1662; rebuilt 1815 [Cong. Yearbook 1871]
[Kelly 1939]
OR   ZC 1779-94, 1806-37 B 1817-37 (RG 4/2035, 584, PRO)
Cop C 1780-1837, 1839-73 M 1840-66 B 1817-37, 1840-75 (DRO); C 1780-1837
     B 1817-37 (S&DFHS)
Cop (Mf) ZC 1779-1837 B 1817-37 (Mf of OR, SLC); ZC 1779-1837 (Printout,
          Mf SLC); Extr C 1780-94, 1807-37 (IGI)

CHEDINGTON St James [Beaminster Forum and Redhone Hundred; Beaminster
Union] [178] Erected 1840-41. United 1971 with SOUTH PERROTT, MOSTERTON.
Now with BEAMINSTER Area benefice. Redundant 1981. Sold 1983 for use as
residence and workshop.
OR   C 1813-1979 M 1756-1812, 1837-1980 B 1813-1974 Banns 1756-1812,
     1851-1975 (DRO) Noted in 1831: C 1809-12 M 1756-1812 B 1810-12. 'No
     other Registers can be found'.
BT   CMB 1731-95, 1798-1811, 1813-20, 1824-35, 1837, 1840-78 (W&SRO)
Cop M 1756-1812 (Ptd Phil 5: 1910; & on CD-ROM); CB 1813-37 (I, DRO, PRI);
     C 1731-1878 M 1731-1846 from BT (VRI); M 1758-1810 (DRO, SG);
     M 1712-1835 from BT (DRO); M 1756-1812 (Boyd); M 1790-1812 (Pallot);
     M 1758-1812 from OR, 1732-56, 1813-35 from BT, 1665 from Hutchins
     (DMI); B 1813-37 (DBI)
Cop (Mf) C 1813-1979 M 1756-1812, 1837-1967, 1975-76, 1980 B 1813-1975
          Banns 1851-1975 (Mf, SG); M 1756-1812 (Mf of Phil, SLC);
          CB 1731-1878 M 1731-1846 (Mf of BT, DRO, SLC); Extr C 1731-1878
          M 1731-1846 from BT (IGI)
MI   (S&DFHS); (DFHS); (DRO); Old and new cy 1983 (SG)

CHELBOROUGH, EAST or LUCCOMBE or LEWCOMBE St James [Tollerford Hundred; Beaminster Union] [83] Now with MELBURY benefice.
OR C 1682-1715, 1720-39, 1745-1812 M 1690-1760 1787-1950 B 1690-1712, 1728-66, 1771-1812 (DRO)
BT CMB 1733-40, 1743, 1748-55, 1757, 1760-65, 1768-78, 1781-1879 (W&SRO)
Cop M 1690-1812 (Ptd Phil 5: 1910; & on CD-ROM); C 1682-1771 M 1690-1837 B 1690-1771 (DRO); C 1787-94 M 1690-1837 (PRI); C 1733-1879 M 1733-1846 from BT (VRI); M 1690-1727, 1734, 1742-60, 1787-95, 1800-37 (SG); M 1733-87 from BT (DRO); M 1690-1812 (Boyd); M 1790-1812 (Pallot); M 1690-1760, 1788-1837 from OR, 1733-88 from BT (DMI); B 1700-1812 (DBI)
Cop (Mf) M 1690-1812 (Mf of Phil, SLC); CB 1733-1879 M 1733-1846 (Mf of BT, DRO, SLC); Extr C 1733-1879 M 1733-1846 from BT (IGI)
MI (S&DFHS); (DFHS); (DRO); cy 1680-1863 (SG)

CHELBOROUGH, WEST St Andrew [Tollerford Hundred; Beaminster Union] [62] Rebuilt *c.*1640. Now with MELBURY benefice.
OR C 1663-1996 M 1673-1805, 1811-35, 1838-1984 B 1662/3-1999 (DRO)
BT CMB 1732-77, 1782-1879 (W&SRO)
Cop M 1673-1811 (Ptd Phil 4: 1909; & on CD-ROM); M 1673-1758, 1782-1835 (DRO, SG); M 1673-1835 (PRI); M 1805-15 from BT (DRO); M 1676-1812 (Boyd); M 1790-1812 (Pallot); M 1673-1835 from OR, 1755-57, 1805-15 from BT (DMI); B 1813-37 (DBI)
Cop (Mf) M 1673-1812 (Mf of Phil, SLC); CB 1732-1879 M 1732-1835 (Mf of BT, DRO, SLC); Extr C 1731-1879 M 1732-1812 from BT (IGI)
MI (S&DFHS); (DFHS); (DRO)

CHESELBOURNE St Martin [Whiteway Hundred; Cerne Union] [352]   Now with MILTON ABBAS, HILTON, MELCOMBE HORSEY.
OR C 1644-1992 M 1664-1992 B 1653-1992 Banns 1754-94, 1823-1939, 1981 (DRO)
BT CMB 1731-1879 (W&SRO)
Cop M 1664-1838 (DRO); C 1784-1837 B 1813-37 (I, DRO); C 1644-1783 M 1664-1811 B 1653-1784 (SG); C 1731-1879 M 1731-1859 from BT (VRI); CB 1813-37 M 1664-1838 (PRI); M 1664-70, 1675, 1680-87, 1697-1838 (SG); M 1731-54, 1812-28 from BT (DRO); M 1664-1812 (Boyd); M 1664-1838 from OR, 1731-95, 1812 from BT (DMI)
Cop (Mf) CB 1731-1879 M 1731-1859 (Mf of BT, DRO, SLC); Extr C 1731-1879 M 1731-1859 from BT (IGI)
MI (S&DFHS); (DFHS); (DRO)

CHESELBOURNE (Prim Meth) Erected 1866 [1882 Return] [Kelly 1903]

CHESIL or CHESILTON *see* PORTLAND

CHETNOLE   *see* YETMINSTER

CHETTLE St Mary [Monkton Up Wimborne Hundred; Wimborne and Cranborne Union; Blandford Union 1894-1930] [129] Now with TOLLARD ROYAL, FARNHAM, GUSSAGE ST MICHAEL, GUSSAGE ALL SAINTS, ASHMORE.
OR C 1538/9-1812 M 1539-1746, 1753-1931 B 1539-1814 Banns 1754-1825 (DRO)
BT CMB 1732-1879 (W&SRO)
Cop C 1538-1989 M 1539-1931 B 1537-1749 1754-1989 Banns 1754-1825 (DRO); C 1538-1812 M 1538-1814 B 1539-1814 (SG); CB 1537-1749, 1753-1989 M 1737-1749, 1754-1931 (I, SG); C 1753-1837 M 1754-1837 (PRI); M 1732-54 from BT (DRO); M 1539-1645, 1660-1836 (SG); M 1539-1836 from OR, 1732-54 from BT (DMI); B 1754-1991 (DBI); CMB 1732-1879 from BT (Pine: CD 3)

CHETTLE cont.
Cop (Mf) CB 1732-1879 M 1732-1846 (Mf of BT, DRO, SLC); Extr C 1732-1879
        M 1732-1848 from BT (IGI)
MI   (S&DFHS); (DFHS); (DRO)

CHICKERELL or WEST CHICKERELL St Mary [part Culliford Tree Hundred, part
Sutton Poyntz Liberty; Weymouth Union] [430] With hamlets of East
Chickerell, Charlestown, Putton. Now with FLEET. see also WEYMOUTH St
Edmund.
OR   C 1699-1930 M 1723-1960 B 1723-1891 Banns 1823-1990 (DRO) Noted in
     1831: C 1724+ MB 1723+
BT   CMB 1731-64, 1767-82, 1787-1879 (W&SRO)
Cop M 1723-1812 (Ptd Phil 7: 1914; & on CD-ROM); C 1699-1930 M 1723-1941
     B 1723-1891 (DRO); C 1699-1837 M 1723-1837 B 1723-1838 (PRI):
     M 1723-1837 (SG); M 1723-1812 (Boyd); M 1790-1812 (Pallot); M 1723-1837
     from OR (DMI); B 1654-1838 (DBI); CMB 1731-1879 from BT (Pine: CD 2)
Cop (Mf) M 1723-1812 (Mf of Phil, SLC); CB 1731-1879 M 1731-1847 (Mf of BT,
         DRO, SLC); Extr C 1731-1879 M 1731-1847 from BT (IGI)
MI   (S&DFHS); (DFHS); (DRO); war memorial (SG)

CHICKERELL (Part Bapt) Putton Chapel, Charlestown, Chickerell [1882 Return]
[Kelly 1939]

CHICKERELL (Ind/Cong) Out-station of WEYMOUTH [Cong. Yearbook 1871]
[Harrod 1865] [1882 Return] [Kelly 1939]
OR   M 1925-69 (DRO)

CHICKERELL (Wes) North Square. Erected 1865 [1882 Return]; [Kelly 1903];
(Meth) [Kelly 1939] Weymouth Circuit

CHICKERELL ('Who object to be designated') Old school-room, corner of the
High Street leading to Fleet [1882 Return]; = ? (Brethren) n.d. [Kelly
1903, 1939]

CHIDEOCK St Giles [Whitchurch Canonicorum Hundred; Bridport Union] [838]
Chapelry in WHITCHURCH CANONICORUM; separate parish 1886. Now with GOLDEN
CAP Team Benefice.
OR   C 1654-1898 M 1654-1995 B 1654-1984 Banns 1754-1814 1890-1987 (DRO)
BT   CMB 1731-1811, 1813-36, 1847-80 (W&SRO)
Cop M 1654-1812 (Ptd Phil 2: 1907; & on CD-ROM); CB 1652-1770 (SG);
     CB 1701-1812 (DCM); C 1654-75, 1743-1837 B 1654-1837 (I, DRO);
     C 1790-1837 MB 1813-37 (PRI); M 1654-1837 (DRO, SG); M 1654-1812
     (Boyd); M 1790-1812 (Pallot); M 1654-1837 from OR, 1753 from BT (DMI);
     B 1750-1837 (DBI); CMB 1731-1880 from BT (Pine: CD 2);
     Extr CMB 1743-1812 M 1820-30 B 1703-10 (I, SG)
Cop (Mf) M 1654-1812 (Mf of Phil, SLC); CB 1731-1880 M 1731-1836 (Mf of
         BT, DRO, SLC); Extr C 1731-1880 M 1731-1836 from BT (IGI)
MI   (S&DFHS); (DFHS); (DRO); (SG); (Mf, SLC)

CHIDEOCK (RC) Chideock Castle, Arundel and (from 1804) Weld families.
Closed c.1740; services held in a farm-house owned by Welds. Chapel 1811
Chideock Manor House. Served by Benedictine monks 1853-64. Our Lady of
Martyrs and St Ignatius erected 1872-74. Now served from BEAMINSTER. Weld
mausoleum and private cemetery.
OR   C 1788-1838 DB 1810-39 destroyed in fire. CMB 1837+ (Inc, Bridport);
     Confirmations 1859, 1865, 1869, 1874, 1876, 1879, 1883, 1887, 1890,
     1893+ (PDA); M 1982-90 (DRO)
Cop C 1788-1838 DB 1810-39 (DRO, SG, Cath FHS collection at Catholic
     Central Library, Lancing Street, London NW1 1ND); B 1810-39 (DBI)

CHIDEOCK (Bapt) Licences to Peter Jule, and for house of Robert Scott, both of Chideockford, 1672

CHIDEOCK (Cong) Licence for house of Thomas Beer, 1672

CHIDEOCK (Wes) n.d. [Kelly 1903]

CHILCOMBE St Mary [Uggscombe Hundred; Bridport Union] [35] United 1954 with BURTON BRADSTOCK, SHIPTON GEORGE. Now with BRIDE VALLEY benefice.
OR   C 1748-1984, 1993 M 1748-1803, 1813-28, 1840-1950 B 1752-1807, 1825-1932, 1990 Banns 1828-1913, 1950 (DRO) Noted in 1831: 'Previous to 1748 the entries were made in the Registers of Askerswell'.
BT   CMB 1748-1836, 1843, 1848-78 (W&SRO)
Cop C 1813-37 B 1813-1990 (I, DRO); C 1748-1837 M 1748-1828 B 1819-1990 (PRI); M 1748-75, 1794-1803, 1813-28 (DRO, SG); M 1748-1813, 1828-40 from BT (DRO); M 1748-1828 from OR, 1748, 1803-13, 1828-40 from BT (DMI); B 1813-37 (DBI); CMB 1748-1878 from BT (Pine: CD 1)
Cop (Mf) CB 1748-1878 M 1748-1828 (Mf of BT, DRO, SLC); Extr C 1748-1878 M 1748-1828 from BT (IGI)
MI   (S&DFHS); (SG)

CHILD OKEFORD   see OKEFORD, CHILD

CHILDHAY   tithing of BROADWINDSOR

CHILFROME Holy Trinity [Tollerford Hundred; Dorchester Union] [111] Now with MELBURY benefice.
OR   C 1695-2000 M 1709-1834, 1839-1993 B 1678-1995 Banns 1754-1811 1828-1925 (DRO) Noted in 1831: CMB 1709+
BT   CMB 1731-1830, 1833-39, 1845-79 (W&SRO)
Cop M 1709-1812 (Ptd Phil 1: 1906; & on CD-ROM); C 1695-1750 M 1709-15, 1733-41, 1754-1816, 1822-34 B 1678-1750 (SG); C 1769-1812 M 1709-1834 B 1701-1992 (PRI); M 1709-1834 B 1678-1707 (DRO); M 1731-54 from BT (DRO); M 1709-1812 (Boyd); M 1790-1812 (Pallot); M 1709-1834 from OR, 1731-54, 1812 from BT (DMI); B 1678-1903, 1907-21, 1926-37, 1941, 1946-51, 1958-95 (NBI); B 1678-1821 (DBI); CMB 1731-1879 from BT (Pine: CD 1)
Cop (Mf) M 1709-1812 (Mf of Phil, SLC); CB 1731-1879 M 1731-1866 (Mf of BT, DRO, SLC); Extr C 1731-1879 M 1732-1866 from BT (IGI)
MI   (DFHS); (DRO)

CHISWELL   see PORTLAND

CHRISTCHURCH [Hampshire] Joined Dorset 1974
OR   see NIPR Vol.8 Part 6 Hampshire

CHURCH HOPE   see PORTLAND

CHURCH KNOWLE St Peter [Hasilor Hundred; Wareham and Purbeck Union] [438] Included tithings of Bradle and Creech. Now with CORFE CASTLE, KIMMERIDGE, STEEPLE, TYNEHAM.
OR   C 1547-1961 M 1560-1837 B 1558-1712, 1734, 1739-1917 Banns 1823-1935 (DRO)
BT   CMB 1733-1839, 1847-79 (W&SRO)
Cop C 1547-1837 M 1560-1837 B 1558-1837 (DRO); C 1547-1739 B 1558-1785 (S&DFHS); C 1785-1837 M 1560-1837 B 1813-37 (PRI); C 1733-1879 M 1733-1839 from BT (VRI); M 1560-1837 (SG); M 1738, 1753 from BT (DRO); M 1560-1837 from OR, 1738-53 from BT (DMI); B 1558-1837 (DBI)

CHURCH KNOWLE cont.
Cop (Mf) CB 1733-1879 M 1733-1839 (Mf of BT, DRO, SLC); Extr C 1731-1879
        M 1731-1839 from BT (IGI)
MI   (S&DFHS); (DFHS); (DRO)

CHURCH KNOWLE (Wes) Creech [1882 Return]

CLENSTONE WINTERBORNE see WINTERBORNE CLENSTONE

CLIFTON MAYBANK or MAUBANK [Yetminster Hundred; Sherborne Union] [60]
Peculiar of the Dean of Sarum. United 1824 with BRADFORD ABBAS.
'No church'. Rectory annexed to BRADFORD ABBAS [Kelly 1939]
OR   see BRADFORD ABBAS
Cop   M 1715-33 from BRADFORD ABBAS register (DMI)

COLEHILL St Michael and All Angels. Civil parish created 1896 from HOLT.
Church erected 1893-95. Ecclesiastical parish created 1903 from WIMBORNE
MINSTER, HAMPRESTON, NEW BOROUGH AND LEIGH [Wimborne and Cranborne Union
1896-1930]
OR   C 1903-74 M 1904-94 B 1903-09, 1918-92 Banns 1904-89 (DRO)
MI   War memorial (S&DFHS); (DFHS); (DRO); (SG)

COLEHILL (Meth) Wimborne Circuit

COMPTON ABBAS or COMPTON ABBAS EAST   St Mary the Virgin [Sixpenny Handley
Hundred; Shaftesbury Incorporation/Union] [401] Rebuilt 1866-67. Remains of
old church redundant 1982. Society for the Protection of Ancient Buildings.
Now with SHASTON benefice.
OR   C 1640-44, 1651-1870 M 1640-41, 1659-1985 B 1640-44, 1659-1940
      Banns 1754-1814, 1824-72 (DRO)
BT   CMB 1731-1879 (W&SRO)
Cop   C 1640-1837 M 1640-1837 B 1640-44, 1659-1723/4, 1813-37 (DRO);
      C 1724-1837 M 1640-1837 B 1813-37 (PRI); C 1731-1879 M 1731-1848 from
      BT (VRI); M 1731-54 from BT (DRO); M 1640-41, 1660-1752, 1754-1837
      (SG); M 1539-1811 (Phil Ms at SG); M 1640-1837 from OR, 1731-54 from BT
      (DMI); B 1724-1837 (DBI)
Cop (Mf) M 1539-1811 (Mf of Phil Ms, SLC); CB 1731-1869 M 1731-1848
        C 1870-79 B 1869-79 (Mf of BT, DRO, SLC); Extr C 1731-1879
        M 1731-1848 from BT (IGI)
MI   (S&DFHS); (DFHS); (DRO); (SG); Old cy 1901 (*Ye Olde Mortality* 3: Ms,
      SG)

COMPTON ABBAS (Wes) n.d. [1882 Return] [Kelly 1903]

COMPTON ABBAS (Prim Meth) [1882 Return]

COMPTON ABBAS WEST or WEST COMPTON St Michael [Cerne, Totbury and Modbury
Hundred; Dorchester Union] [69] Rebuilt 1867. Redundant 1983. Sold for use
as monument and occasional services.
OR   C 1538-1978 M 1539-1811, 1816-1977 B 1539-1972 (DRO)
BT   CMB 1745-79, 1783-1844, 1847-79 (W&SRO)
Cop   C 1538-1798, 1813-37 M 1539-1837 (DRO); C 1538-1798 M 1539-1644,
      1652-76, 1685-1840 B 1539-1794 (SG); C 1745-1879 M 1745-1859 from BT
      (VRI); C 1813-37 M 1539-1837 B 1814-38 (PRI); C 1558-1798 (S&DFHS);
      M from BT 1745-54, 1805-16 (DRO); M 1539-1812 (Boyd); M 1539-1811,
      1816-37 from OR, 1745-54, 1811-16 from BT (DMI); B 1813-37 (I, DRO);
      B 1814-1972 (DBI)

COMPTON ABBAS WEST cont.
Cop (Mf) CB 1745-1879 M 1745-1859 (Mf of BT, DRO, SLC); Extr C 1745-1879
M 1745-1859 from BT (IGI)
MI (S&DFHS); (DFHS); (DRO); (SG)

COMPTON VALENCE or EAST COMPTON   St Thomas of Canterbury or St Thomas à
Becket [Frampton Liberty; Dorchester Union] [104] Included in Peculiar of
Manor and Liberty of Frampton. Now with THE WINTERBORNES AND COMPTON
VALENCE benefice.
OR   C 1655/6-1992 M 1657-67, 1677-1988 B 1655-1992 Banns 1824-1973 (DRO)
BT   CMB 1732-1879 (W&SRO)
Cop   CB 1655-1837 M 1657-1836 (DRO); CMB 1655-1812 (SG); C 1790-1837
M 1657-1836 B 1813-37 (PRI); C 1732-1879 M 1732-1860 from BT (VRI);
M 1657-58, 1664-67, 1677-84, 1698-1704, 1709-29, 1735-89, 1797,
1807-25, 1830-36 (SG); M 1732-54 from BT (DRO); M 1657-1836 from OR,
1732-54, 1800-12 from BT (DMI); B 1655-1837 (DBI)
Cop (Mf)   CB 1732-1879 M 1732-1860 (Mf of BT, DRO, SLC); Extr C 1732-1879
M 1732-1860 from BT (IGI)

COMPTON, EAST   *see* COMPTON VALENCE

COMPTON, NETHER St Nicholas [Sherborne Hundred; Sherborne Union] [415]
Peculiar of the Dean of Sarum until 1847. Now with QUEEN THORNE benefice.
OR   C 1538-41, 1561-1662, 1691-1879 M 1541, 1561-1647, 1655-62, 1716-1837
B 1538-41, 1561-1647, 1655-1994 Banns 1754-1820 (DRO) Noted in 1831:
CB 1776+ M 1754+
BT   CMB 1579-82, 1594-97, 1600-18, 1672-80, 1684-98, 1700-01, 1704-1812,
1815-80 (W&SRO)
Cop   C 1538-1776, 1813-79 M 1541-1680, 1696-1837 B 1538-1776, 1813-37
(DRO); C 1579-1880 M 1579-1837 from BT (VRI); C 1696-1837 M 1541-1680
B 1813-37 (PRI); C 1579-1644, 1655-62, 1672-92, 1696-99,
1716-37, 1744-1837 (SG); M 1579-1759 from BT (DRO); M 1541-1837 from
OR, 1579-1759 from BT (DMI); B 1538-1776 (DBI)
Cop (Mf)   CB 1579-1880 M 1579-1837 (Mf of BT, DRO, SLC); Extr C 1579-1880
M 1579-1836 from BT (IGI)
MI   (S&DFHS); (DFHS); (DRO); Ch cy 1973 (SG)

COMPTON, NETHER (Presb/Ind/Cong) f 1662 [*Cong. Yearbook* 1871] [Kelly 1939]
Halfway House, Stallen.
OR   C 1856-79 B 1865-1907, 1961 (DRO)
MI   (S&DFHS); Ch cy 1973 (SG)

COMPTON, OVER St Michael [Sherborne Hundred; Sherborne Union] [139]
Peculiar of the Dean of Sarum until 1847. Now with QUEEN THORNE benefice.
OR   C 1726-1995 M 1726-1837 B 1726-1995 (DRO) Noted in 1831: No.I
Bap.Marr.Bur. 1538-1778 'interrupted by No.II Bap.Bur 1726-1812.
No.III Marr 1754-1812'.
BT   CMB 1579-82, 1586-88, 1594-96, 1601-19, 1622, 1625-40, 1671-1703,
1706-1880 (W&SRO)
Cop   C 1726-1812 M 1726-1837 B 1726-1812 (DRO); CB 1813-37 (I, DRO);
C 1579-1880 M 1579-1836 from BT (VRI); M 1726-1837 B 1813-37 (PRI);
M 1726-1837 (SG); M 1579-1726 from BT (DRO); M 1726-1837 from OR,
1579-1754 from BT (DMI); B 1726-1995 (DBI)
Cop (Mf)   CB 1579-1880 M 1579-1836 (Mf of BT, DRO, SLC); Extr C 1579-1880
M 1579-1836 from BT (IGI)
MI   (S&DFHS); (DFHS); (DRO); Ch cy 1975 (SG)

COMPTON, OVER (Cong) Licence to Robert Bartlet, house of James Hanne, 1672

COMPTON, OVER (Presb) Licence for house of William Bartlett, 1672

COMPTON, WEST *see* COMPTON ABBAS WEST

COOMBE   *see* SHERBORNE

COOMBE ALMER tithing of STURMINSTER MARSHALL

COOMBE KEYNES Holy Rood [Winfrith Hundred; Wareham and Purbeck Union] [113] Rebuilt 1860. United 1974 with WOOL, EAST BURTON. Now with WOOL AND EAST STOKE BENEFICE. Church redundant 1974. Sold 1980 for use as monument and community purposes.
OR   C 1585-1736, 1744-1973 M 1583-1654, 1663-1714, 1746-1975 B 1586-1686, 1695-98, 1714-22, 1729, 1733, 1747-1810 Banns 1756-1811, 1903-67 (DRO)
         see also WOOL
BT   CMB 1731-1879 (W&SRO)
Cop CMB 1585-1837 (DRO, W&SRO, SG); C 1731-1879 M 1731-1855 from BT (VRI);
         Coombe Keynes and Wool C 1592-96, 1625-29, 1644-50, 1690-93, 1722
         M 1583-1750, 1811 (SG); C 1813-37 M 1583-1836 B 1714-1837 (PRI);
         M 1731-1839 from BT (DRO); M 1756-1811 from OR, 1731-1839 from BT,
         and see WOOL for 1583-1754 (DMI); B 1586-1837 (DBI); Extr B 1558-1793,
         1810 (SG)
Cop (Mf) CB 1731-1879 M 1731-1855 (Mf of BT, DRO, SLC); Extr C 1731-1879
         M 1731-1855 from BT (IGI)
MI   Ch (SG)

CORFE CASTLE St Edward the Martyr [Corfe Castle Hundred; Wareham and Purbeck Union] [1712] Royal Peculiar until 1847. Included chapelry of KINGSTON (separate parish 1877). Now with CHURCH KNOWLE, KIMMERIDGE, STEEPLE, TYNEHAM.
OR   C 1653-1889 M 1695-1963 B 1653-1750, 1756-59, 1773-1948 Banns 1903-51
         (DRO)
BT   CMB 1813-40, 1846-79 (W&SRO)
Cop C 1653-1837 M 1695-1839 B 1695-1837 (DRO); C 1693-1837 MB 1695-1837
         (SG); C 1773-1837 MB 1813-37 (PRI); C 1837-79 M 1813-47 from BT (VRI);
         M 1695-1837 from OR, 1602-69 from M licences (DMI); B 1813-37 (DBI)
Cop (Mf) CB 1813-79 M 1813-47 (Mf of BT, DRO, SLC); Extr C 1837-79
         M 1813-47 from BT (IGI)
MI   (S&DFHS); (DFHS); (DRO)

CORFE CASTLE Chapel-of-ease at Bushey [Harrod 1865]

CORFE CASTLE St James, Kingston. Chapelry in CORFE CASTLE; separate parish 1877. Old church 1833; 'used for weddings and burials' [Kelly 1903]; redundant by 1933 when in use as church hall. Sold for residential use 1977. St James erected 1873-80. Now with LANGTON MATRAVERS, WORTH MATRAVERS.
OR   M 1865-1967 (DRO)
BT   CB 1877-80. For earlier transcripts *see* CORFE CASTLE (W&SRO)
Cop C 1877-80 from BT (VRI)
Cop (Mf) CB 1877-80 (Mf of BT, DRO, SLC); Extr C 1877-80 from BT (IGI)
MI   (S&DFHS); (DFHS); (DRO); Old cy *c.*1978 (SG)

CORFE CASTLE (Bapt) Licence to John Maynard of Corfe, 1672

CORFE CASTLE (Ind/Cong, now Cong Fed) Erected 1800 [*Cong. Yearbook* 1871] [Kelly 1939]; Old Independent Chapel and Schoolroom, West Street [1882 Return]; New Independent Chapel, East Street [1882 Return]; (Cong Fed) East Street f 1835
OR   ZC 1810-37 (RG 4/458, PRO) *and see* POOLE (RG 4/1230, PRO)
Cop   C 1810-37 (DRO, S&DFHS)
Cop (Mf) ZC 1810-37 (Mf of OR, SLC); ZC 1810-37 (Printout, Mf SLC);
          Extr C 1810-37 (IGI)

CORFE CASTLE (Wes) f by 1774. Preaching house by 1776 [Biggs] [1882 Return] [Kelly 1903]

CORFE CASTLE (Wes) Kingston. House occupied by John Paine registered 1798 [Biggs] Preaching Room [1882 Return] [Kelly 1903]
OR   *see* POOLE (RG 4/1230, PRO)

CORFE CASTLE (Wes) Rempstone Heath [1882 Return]

CORFE CASTLE (S of F) Corfe Castle Monthly Meeting
Cop   C 1661-1725 M 1672-1724 B 1668-1725 (DRO); B 1668-1725 (DBI)

CORFE CASTLE Corfe Castle Cemetery (Corfe Castle Parish Council)

CORFE HILLS *see* CANFORD MAGNA, Broadstone

CORFE MULLEN St Nicholas, until 1870s, then St Hubert [Cogdean Hundred; Wimborne and Cranborne Union] [603] Chapelry in STURMINSTER MARSHALL. Separate parish 1858.
OR   C 1651-1984 M 1652-61, 1670-1992 B 1652-61, 1670-78, 1756-1928, 1939,
      1948 Banns 1763, 1774, 1777, 1779-1905, 1942-57 1990-94 (DRO)
      and see STURMINSTER MARSHALL
BT   CMB 1813-80 (W&SRO)
Cop   C 1651-1840 M 1628-1840 B 1652-1840 (DRO); C 1651-1840 MB 1652-1840
      (SG); M 1711-44 from Sturminster Marshall register (SG); C 1813-80
      M 1813-49 from BT (VRI); C 1740-1837 MB 1813-37 (PRI); M 1652-1838 from
      OR (DMI); B 1652-1840 (DBI)
Cop (Mf) CB 1813-80 M 1813-45 (Mf of BT, DRO, SLC); Extr C 1813-80
          M 1813-49 from BT (IGI)
MI   (S&DFHS); (DFHS); (DRO)

CORFE MULLEN St Nicholas of Jerusalem. Consecrated 1997, in parish of St Hubert.

CORFE MULLEN (Bapt) Chapel in the Valley, Newtown Road. Erected 1813. Rebuilt 1879, 1986
MI   (Ptd NQSD 10: 1907: 130-32)

CORFE MULLEN (FIEC) Central Hall Evangelical Free Church, Wareham Road. (Undenominational) Central Hall 1923 [Kelly 1939]

CORFE MULLEN (Wes) Lambs Green [1882 Return] [Kelly 1903]; Meth [Kelly 1939]
OR   *see* Christchurch Circuit C 1833-71, 1885-1911 (HRO)

CORFE MULLEN (Prim Meth) [1882 Return] [Kelly 1903]; Meth [Kelly 1939]

CORFE MULLEN (Meth) Wareham Road. Poole and Swanage Circuit.

CORFE MULLEN (Meth) Wimborne Circuit

57

CORFE MULLEN (Meth) Corfe Mullen Methodist Church, Brackendale, Rushull Lane.

CORSCOMBE St Mary [Beaminster Forum and Redhone Hundred; Beaminster Union] [714] *see also* TOLLER WHELME. Now with MELBURY benefice.
OR C 1595-1636, 1653-1847 M 1595-1602/3, 1610-42, 1662-1837 B 1595-1604, 1609-33, 1653-55, 1660-1878 Banns 1754-1812, 1823-1944 (DRO)
BT CMB 1731-1838, 1847-80; including TOLLER WHELME 1871-80 (W&SRO)
Cop M 1595-1837 (Ptd Phil 7: 1914; & on CD-ROM); C 1595-1812 M 1595-1837 (DRO); CB 1813-37 (I, DRO); CMB 1595-1742 (I, SG); C 1731-1880 M 1731-1837 from BT (VRI); C 1740-1837 M 1800-37 B 1813-37 (PRI); M 1595-1602, 1610-42, 1660-64, 1670-1837 (SG); M 1595-1837 (Boyd); M 1790-1837 (Pallot); M 1595-1837 from OR (DMI); B 1750-1837 (DBI)
Cop (Mf) M 1595-1837 (Mf of Phil, SLC); CB 1731-1880 M 1731-1837 (Mf of BT, DRO, SLC); Extr C 1731-1880 M 1731-1837 from BT (IGI)
MI (S&DFHS); (DFHS); (DRO); Cy (SG)

CORSCOMBE St John, Toller Whelme. Erected 1870-71. Parish created 1871 from CORSCOMBE.
OR M 1872-1932 Banns 1872-1932 (DRO)
BT *see* CORSCOMBE for 1871-80
MI (S&DFHS); (DFHS)

CORTON *see* PORTESHAM

CORYATES *see* PORTESHAM

COWGROVE tithing of WIMBORNE MINSTER [728]

CRANBORNE St Mary and St Bartholomew [part Cranborne hundred, part Monkton Up Wimborne Hundred; Wimborne and Cranborne Union] [2158 including tithings of Blagdon and Monkton up Wimborne] Included also chapelry of BOVERIDGE, chapelry of ALDERHOLT (separate parish 1849) and hamlets of VERWOOD and THREE LEGGED CROSS. Now with BOVERIDGE, EDMONDSHAM, WIMBORNE ST GILES, WOODLANDS.
OR C 1602-51, 1659, 1664-1962 M 1602-48, 1670-1985 B 1602-50, 1668-1931 Banns 1754-1822, 1862-1965 (DRO)
BT CMB 1731-78, 1780-1841, 1847-79 (W&SRO)
Cop CMB 1602-1837 (DRO); CB 1602-1837 (I, SG); C 1785-1837 M 1718-1837 B 1813-37 (PRI); C 1731-1879 M 1731-1841 from BT (VRI); M 1731-54 from BT (DRO); M 1602-1717 (Boyd); M 1602-1837 from OR, 1731-54 from BT (DMI); B 1718-1837 (DBI); Extr C 1678-1711 (I, SG)
Cop (Mf) CB 1731-1879 M 1731-1841 (Mf of BT, DRO, SLC); Extr C 1731-1879 M 1731-1841 from BT (IGI)
MI (S&DFHS); (DFHS); (DRO)

CRANBORNE St James, Alderholt. Chapelry in CRANBORNE. Separate parish 1849 [Wimborne and Cranborne Union 1894-1930]
OR C 1849-1960 M 1849-1983 B 1849-1964 Banns 1849-1958 (DRO)
BT *see* CRANBORNE
MI (S&DFHS); (DFHS); (DRO); Ch, cy, war memorial (SG)

CRANBORNE St Aldhelm, Boveridge. Chapel-of-ease erected 1838. Now with CRANBORNE. Church redundant 1980. Sold for residential use 1982.
OR *see* CRANBORNE

CRANBORNE St Michael and All Angels, Verwood. Hamlet of Verwood in Cranborne. Chapel-of-ease erected 1829. Rebuilt 1886. United 1887 with hamlet of West Moors in WEST PARLEY, as a separate parish. Separated from West Moors 1922.
OR   C 1840-1964 M 1887-1980 B 1840-1940 Banns 1887-1985 (DRO)
BT   *see* CRANBORNE
Cop C 1840-1922 (DRO); B 1840-1940 Banns 1887-1901 (I, DRO); B 1840-1940 (DBI)
MI   (S&DFHS); (DFHS); (DRO)

CRANBORNE All Saints, Three Legged Cross, Verwood. Iron mission church erected 1893. Daughter church of St Michael's. Demolished 1992. Church centre erected 1994
OR   M 1981-91 (DRO)

CRANBORNE Monkton up Wimborne. Iron mission church erected 1890 [Kelly 1939]. Listed under WIMBORNE ST GILES [Kelly 1903]
MI   (S&DFHS); (DRO)

CRANBORNE (Bapt) Verwood n.d. [Kelly 1903]

CRANBORNE (Ind/Cong, now URC) Verwood Congregational Church f 1802. Rebuilt 1819. New chapel Manor Road erected 1877 (now a library) [1882 Return] New building 1906 [Kelly 1939]
OR   C 1816-3? (location unknown)
Cop C 1816-77 (DRO)

CRANBORNE (Cong now URC) Ringwood Road, Three Legged Cross f 1830. Erected 1832. New building 1890-91 [Kelly 1939]

CRANBORNE (Ind/Cong) Alderholt Chapel [1882 Return] Rebuilt 1923 ? [Kelly 1939]

CRANBORNE (Cong) Cripplestyle Chapel, Alderholt. Erected 1807 [*Cong. Yearbook* 1871] [1882 Return] Rebuilt ? 1888 [Kelly 1939]

CRANBORNE (Wes) f by 1766. House called The Kneel ? owned by Reuben Small, registered 1799 [Biggs] A building [1882 Return] [Kelly 1903]
OR   *see* POOLE (RG 4/1230, PRO)

CRANBORNE (Wes) Verwood [1882 Return]

CRANBORNE (Wes) 'Crindall' [1882 Return]; Crendell, Wimborne Circuit

CRANBORNE (Prim Meth) Ebenezer [1882 Return] [Kelly 1903]
OR   C 1898-1926 *see* Woodfalls records, Wiltshire (W&SRO)
Cop (Mf) C 1898-1926 (Mf of OR, SLC)

CRANBORNE (Prim Meth/Meth) Verwood. Erected 1876. Replaced 1909. = ? Vicarage Road. Wimborne Circuit

CRANBORNE (Prim Meth) Three Legged Cross [Kelly 1903]; Meth [Kelly 1939]

CRANBORNE (Plymouth Brethren) Three Legged Cross [Kelly 1939]

CRANBORNE POOR LAW UNION workhouse at WIMBORNE

CREECH   tithing of CHURCH KNOWLE [204] partly in STEEPLE *q.v.*

CREEKMOOR *see* CANFORD MAGNA

CRENDELL   hamlet of CRANBORNE

CRICHEL, LONG St Mary [Knowlton Hundred; Wimborne and Cranborne Union]
[138] Rebuilt 1852. United 1960 with MOOR CRICHEL. Now with WITCHAMPTON,
STANBRIDGE.
OR   C 1663-1729, 1734/5-1809 M 1663-1729, 1735-1837 B 1663-1729, 1735-1810
     Banns 1756-76, 1824-65, 1887-1970 (DRO)
BT   CMB 1731-77, 1781-84, 1788-1879 (W&SRO)
Cop C 1731-1879 M 1731-1836 from BT (VRI); C 1813-91 M 1837-91 B 1813-40
     (PRI); M 1663-1891 CB 1813-91 (DRO); M 1663-1837 (SG); M 1663-1837
     from OR, 1731-54, 1811-12 from BT (DMI); B 1813-91 (DBI)
Cop (Mf) CB 1731-1879 M 1731-1836 (Mf of BT, DRO, SLC); Extr C 1731-1879
         M 1731-1836 from BT (IGI)
MI   (S&DFHS); (DFHS); (DRO)

CRICHEL, MORE or MOOR CRICHEL St Mary [Badbury Hundred; Wimborne and
Cranborne Union] [304] United 1960 with LONG CRICHEL. Redundant 1973 for
use as monument.
OR   C 1664-1792, 1813-1945 M 1664-1958 B 1664-1792, 1813-88
     Banns 1824-1947 (DRO)
BT   CMB 1731-32, 1745-1846 C 1847-79 (W&SRO)
Cop CB 1813-37 M 1664-1836 (PRI); C 1813-37 B 1813-88 (I, DRO);
     M 1664, 1672-73, 1681-1836 (DRO, SG); M 1654-1836 from OR (DMI);
     B 1813-37 (DBI)
Cop (Mf) CB 1731-1879 M 1731-1839 (Mf of BT, DRO, SLC); Extr C 1731-1879
         M 1731-1839 from BT (IGI)

CRIPPLESTYLE *see* CRANBORNE

CRIPTON   tithing of WINTERBORNE CAME

CRITCHELL   *see* CRICHEL

CROSSWAYS Civil parish formed 1983 from parts of WOODSFORD, OWERMOIGNE,
WATERCOMBE, WARMWELL, WEST KNIGHTON. Site of RAF Woodsford 1937; renamed
RAF Warmwell 1938. Closed 1946

CROSSWAYS (Wes) Weymouth Circuit
OR   M 1931-83 (DRO)

DALWOOD St Peter [Fordington Liberty; Axminster Union] [434] Chapelry in
STOCKLAND. Transferred to Devon and Diocese of Exeter in 1830s. Now with
Stockland, Kilmington and Shute (Devon)
OR   C 1568-1644, 1713-1901 M 1568-1650, 1718-36, 1757-1978 B 1585-1655,
     1714-15, 1730-1905 (Devon RO)
BT   CMB 1731-1836 (W&SRO); CB 1837-38 M 1837 (Devon RO)
Cop CM 1731-1836 (VRI)
Cop (Mf) CMB 1731-1836 (Mf of BT, DRO, SLC); Extr C 1568-1644, 1713-1855
         M 1568-1650, 1716-1837 B 1585-1655, 1714-1915 (Mfc, SG);
         Extr CM 1731-1836 from BT (IGI, Devon)

DALWOOD (Presb) Licences for house of John Hooper, and to Zachariah Mayne
for his house, 1672

DALWOOD (Bible Christian/U Meth) Dalwood Circuit
OR   C 1891-1963 (Devon RO)

DALWOOD (Bible Christian/U Meth) Chapel
OR   C 1949-63 (Devon RO)

DEAN   *see* SIXPENNY HANDLEY

DEBERFORD   tithing of BROADWINDSOR

DENLAND   *see* SIXPENNY HANDLEY

DEWLISH All Saints [Dewlish Liberty; Dorchester Union] [361] Former ancient
parish later considered a chapelry of MILBORNE ST ANDREW, with which now
united.
OR   C 1627-72, 1682-84, 1698-1876 M 1634-45, 1655-68, 1700-17, 1725-1957,
     1968-87 B 1616-44, 1653-72, 1681-84, 1697-1993 Banns 1777-1812,
     1823-59 (DRO)
BT   CMB 1732-1832, 1845-80 (W&SRO)
Cop C 1627-1837 M 1633-1837 B 1616-1837 (DRO); CMB 1616-47, 1652-72,
     1681-84, 1697-1719, 1717-1812 (I, SG); C 1732-1832, 1844-80 M 1732-1832
     from (VRI); C 1783-1837 M 1812-37 B 1813-37 (PRI); M 1633-1837 from
     OR, 1751-58 from BT (DMI); B 1616-1837 (DBI)
Cop (Mf) CB 1732-1832, 1844-80 M 1732-1832 (Mf of BT, DRO, SLC);
          Extr C 1732-1832, 1844-80 M 1732-1832 from BT (IGI)
MI   (S&DFHS); (DFHS); (DRO); (SG) Extr: Pratt (Ms, SG)

DEWLISH (Wes) Erected 1859 [1882 Return] [Kelly 1903]; Meth [Kelly 1939]
Dorchester Circuit

DORCHESTER Borough [3033] Civil parish created 1927 by uniting DORCHESTER
ALL SAINTS with DORCHESTER ST PETER. Ecclesiastical parish created 1973 by
uniting DORCHESTER St Peter, All Saints, Holy Trinity, FROME WHITFIELD,
FORDINGTON, WEST FORDINGTON. Now includes DORCHESTER churches, WINTERBORNE
MONKTON and WINTERBORNE HERRINGSTON

DORCHESTER All Saints, High East Street [Uggscombe Hundred; Dorchester
Union 1836-1927] [667] Rebuilt 1613 and 1843-45. United 1962 with
DORCHESTER St Peter. Church redundant 1970. Sold 1972 to Dorchester Borough
Council as museum. Parish abolished 1973 to form part of DORCHESTER parish.
OR   C 1653/4-1970 M 1654-1970 B 1654-1881 Banns 1754-84, 1825-1901 (DRO)
BT   CMB 1731-1812, 1814-36, 1842-79 (W&SRO)
Cop C 1653-1812 M 1654-1845 B 1654-1759 (DRO); CB 1653-1812 M 1654-57,
     1663-1845 (SG); CMB 1813-37 (I, DRO); C 1686-1812 M 1654-1836
     B 1686-1812 (Ms, SLC); C 1759-1837 MB 1813-37 (PRI); C 1814-80 from BT
     (VRI); M 1654-1845 from OR (DMI); B 1654-1837 (DBI)
Cop (Mf) C 1813-94 M 1813-1935 B 1813-81 Banns 1825-1901 (Mf, SG);
          C 1686-1812 M 1654-1836 B 1686-1812 (Mf of Ms, SLC); CB 1731-1880?
          M 1731-1836 (Mf of BT, DRO, SLC); C 1653-1812 M 1654-1836
          (Printout, Mf SLC); Extr C 1653-1880 M 1654-1836 (IGI)

DORCHESTER Holy Trinity, High West Street [Uggscombe Hundred; Dorchester
Union 1836-1927] [1269] United 1610 with FROME WHITFIELD. Rebuilt 1824 and
1875-76. Abolished 1973 to form part of DORCHESTER parish. Building handed
over to RC church 1976.
OR   C 1559-1974 M 1560-1975 B 1559/60-1874 Banns 1853-1974 (DRO) Noted in
     1831: CMB 1653+
BT   CMB 1739-1879 (W&SRO)

DORCHESTER Holy Trinity cont.
<u>Cop</u> M 1560-1812 (Ptd Phil 7: 1914; & on CD-ROM); C 1559-1812 M 1560-1837
B 1653-1722 (DRO); C 1559-1805 M 1560-1837 B 1559-1799 (SG);
C 1722-1837 MB 1813-37 (PRI); CB 1813-37 (I,DRO); C 1739-1879
M 1739-1837 from BT (VRI); M 1739-52 from BT (DRO); M 1560-1812 (Boyd);
M 1790-1812 (Pallot); M 1560-1837 from OR, 1739-54 from BT (DMI);
B 1653-1837 (DBI); Extr CM from BT (IGI)
<u>Cop (Mf)</u> C 1800-1921 M 1791-1922 B 1800-74 Banns 1853-76 (Mf, SG);
M 1560-1812 (Mf of Phil, SLC); CB 1739-1879 M 1739-1837 (Mf of BT,
DRO, SLC); Extr C 1739-1879 M 1739-1837 from BT (IGI)

DORCHESTER St Peter, High West Street [Uggscombe Hundred; Dorchester Union
1836-1927] [1097] United 1962 with DORCHESTER All Saints. Abolished 1973 to
form part of DORCHESTER parish.
<u>OR</u> C 1653-1951 M 1653-1973 B 1653-1883 Banns 1754-94, 1897-1979 (DRO)
<u>BT</u> CMB 1730-34,1737-1879 (W&SRO)
<u>Cop</u> C 1653-1812 M 1754-1837 B 1653-1812 (DRO); C 1653-1802 M 1653-1812
B 1653-1812 (SG); CB 1813-37 (DRO); C 1730-1879 M 1730-1847 from BT
(VRI); C 1721-1837 MB 1813-37 (PRI); M 1653-1812 (Boyd); M 1653-1837
from OR (DMI); B 1800-12 (SG); B 1800-37 (DBI)
<u>Cop (Mf)</u> C 1800-1920 M 1795-1919 B 1800-77, 1882-83 (Mf, SG); CB 1730-1879
M 1730-1847 (Mf of BT, DRO, SLC); Extr C 1730-1879 M 1730-1847
from BT (IGI)
<u>MI</u> (Ptd A Metcalfe *A popular and illustrated guide to St Peter's Church,
Dorchester*: 1907)

DORCHESTER St George, Fordington [Fordington Liberty; Dorchester Union
1836-1900] [2030; increase in population by 755 since 1821 ascribed to
establishment of a cloth factory] Peculiar of the Prebend of Fordington,
Sarum Cathedral until 1847. Abolished 1973 to form part of DORCHESTER
parish.
<u>OR</u> C 1705-1968 M 1705-1970 B 1705-1973 Banns 1754-97, 1852-80, 1894-1964
(DRO) No earlier registers noted in 1831.
<u>BT</u> CMB 1577-79, 1585-88, 1591-94, 1603-09, 1614-34, 1638-39, 1664-72,
1675, 1678-1703, 1706-09, 1734-43, 1746-1826, 1829-39, 1842-79 (W&SRO)
<u>Cop</u> M 1577-1812 (Ptd Phil 4: 1909; & on CD-ROM); C 1813-37 B 1705-1803
(I. DRO); C 1577-1879 M 1577-1836 from BT (VRI); C 1577-1812
M 1575-1776 B 1564-1812 (SG); CMB 1813-37 (PRI); M 1577-1812 (Boyd);
M 1790-1812 (Pallot); M 1705-1838 from OR, 1577-1704 from SG copy
(DMI); B 1813-37 (DBI)
<u>Cop (Mf)</u> M 1577-1812 (Mf of Phil, SLC); CB 1577-1879 M 1577-1836 (Mf of BT,
DRO, SLC); Extr C 1577-1879 M 1577-1838 from BT (IGI)

DORCHESTER Christchurch, later St Mary, West Fordington. Christ Church
erected 1846. Parish formed 1847 from FORDINGTON. St Mary, newly erected,
replaced Christchurch as parish church 1929. Christchurch demolished
*c.*1931. Parish abolished 1973 to form part of DORCHESTER parish.
<u>OR</u> C 1847-1962 M 1847-1987 Banns 1847-1985 (DRO)
<u>BT</u> CMB 1847-79; for earlier transcripts *see* FORDINGTON (W&SRO)
<u>Cop</u> C 1847-79 from BT (VRI)
<u>Cop (Mf)</u> C 1847-79 (Mf of BT, DRO, SLC); Extr C 1847-79 from BT (IGI)

DORCHESTER St Francis, The Friary, Hillfield Road (Society of St Francis)

DORCHESTER (RC) Our Lady Queen of Martyrs and St Michael, High West Street.
f 1867. Former church at Wareham re-built here 1906-07. Closed 1976, and
Holy Trinity parish church taken over by RCs.
<u>OR</u> C 1871+ M 1884+ DB 1871+ Confirmations 1899+ (Inc). For earlier
entries *see* WEYMOUTH. Confirmations 1872, 1876, 1892-1933 (PDA)

DORCHESTER (Part Bapt) Dorford Chapel, Bridport Road f 1648. High East Street [Harrod 1865] Durngate Street [1882 Return] Rebuilt 1914 [Kelly 1939] SBA

DORCHESTER (Bapt) Licences to John Dibman and Francis Gie of Dorchester, 1672

DORCHESTER (Bapt) f 1830. Western Association [*Bapt. Handbook* 1861] =? Salisbury Street. Erected 1833

DORCHESTER (Bapt) High West Street. Erected 1912-14

DORCHESTER (Ind/Cong now URC/Meth) f 1662 Durngate Street. Later South Street, Rebuilt 1856-57 [*Cong. Yearbook* 1871] [1882 Return] [Kelly 1939] Now Charles Street.
OR   ZC 1788-1837 (RG 4/346, PRO); C 1837-1980, membership records and minutes 1828-88 (DRO)
Cop (Mf) ZC 1788-1837 (Mf of OR, SLC); C 1788-1837 (Printout, Mf SLC); C 1837-1951 membership records and minutes 1828-88 (Mf of OR, SLC); Extr C 1788-1837 (IGI)

DORCHESTER (Cong) Licence for house of John Ingram, Fordington; licences to William Ben for house of Philip Stansby, Dorchester; to Joshua Churchill for his house at Dorchester and that of Benjamin Devenish at Fordington; to Benjamin Way for the house of William Hayden, Dorchester, 1672

DORCHESTER (Presb/Unit) Pease Lane (Colliton Street) f 1662. Rebuilt 1720. Closed 1975. Demolished
OR   ZC 1750-1836 (RG 4/459, 345, PRO)
Cop C 1750-1836 (DRO, S&DFHS)
Cop (Mf) C 1750-1836 (Mf of OR, SLC); C 1750-1836 (Printout, Mf SLC); Extr C 1750-1836 (IGI)

DORCHESTER (Presb) Licences for houses of William Twiste, George Hammond and Jasper Samways; licence to George Hammond for house of John West and John Marsh, 1672

DORCHESTER (Lady Hunt Conn) Room in Grey House Yard, South Street. United 1826 with Durngate Street Cong Chapel.
OR   ZC 1822-26 (RG 4/2408, PRO)
Cop C 1822-26 (DRO, S&DFHS)
Cop (Mf) C 1822-26 (Mf of OR, SLC); C 1822-26 (Printout, Mf SLC); Extr C 1822-26 (IGI)

DORCHESTER (Wes) Circuit. Formed from WEYMOUTH Circuit 1831.
OR   C 1796-1831, 1838-1921 (DRO)
Cop (Mf) C 1838-1921 (Mf of OR, SLC)

DORCHESTER (Wes) North Square. Durngate [Harrod 1865] South Street. Erected 1875 [Kelly 1939] Dorchester Circuit
OR   ZC 1831-37 (RG 4/2409, PRO); M 1929-79 (DRO)
Cop C 1831-37 (DRO, S&DFHS)
Cop (Mf) ZC 1831-37 (Mf of OR, SLC); ZC 1831-37 (Printout, Mf SLC); Extr C 1831-37 (IGI)

DORCHESTER (Wes) Fordington. Dorchester Circuit
OR   M 1981-82 (DRO)

DORCHESTER (Prim Meth) Dorchester Circuit. From 1864 part of WEYMOUTH Circuit
OR   C 1861-86, 1891-1932 (DRO)

DORCHESTER (Prim Meth) Durngate Street. Erected 1875 [1882 Return] [Kelly 1903]
OR   C 1869-73 (DRO)

DORCHESTER Independent Free Christian Church, Fordington

DORCHESTER (Christadelphians) A building belonging to Mr William Vernon, Fordington Green [1882 Return]

DORCHESTER (Brethren) Building belonging to Mr J.R.Taylor, Princes Street [1882 Return]; East Parade erected 1896 [Kelly 1903]

DORCHESTER Poor Law Union Workhouse. Hospital erected 1616, South Street. Demolished 1836. New building Damers Road 1836. Chapel erected c.1900. Became Damers Hospital 1948.

DORCHESTER Prison. Erected 1795 [Kelly 1903]

DORCHESTER Cemetery, Weymouth Avenue 1856 (Dorchester Joint Burial Committee, Dorchester Town Council)
BT   B 1857-79 (W&SRO)
Cop (Mf)   B 1857-79 (Mf of BT, DRO)

DORCHESTER Fordington Cemetery (Dorchester Joint Burial Committee, Dorchester Town Council)

DORSET (S of F) Dorset Quarterly Meeting f 1668. United 1804 with Hampshire QM, Dissolved 1855.
OR   Z 1648-1794, 1804-37 M 1664-1795, 1805-36 B 1658-1794, 1804-37
     (RG 6/196, 572-73, 623-25, 649, 943, 1032, 1147-48, 1483, 1611, PRO)
     Some records but no registers at HRO.
Cop   C 1648-1836 M 1668-1836 B 1659-1836: digest copy (DRO, HRO);
     B 1776-1837 (DBI); ZMB 1649-1729 (Ts, Hist.Soc.of Pennsylvania,
     Philadelphia)
Cop (Mf)   ZMB 1776-1837 (Mf of RG 6/624, 1147, 625, 1148, 196, 572, 573,
           SLC); ZMB 1648-1804 (Mf of RG 6/649, 623, 1032, SLC);
           ZMB 1673-1795 (Mf of RG 6/1611, 943, 1483, SLC); ZMB 1635-1837
           (Transcript of digest registers, Mf SG, SLC); ZMB 1649-1729 (Mf of
           Ts, SLC); M 1658-1836 from meetings throughout the county, from
           records at DRO (DMI)

DOTTERY   see LODERS

DRIMPTON   see BROADWINDSOR

DUNGEON HILL   Modern benefice including BUCKLAND NEWTON, GLANVILLES
               WOOTTON< HOLNEST, LONG BURTON, PULHAM.

DUNTISH   tithing of BUCKLAND NEWTON

DURWESTON St Nicholas [Pimperne Hundred; Blandford Union] [418] United 1381 with KNIGHTON. Now with PIMPERNE, STOURPAINE, BRYANSTON.
OR C 1730-1884 M 1731-1837 B 1731-1915 Banns 1754-99, 1805-07, 1823-34, 1903-74 (DRO)
BT CMB 1731-40, 1744-1837, 1847-78 (W&SRO)
Cop C 1730-1899 MB 1731-1899 (DRO, DCM, SG); C 1730-1837 MB 1813-37 (PRI);
    C 1731-1878 M 1731-1837 from BT (VRI); M 1731-1837 from OR (DMI);
    B 1813-47 (DBI)
Cop (Mf) CB 1731-1878 M 1731-1837 (Mf of BT, DRO, SLC); Extr C 1731-1878
        M 1731-1837 (IGI)
MI (S&DFHS); (DFHS); (DRO)

DURWESTON (Prim Meth) In former parish newsroom [Kelly 1903, 1939]

EAST BURTON   *see* BURTON, EAST

EAST CHALDON   *see* CHALDON HERRING

EAST CHELBOROUGH   *see* CHELBOROUGH, EAST

EAST CHICKERELL   *see* CHICKERELL

EAST COMPTON   *see* COMPTON VALENCE

EAST HOLME   *see* EAST STOKE

EAST HOWE   *see* CANFORD MAGNA

EAST LANGTON   *see* LANGTON MATRAVERS

EAST LULWORTH   *see* LULWORTH, EAST

EAST MORDEN   *see* MORDEN

EAST ORCHARD   *see* ORCHARD, EAST

EAST PULHAM   *see* PULHAM

EAST STOKE   *see* STOKE, EAST

EAST STOUR   or EAST STOWER *see* STOUR, EAST

EAST WOODYATES   *see* WOODYATES, EAST, PENTRIDGE

EASTON   *see* PORTLAND

EDMONDSHAM St Nicholas [part Bindon Liberty, part Cranborne Hundred; Wimborne and Cranborne Union] [271] Now with CRANBORNE, BOVERIDGE, WIMBORNE ST GILES, WOODLANDS.
OR C 1573/4-1646/7, 1669-71, 1677-1951 M 1573-1645, 1672-1990
    B 1573-1646, 1672-1996 (DRO) Noted in 1831: CMB 1677+
BT CMB 1731-1835, 1840-79 (W&SRO)
Cop C 1573-1647, 1677-1837 M 1573-1837 B 1573-1672, 1750-1837 (DRO);
    C 1761-1837 M 1573-1837 B 1813-37 (PRI); C 1573-88 (I, SG); C 1731-1879
    M 1731-1840 from BT (VRI); M 1573-1645, 1672-1837 (SG); M 1573-1836
    from OR, 1776-96 from BT (DMI); B 1750-1837 (DBI)
Cop (Mf) CB 1731-1879 M 1731-1840 (Mf of BT, DRO, SLC); Extr C 1731-1879
        M 1731-1840 from BT (IGI)
MI (S&DFHS); (DFHS); (DRO); Ch cy 1967 (SG)

EDMONDSHAM (Prim Meth) Erected 1848 [1882 Return] [Kelly 1903]; Meth [Kelly 1939]
OR   C 1898-1926 *see* Woodfalls records, Wiltshire (W&SRO)
Cop (Mf)   C 1898-1926 (Mf of OR, SLC)

ENMORE GREEN *see* MOTCOMBE

ENSBURY   *see* CANFORD MAGNA

EVERSHOT St Osmund [Tollerford Hundred; Beaminster Union] [569] Chapelry in FROME ST QUINTIN. Now with MELBURY benefice.
OR   C 1694-1876 M 1694-1775, 1783-1841 B 1694-1717, 1722-1899
     Banns 1754-75, 1824-74, 1879-1973 (DRO) Noted in 1831: 'marriages
     irregularly scattered'.
BT   CMB 1732-1812, 1814-79 (W&SRO)
Cop C 1694-1717, 1722-61, 1787-1837 M 1694-1841 B 1722-58, 1813-37 (DRO);
     C 1732-1879 M 1736-1840 from BT (VRI); C 1787-1837 M 1694-1831
     B 1813-37 (PRI); M 1694-1841 (SG); M 1776-96 from BT (DRO); M 1694-1836
     from OR, 1776-96 from BT (DMI); B 1722-1837 (DBI)
Cop (Mf) CB 1732-1879 M 1736-1840 (Mf of BT, DRO, SLC); Extr C 1732-1879
          M 1738-1840 from BT (IGI)

EVERSHOT (Gospel Hall) [Kelly 1939]

EWERNE *see* IWERNE (COURTNEY, MINSTER, STEEPLETON)

EYPE   *see* SYMONDSBURY

FARNHAM St Laurence [Cranborne Hundred; Wimborne and Cranborne Union 1835-94; Blandford Union 1894-1930] [314 including tithing of Farnham Tollard 220] Now with TOLLARD ROYAL, GUSSAGE ST MICHAEL, GUSSAGE ALL SAINTS, ASHMORE, CHETTLE.
OR   C 1737-1974 M 1737-53, 1761-62, 1784-90, 1813-1961 B 1737-1809,
     1813-1992 (DRO) Noted in 1831: CMB 1647-1731, 1737+
BT   CMB 1731-1879 (W&SRO)
Cop C 1737-1837 B 1813-37 (I, DRO); C 1731-1879 M 1734-1845 from BT (VRI);
     C 1737-1837 MB 1813-37 (PRI); M 1737-62, 1784-91. 1813-37 (DRO, SG);
     M 1732-88 from BT (DRO); M 1737-1837 from OR, 1731-37, 1812 from BT
     (DMI); B 1813-37 (DBI)
Cop (Mf) CB 1731-1879 M 1734-1845 (Mf of BT, DRO, SLC); Extr C 1731-1879
          M 1734-1845 from BT (IGI)
MI   (S&DFHS); (DFHS); (DRO)

FARNHAM (Wes) Erected 1865 [Kelly 1903]; Meth [Kelly 1939]

FARRINGDON *see* IWERNE COURTNEY

FERNDOWN   *see* HAMPRESTON

FIDDLEFORD hamlet of OKEFORD FITZPAINE; formerly in CHILD OKEFORD

FIFEHEAD MAGDALEN St Mary Magdalene (Redland Hundred; Sturminster Union] [241] Now with GILLINGHAM benefice.
OR   C 1565-1992 M 1565-1993 B 1564/8-1990 Banns 1825-1994 (DRO)
BT   CMB 1598-1600, 1731-84, 1788-1879 (W&SRO)
Cop C 1565-1683, 1744-1837 M 1565-1839 B 1564/5-1683/4, 1813-37 (DRO);
     C 1598-1879 M 1598-1846 from BT (VRI); C 1744-1837 MB 1813-37 (PRI);
     M 1598-1753 from BT (DRO); M 1565-1839 (SG); M 1565-1839 from OR,
     1598-1600, 1731-54 from BT (DMI); B 1564-1837 (DBI)

FIFEHEAD MAGDALEN cont.
Cop (Mf) CB 1598-1879 M 1598-1846 (Mf of BT, DRO, SLC); Extr C 1598-1879
        M 1598-1846 from BT (IGI)
MI   (S&DFHS); (DFHS); (DRO)

FIFEHEAD NEVILLE or FIFEHIDE NEVILLE All Saints [Pimperne Hundred;
Sturminster Union] [101] Now with HAZLEBURY BRYAN AND THE HILLSIDE PARISHES
benefice.
OR   C 1573-1640, 1646-51, 1670-1999 M 1573-1640, 1670-1710, 1718-1807,
     1815-1996 B 1573-1640, 1670-1998 Banns 1754-81, 1828-1934, 1968, 1971
     (DRO)
BT   CMB 1731-1879 (W&SRO)
Cop C 1573-1711, 1741-1812 M 1573-1807 B 1573-1711, 1813-1934 (DRO);
     CB 1573-1711 M 1573-1640, 1670-1807 (SG); C 1731-1879 M 1731-1839 from
     BT (VRI); M 1731-54 from BT (DRO); C 1741-1812 M 1813-39 (PRI);
     M 1573-1807 from OR, 1731-54, 1809-37 from BT (DMI); B 1813-1934 (SG);
     B 1722-1934 (DBI); Extr CB 1703-1800 M 1573-1640, 1670-1807 (SG)
Cop (Mf) CB 1731-1879 M 1731-1839 (Mf of BT, DRO, SLC); Extr C 1731-1879
        M 1731-1839 from BT (IGI)

FIFEHEAD NEVILLE (Prim Meth) Erected 1882 [Kelly 1903]; Meth [Kelly 1939]

FIFEHEAD ST QUINTIN or LOWER FIFEHEAD. tithing of BELCHALWELL

FIFEHEAD SYDLING tithing of SYDLING ST NICHOLAS

FIFEHEAD, LOWER tithing of BELCHALWELL

FISHPOND see WHITCHURCH CANONICORUM

FLEET Holy Trinity [Uggscombe Hundred; Weymouth Union] [122] Old church
destroyed in storm 1824, except chancel. Rebuilt 1827-29. Now with
CHICKERELL.
OR   C 1663-1993 M 1664-1721, 1732-54, 1759, 1813-35, 1942-88 B 1664-1995
     (DRO)
BT   CMB 1731-62, 1776-1829, 1834-45, 1847-79; see also UPWEY 1799 (W&SRO)
Cop M 1664-1753 (Ptd Phil 6: 1912; & on CD-ROM); C 1663-1993 M 1664-1988
     B 1664-1995 (DRO); CM 1663-1812 B 1664-1809 (SG); C 1813-38 M 1798-1841
     B 1798-1840 (PRI); C 1731-1879 M 1731-1849 from BT (VRI); M 1664-1721,
     1732-52, 1756-60, 1777-1803, 1809-23, 1831-35 (SG); M 1731-55 from BT
     (DRO); M 1663-1753 (Boyd); M 1664-1753, 1756-1835 from OR, 1731-56 from
     BT (DMI); B 1798-1994 (DBI)
Cop (Mf) M 1664-1753 (Mf of Phil, SLC); CB 1731-1879 M 1731-1849 (Mf of BT,
        DRO, SLC); Extr C 1731-1879 M 1731-1849 from BT (IGI)
MI   (S&DFHS); (DFHS); (DRO); old and new churches (SG)

FOLKE St Lawrence [Sherborne Hundred; Sherborne Union] [281] Peculiar of
the Dean of Sarum until 1847. Rebuilt 1628. United 1972 with NORTH WOOTTON,
HAYDON. Now with THE CAUNDLES WITH FOLKE AND HOLWELL benefice.
OR   C 1538-1906 M 1538-1991 B 1538-1993 Banns 1755-82, 1823-1924 (DRO)
BT   CMB 1586-88, 1595-1619, 1626-38, 1664, 1669-99, 1701-05, 1708-1812,
     1814-27, 1847-78 (W&SRO)
Cop C 1538-1837 M 1538-1837 B 1538-1837 (DRO); C 1586-1878 M 1586-1837
     from BT (VRI); C 1750-1837 M 1538-1837 B 1813-37 (PRI); M 1586-1755
     from BT (DRO); M 1538-1837 (SG); M 1538-1837 from OR, 1586-1755 from
     BT (DMI); B 1538-1837 (DBI)
Cop (Mf) CB 1586-1878 M 1586-1837 (Mf of BT, DRO, SLC); Extr C 1586-1878
        M 1586-1837 from BT (IGI)

FOLKE (Presb) Licence for house of Robert Bullen, 1672

FOLKE (Wes) Alweston [Kelly 1903]

FOLKE (Prim Meth) Alweston [1882 Return]; Meth [Kelly 1939]

FONTMELL MAGNA or GREAT FONTMELL St Andrew [Sixpenny Handley Hundred; Shaftesbury Incorporation/Union] [743 including including tithing of Hartgrove 187] Included chapelry of WEST ORCHARD, transferred to EAST ORCHARD with MARGARET MARSH 1952. Now with IWERNE COURTNEY, IWERNE STEEPLETON, SUTTON WALDRON.
OR C 1653-1993, M 1654-1993 B 1653/4-1948 Banns 1653-57, 1754-1822, 1824-65 (DRO)
BT CMB 1731-1834, 1841-79 (W&SRO)
Cop C 1653-86/7, 1769-1837 M 1654-1837 B 1813-37 (DRO); C 1769-1837 MB 1813-37 (PRI); C 1731-1879 M 1731-1848 from BT (VRI); M 1654-1837 (SG); M 1731-54 from BT (DRO); M 1654-1837 from OR, 1697-98, 1731-54 from BT (DMI); B 1813-37 (DBI)
Cop (Mf) CB 1731-1879 M 1731-1848 (Mf of BT, DRO, SLC); Extr C 1731-1879 M 1731-1848 from BT (IGI)
MI (S&DFHS); (DFHS); (DRO); Cy 1909 (*Ye Olde Mortality* 9: Ms, SG)

FONTMELL MAGNA (Wes) f by 1782. Building in occupation of John Monkton registered 1795; a building registered 1797 [Biggs] Rebuilt 1830 [1882 Return] [Kelly 1939] North Dorset Circuit

FONTMELL MAGNA (Wes) Hartgrove [1882 Return]

FONTMELL MAGNA (Wes) Bedchester [1882 Return]

FORDINGTON, WEST FORDINGTON see DORCHESTER

FORTUNESWELL see PORTLAND

FRAMPTON St Mary [Frampton Liberty; Dorchester Union] [370] Peculiar of Manor and Liberty of Frampton (which included Bettiscombe, Bincombe, Compton Valence) Now with BRADFORD PEVERELL, STRATTON, SYDLING ST NICHOLAS
OR C 1627-1803, 1813-86 M 1632-1993 B 1627-1803, 1813-1943 Banns 1655/6-1658/9 (DRO) Noted in 1831: CMB 1654+
BT CMB 1731-1802, 1805-36, 1844-78 (W&SRO)
Cop C 1627-53, 1738-1837 M 1628-1837 B 1627-53, 1813-36 (DRO); CMB 1627-1812 (I, SG); C 1731-1878 M 1731-1845, 1857-59 from BT (VRI); C 1738-1837 MB 1813-37 (PRI); M 1628-1837 (SG); M 1628-1836 from OR, 1752-53 from BT (DMI); B 1813-37 (DBI)
Cop (Mf) CB 1731-1878 M 1731-1845 (Mf of BT, DRO, SLC); Extr C 1731-1878 M 1731-1845, 1857-59 from BT (IGI)

FRIERMAYNE Ancient parish united 1563 with WEST KNIGHTON.

FROME BILLET Ancient parish united 1470 with WEST STAFFORD.

FROME ST QUINTIN or LITTLE FROME St Quintin [Tollerford Hundred; Cerne Union] [143] Now with MELBURY benefice.
OR C 1661-1796 M 1653-99, 1706-64, 1815-37 B 1654-1796 Banns 1824-70 *and see* MELBURY BUBB banns 1889-1925 (DRO)
BT CMB 1731-1879 (W&SRO)

FROME ST QUINTIN cont.
Cop C 1661-1787 M 1653-1764, 1815-37 B 1654-1786, 1813-37 (DRO);
      C 1731-1879 M 1731-1879 from BT (VRI); MB 1813-37 (PRI); M 1653-66,
      1673, 1678, 1682-85, 1697-99, 1705-09, 1722-28, 1733-43, 1752-53,
      1760-64, 1815-37 (SG); M 1764-97 from BT (DRO); M 1653-99, 1705-64,
      1815-37 from OR, 1731-1815 from BT (DMI); B 1813-37 (DBI)
Cop (Mf) CB 1731-1879 M 1731-1839 (Mf of BT, DRO, SLC); Extr C 1731-1879
          M 1731-1839 from BT (IGI)
MI   (S&DFHS); (DFHS); (DRO)

FROME ST QUINTIN Chantmarle (House) Chapel 1612

FROME VAUCHURCH St Mary [Tollerford Hundred; Dorchester Union] [135]
United 1925 with MAIDEN NEWTON. Now with MELBURY benefice.
OR   C 1654-1812 M 1667-1835, 1841-1924 B 1642-1812 Banns 1756-1810,
      1825-1924 (DRO)
BT   CMB 1732-1879 (W&SRO)
Cop M 1667-1812 (Ptd Phil 3: 1908; & on CD-ROM); C 1654-1812 M 1667-1835
      B 1642-1812 (DRO); C 1662-1812 M 1667-1837 B 1642-1837 (I, DRO);
      M 1732-56 B 1813-37 from BT (DRO); C 1738-1812 M 1667-1835 (PRI);
      C 1731-1879 from BT (VRI); M 1667-1835 (SG); M 1667-1775 (Boyd);
      M 1790-1812 (Pallot); M 1667-1835 from OR, 1732-56, 1811-37 from BT
      (DMI); B 1813-1998 (NBI); B 1813-37 (DBI); Extr CMB 1643-1869 (SG)
Cop (Mf) M 1667-1812 (Mf of Phil, SLC); CB 1732-1879 M 1732-1865 (Mf of
          BT,DRO, SLC); Extr C 1731-1879 M 1732-1865 from BT (IGI)

FROME VAUCHURCH 'At Tollerford, which gives its name to the Hundred, was
anciently a chapel' [Kelly 1903]

FROME WHITFIELD [George Hundred until 1610, when united with DORCHESTER
Holy Trinity]

GILLINGHAM Modern benefice including BUCKHORN WESTON, FIFEHEAD MAGDALEN,
GILLINGHAM, LANGHAM, MILTON, KINGTON MAGNA, EAST STOUR, WEST STOUR, STOUR
PROVOST, STOUR ROW, TODBER.

GILLINGHAM St Mary the Virgin [Gillingham Liberty; Shaftesbury
Incorporation/Union] [2520 excluding chapelries] Royal Peculiar until 1847.
Included chapelries of MOTCOMBE (separate parish, with ENMORE GREEN, 1883);
BOURTON (separate parish 1847); EAST STOUR, WEST STOUR. Now with GILLINGHAM
benefice.
OR   C 1564/5-1980 M 1559-1700, 1723-1991 B 1559-1992 Banns 1754-97,
      1949-73 (DRO)
BT   CMB 1718-19, 1734-35, 1739-44, 1748, 1751, 1774-1879 (W&SRO)
Cop C 1787-1837, 1952-79 M 1559-1838 B 1559-1735, 1813-37 (DRO);
      C 1787-1837 MB 1813-37 (PRI); C 1718-1879 M 1718-1836 from BT (VRI);
      M 1559-1838 from OR (DMI); B 1787-1837 (DBI)
Cop (Mf) CMB 1718-1812 CB 1813-79 M 1813-38 (Mf of BT, DRO, SLC);
          Extr C 1718-1879 M 1718-1838 from BT (IGI)
MI   (DFHS); (DRO)1 EXtr Ch (Ptd Gent.Mag. 1814: 1 113); Cy 1905 (*Ye Olde
        Mortality* 9: Ms, SG)

GILLINGHAM St George, Bourton [Gillingham Liberty; Mere Union 1835-94;
Shaftesbury Union 1894-1930] [810] Erected 1812; rebuilt 1878-79. Chapelry
in GILLINGHAM, separate parish 1847. Now with UPPER STOUR benefice
[Wiltshire]
OR   C 1812-1990 M 1837-1990 B 1813-1989 Banns 1848-1990 (DRO)
      Noted in 1831: CB 1810-12.
BT   CMB 1813-79; for earlier transcripts *see* GILLINGHAM (W&SRO)

GILLINGHAM St George, Bourton cont.
Cop CB 1813-37 (DRO, PRI); C 1813-79 from BT (VRI); M 1813-37, 1846 from
BT (DMI); B 1813-50 (DBI)
Cop (Mf) CB 1813-79 (Mf of BT, DRO, SLC); Extr C 1813-79 from BT (IGI)

GILLINGHAM St Simon and St Jude, Milton on Stour. Consecrated 1860
[Kelly 1939]. Now with GILLINGHAM benefice.
OR M 1884-1992 B 1887-1992 (DRO)
MI (S&DFHS); (DFHS); (DRO); (SG)

GILLINGHAM St George, Langham Lane. Chapel-of-ease erected 1921. Now with
GILLINGHAM benefice.

GILLINGHAM (RC) St Benedict, Rolls Bridge. Erected 1907

GILLINGHAM (Bapt) f 1839 [*Bapt. Handbook* 1861] Erected 1840; rebuilt 1892
[Kelly 1939]
MI Cy 1905 (*Ye Olde Mortality* 8: Ms, SG)

GILLINGHAM (Part Bapt) Newbury [1882 Return]

GILLINGHAM (Bapt) Bourton f 1834. Bristol Association [*Bapt. Handbook* 1861]
[Harrod 1865] [Kelly 1903, 1939]

GILLINGHAM (Presb) Licence for house of Robert Berren, 1672

GILLINGHAM (Wes) Shaftesbury and Gillingham Circuit. Includes parishes of
Alvediston, Cann, Donhead St Mary, Motcombe, Shaftesbury, Tisbury, Tollard
Royal, West Tisbury [Dorset and Wilts]
OR Gillingham section C 1850-1967; Shaftesbury Section C 1843-1906 (DRO)
Cop (Mf) C 1843-1932 (Mf of OR, SLC)

GILLINGHAM (Wes) Preaching house registered 1792 [Biggs]
OR ZC 1796-1824 (RG 4/460, PRO)
Cop (Mf) ZC 1796-1824 (Mf of OR, SLC); C 1796-1824 (Printout, Mf SLC);
Extr C 1796-1824 (IGI)

GILLINGHAM (Wes) New Wesleyan Methodist Church [1882 Return]

GILLINGHAM (Wes) Huntingford Chapel [1882 Return]

GILLINGHAM (Wes) Bourton. [Harrod 1865] Rebuilt 1882 [Kelly 1903];
erected 1888 [Kelly 1939]

GILLINGHAM (Prim Meth) Shaftesbury and Gillingham Circuit
OR *see* MOTCOMBE

GILLINGHAM (Prim Meth) Chapel [Harrod 1865] [1882 Return] [Kelly 1903]

GILLINGHAM (Prim Meth) Cottage occupied by Elizabeth Harrison, Weaverland
Lane [1882 Return]

GILLINGHAM (Prim Meth) Queen Street
OR C 1936-63 (DRO)
Cop (Mf) C 1873-1950 kept by Queen Street chapel, Gillingham (Mf of OR,
SLC)

GILLINGHAM (Meth)
OR *see* Frome Meth Circuit (Somerset) C 1837-81 (SRO)

GILLINGHAM (Meth) High Street. North Dorset Circuit

GILLINGHAM (Christians) Temperance Hall [1882 Return]

GILLINGHAM Gillingham Cemetery 1953. (Gillingham Town Council)

GLANVILLES WOOTTON or WOOTTON GLANVILLE   St Mary the Virgin [Buckland Newton Hundred; Cerne Union] [331] Included tithing of Wootton Newland. United 1929 with HOLNEST and parts of LONG BURTON, HAYDON. Now with DUNGEON HILL benefice.
OR   C 1549-1650,   1659-1886   M   1546-1642,   1656-1997   B   1578-1643,
    1667-1724/5, 1732/3-1813 Banns 1754-1812, 1824-1908 (DRO)
BT   CMB 1731-1879 (W&SRO)
Cop   C 1549-1837 M 1546-1837 B 1578-1684 (DRO); CMB 1546-1731 (I, SG);
    C 1731-1879 M 1731-1846 from BT (VRI); C 1740-1837 M 1813-37 (PRI);
    M 1546-52, 1560-83, 1589-1642, 1656-57, 1662-1703, 1708-1837 (SG);
    M 1815-37 from BT (DRO); M 1546-1753, 1755-1837 from OR, 1813-37 from
    BT (DMI); B 1578-1899 (DBI)
Cop (Mf)   CB 1731-1880? M 1731-1846 (Mf of BT, DRO, SLC); Extr C 1731-1880
    M 1731-1846 from BT (IGI)
MI   Ch (Ptd *Miscellanea Genealogica et Heraldica.* series 5: 8: 1932:
    218-19)

GLANVILLES WOOTTON (Wes) n.d. [1882 Return] [Kelly 1903]; Meth [Kelly 1939]

GOATHILL St Peter [Horethorne Hundred (Somerset) until 1895 when transferred to Dorset; Sherborne Union]
OR   *see* NIPR Vol.8 Part 3 Somerset

GODMANSTONE Holy Trinity [Cerne, Totbury and Modbury Hundred; Cerne Union] [152] Now with CERNE ABBAS, MINTERNE MAGNA
OR   C 1654-1812 M 1654-1943, 1953-90 B 1654-1812 Banns 1754-1811 (DRO)
BT   CMB 1731-1832, 1847-79 (W&SRO)
Cop   M 1654-1812 (Ptd Phil 6: 1912; & on CD-ROM); C 1770-1812 M 1654-1836
    (PRI); C 1731-1879 M 1731-1832 from BT (VRI); C 1716-1812 (I, DRO);
    M 1654-64, 1669-81, 1693-1836 (SG); M 1654-1836 (DRO); M 1654-1812
    (Boyd); M 1790-1811 (Pallot); M 1654-1836 from OR, 1731-54, 1812 from
    BT (DMI); B 1654-1837 (DBI)
Cop (Mf)   M 1654-1812 (Mf of Phil, SLC); CB 1731-1879 M 1731-1832 (Mf of BT,
    DRO, SLC); Extr C 1731-1879 M 1731-1832 from BT (IGI)

GOLDEN CAP Team Benefice Includes BETTISCOBE and PILSDON, CATHERSTON LEWESTON, CAARMOUTH, CHIDEOCK, HAWKCHURCH, LYME REGIS, MARSHWOOD, MONKTON WYLD, WHITCHURCH CANONICORUM with STANTON ST GABRIEL and FISHPOND, WOOTTON FITZPAINE.

GOMERSHAY tithing of STALBRIDGE [90]

GOREWOOD [Piddletrenthide Liberty from 1858; Cerne Union] Extra-parochial place; civil parish 1858. From 1933 part of MINTERNE MAGNA.

GREAT CANFORD   *see* CANFORD MAGNA

GREAT FONTMELL   *see* FONTMELL MAGNA

GREAT HINTON   *see* HINTON MARTELL

GREAT KINGTON   *see* KINGTON MAGNA

GREAT MINTERNE   *see* MINTERNE MASNA

GREAT TOLLER   *see* TOLLER PORCORUM

GRIMSTONE   *see* STRATTON

GUSSAGE ALL SAINTS All Saints [Knowlton Hundred; Wimborne and Cranborne Union] [373] Now with TOLLARD ROYAL, FARNHAM, GUSSAGE ST MICHAEL, ASHMORE, CHETTLE.
OR   C 1560-1620, 1625-47, 1653-1889 M 1560-1619, 1625-41, 1654-1993
     B 1560-1619/20, 1625-41, 1653-1993 Banns 1759-90, 1823-1904, 1933 (DRO)
BT   CMB 1732-1808, 1811-44, 1847-78 (W&SRO)
Cop CMB 1560-1840 (SG); CMB 1813-37 (I, DRO); C 1793-1837 MB 1813-37
     (PRI); C 1732-1878 M 1732-1844 from BT (VRI); M 1560-1619, 1625-40,
     1654-1836 (DRO, SG); M 1560-1836 from OR, 1756 from BT (DMI);
     B 1813-37 (DBI)
Cop (Mf) CB 1732-1878 M 1732-1844 (Mf of BT, DRO, SLC); Extr C 1732-1878
         M 1732-1844 from BT (IGI)
MI   (S&DFHS); (DFHS); (DRO)

GUSSAGE ST ANDREW St Andrew Hamlet in SIXPENNY HANDLEY. Erected 13th cent.
Now with SIXPENNY HANDLEY, PENTRIDGE.
OR   C 1785-1992 (DRO) Noted in 1831: 'one book of Bap.1785-1812. This
     Chapel is attached to Handley'
BT   CMB 1766-69, 1775-80, 1783-85, 1788-1811, 1813-34 C 1847-79; for 1835
     see GUSSAGE ST MICHAEL (W&SRO)
Cop C 1813-37 (I, DRO); C 1766-1879 from BT (VRI); C 1785-1837 (PRI);
     M 1766-1834 from BT (DMI)
Cop (Mf) C 1766-1879 B 1766-1811 (Mf of BT, DRO, SLC); Extr C 1766-1879
         from BT (IGI)

GUSSAGE ST MICHAEL or MIDDLE GUSSAGE St Michael [Badbury Hundred; Wimborne and Cranborne Union] [233] *see also WOODLANDS*. Now with TOLLARD ROYAL, FARNHAM, GUSSAGE ALL SAINTS, ASHMORE, CHETTLE.
OR   C 1653/4-1692 1711-1812 M 1654-82, 1711-1995 B 1654-56, 1663-80,
     1711-1811 (DRO)
BT   CMB 1732-84, 1786-1813, 1817-36, 1847-79; 1835 transcript includes
     GUSSAGE ST ANDREW (W&SRO)
Cop C 1653-1850 M 1654-1848 B 1654-1851 (DRO); CMB 1650-1850 (I, SLC);
     C 1732-1836, 1847-79 M 1732-1835 from BT (VRI); C 1729-1837 MB 1813-37
     (PRI); M 1731-41 from BT (DRO); M 1654-82, 1711, 1720-1848 (SG);
     M 1654-1848 from OR, 1731-1816 from BT (DMI); B 1654-1851 (DBI)
Cop (Mf) CB 1732-1836, 1847-79 M 1732-1835 (Mf of BT, DRO, SLC);
         Extr C 1732-1836, 1847-79 M 1732-1835 from BT (IGI)
MI   (S&DFHS); (DFHS); (DRO)

GUSSAGE ST MICHAEL (Wes) Wimborne Circuit. [Harrod 1865] A building
[1882 Return] [Kelly 1903]
OR   M 1958-61, 1966 (DRO)

GUSSAGE [unspecified] (Wes)
OR   *see* POOLE (RG 4/1230, PRO)

HALSTOCK St Mary [Halstock Liberty; Beaminster Union] [554] Peculiar of the Prebend of Lyme Regis and Halstock, Sarum Cathedral until 1847. Rebuilt 1846. Now with MELBURY benefice.
OR   C 1698-1751, 1760-1969 M 1700-74, 1779-1837 B 1693-1913 Banns 1739-74,
     1779-83, 1794-1812, 1824-1936 (DRO)

HALSTOCK cont.
BT CMB 1579-82, 1592-94, 1606-11, 1614-20, 1623-28, 1631-39, 1670-75,
    1678, 1683-86, 1690-91, 1695, 1698-1700, 1703-29, 1735-39, 1743-49,
    1751-52, 1756-1805, 1808-26, 1829-34, 1836-80 (W&SRO)
Cop M 1701-1812 (Ptd Phil 3: 1908; & on CD-ROM); C 1698-1837 M 1700-1837
    B 1698-1837 (DRO); C 1698-1751, 1760-1806, 1810-12 M 1701-1837
    B 1698-1812 (SG); C 1721-1837 M 1808-37 B 1813-37 (PRI); C 1813-65
    (S&DFHS); C 1836-80 from BT (VRI); M 1579-1700, 1774-79 from BT (DRO);
    M 1701-75 (Boyd); M 1790-1812 (Pallot); M 1700-1837 from OR, 1579-1754,
    1774-80, 1782 from BT (DMI); B 1698-1837 (DBI)
Cop (Mf) M 1701-1812 (Mf of Phil, SLC); CB 1579-1834, 1836-80 M 1579-1835
    (Mf of BT, DRO, SLC); Extr C 1579-1880 M 1579-1835 from BT (IGI)
MI (S&DFHS); (DFHS)

HAM CHAMBERLAYNE see HAMPRESTON

HAMMOON St Paul [Pimperne Hundred; Sturminster Union] [54] United 1971 with
CHILD OKEFORD, MANSTON. Now with THE OKEFORD BENEFICE.
OR C 1657-1812 M 1656, 1671-1804, 1813-35 B 1656-1812 Banns 1755-87,
    1825-1963 (DRO)
BT CMB 1731-79, 1782-1840, 1844-45, 1847-80 (W&SRO)
Cop C 1659-1823 M 1656-1861 B 1659-1801 (DRO); C 1731-1880 M 1731-1845
    from BT (VRI); C 1621-1812 M 1813-35 (PRI); M 1656-1837 from OR, 1754,
    1805-12 from BT (DMI); B 1656-1899 (DBI); Extr C 1662-1774 M 1687-1765
    B 1657-1763 (SG)
Cop (Mf) CB 1731-1880 M 1731-1845 (Mf of BT, DRO, SLC); Extr C 1731-1880
    M 1731-1845 from BT (IGI)
MI (S&DFHS); (DFHS); (DRO)

HAMPRESTON Benefice including HAMPRESTON, STAPEHILL, FERNDOWN, GLENMOOR.

HAMPRESTON or HAM CHAMBERLAYNE All Saints [part Cranborne Hundred, part
Westover Liberty (Hampshire), entirely Dorset from 1860s; Wimborne and
Cranborne Union] [883 including Long Ham in Westover Liberty] see also
COLEHILL.
OR C 1617-53, 1678-1937 M 1617-62, 1678-1958 B 1617-52/3, 1678-1920 Banns
    1754-1822, 1885-1972 (DRO)
BT CMB 1731-1844, 1850-80 (W&SRO)
Cop CM 1617-1918 B 1617-1920 (DRO); CB 1617-53 M 1617-62, 1678-1837 (SG);
    C 1765-1840 M 1617-1837 B 1813-43 (PRI); C 1731-1880 M 1731-1844 from
    BT (VRI); M 1617-1837 from OR, 1731-54 from BT (DMI); B 1813-43 (DBI)
Cop (Mf) CB 1731-1880 M 1731-1844 (Mf of BT, DRO, SLC); Extr C 1731-1880
    M 1617-27, 1657-59, 1731-1844 (IGI)
MI (S&DFHS); (DFHS); (DRO)

HAMPRESTON All Saints, Stapehill. Church hall erected 1932. Now part of
HAMPRESTON benefice.

HAMPRESTON St Mary, Ferndown. Mission hall erected late 19th century
[Kelly 1903]; new building 1934 [Kelly 1939] Now part of HAMPRESTON
benefice.
OR 1948+ (Inc)

HAMPRESTON Glenmoor, Ferndown. Now part of HAMPRESTON benefice.

HAMPRESTON (RC) Stapehill, Little Canford. f 1637. School run by Jesuit priests to 1724 and 1750+. Chapel of Holy Cross Abbey (Cistercian Nuns) f 1802; 1989 abbey moved to Whitland, Carmarthenshire. Church of Our Lady of Dolours erected 1851 [1882 Return] Served from WEST MOORS from 1970s.
OR Early volume including CANFORD now missing. CMDB 1856+ (Inc, West Moors); Confirmations 1863, 1868, 1883, 1884, 1888, 1889, 1890, 1893-1931 (PDA)
Cop C 1770-1856 M 1847, 1852-56 Confirmations 1851 D 1851-56 (Ptd CRS 43: 1949)
Cop (Mf) 'Canford Magna and Stapehill' ZC 1772-1856 (Printout, Mf SLC)
MI (S&DFHS); (DFHS); (DRO); (Ptd CRS 43: 119)

HAMPRESTON (Ind/Cong, now URC) Longham Congregational Church, Ringwood Road. f 1820. Erected 1841. Out-station of WIMBORNE [*Cong. Yearbook* 1871]
MI (S&DFHS); (DFHS)

HAMPRESTON (URC: Cong/Bapt) Ferndown, Wimborne Road f 1905. SBA
MI (DRO)

HAMPRESTON (Wes) Longham f by 1766. House of William Neave registered 1795 [Biggs] Chapel [Harrod 1865]

HAMPRESTON (Wes) Stapehill. Wimborne Circuit [Kelly 1903]
OR M 1958-75 (DRO)

HAMPRESTON (Prim Meth) Ferndown [Kelly 1903]

HAMWORTHY *see* STURMINSTER MARSHALL

HANDLEY *see* SIXPENNY HADLEY

HANFORD St Michael [Redland Hundred; Sturminster Union 1858-1930] Erected 1650. Described as extra-parochial in 1831 [10] Redundant 1974. Sold to Hanford School for use as chapel.
OR C 1832-1954 M 1815-35, 1847-1949 B 1815, 1828-74, 1918 Banns 1862-1919, 1949 (DRO) Noted in 1831: CB 1669-1782, 1785-1812 M 1672-1704, 1762-1806; ' No Marr solemnized during the above intervals.' Early registers from 1669 lost between 1927 (when transcribed; see below) and 1977.
BT CMB 1813-74 (W&SRO)
Cop C 1669-1856 M 1672-1836 B 1671-1864 (DRO); C 1669, 1676, 1685-97, 1716, 1745-62, 1782-85, 1793, 1807-12, 1856 M 1672-86, 1692, 1699-1704, 1755, 1760-68, 1774-1806, 1827, 1835-36 B 1671-1864, 1927 (SG); CMB 1813-37 (PRI); C 1813, 1849-57 M 1815-35, 1847 from BT (VRI); M 1672-1704, 1755-81, 1799-1835 (SG); M 1815-36 from OR, 1672-1814, 1836 from SG copy (DMI); B 1675-1864 (DBI)
Cop (Mf) C 1813, 1849-57 M 1815-35, 1847 B 1815-35, 1857-74 (Mf of BT, DRO, SLC); Extr C 1813, 1849-57 M 1815-35, 1847 from BT (IGI)

HARCOMBE *see* WHITCHURCH CANONICORUM

HARTGROVE tithing of FONTMELL MAGNA

HARTLY tithing of MINTERNE MAGNA

HASELBURY BRYAN *see* HAZELBURY BRYAN

HAWKCHURCH St John the Baptist [part Cerne, Totbury and Modbury Hundred, part Uggscombe Hundred; Axminster Union] [886 including tithing of Wyldecourt] Noted in 1831: 'Most part of the parish of HAWKCHURCH, under the name of Phillyholme, is in ...Uggerscombe Hundred'. Transferred 1896 to Devon. Now with GOLDEN CAP Team Benefice [Salisbury Diocese]
OR C 1664-1897 M 1664-1978 B 1664-1967 (Devon RO)
BT CMB 1731-1880 (W&SRO)
Cop M 1664-1812 (Ptd Phil 2: 1907; & on CD-ROM); CB 1663-1851 M 1664-1864 (DRO, SG); CB 1813-37 M 1664-1837 (PRI); C 1731-1880 M 1731-1837 from BT (VRI); M 1813-47 (S&DFHS); M 1731-54 from BT (DRO); M 1669-1812 (Boyd); M 1790-1812 (Pallot); M 1664-1837 from OR, 1731-54 from BT (DMI); B 1809-38 (DBI)
Cop (Mf) M 1664-1812 (Mf of Phil, SLC); CB 1731-1880 M 1731-1837 (Mf of BT, DRO, SLC); Extr C 1731-1880 M 1731-1837 from BT (IGI)
MI (SG)

HAWKCHURCH (Presb) Licences for house of Thomas More, and to John Gill for his house, 1672

HAWKCHURCH (S of F) Hawkchurch Monthly Meeting
OR C 1648-1703/04 B 1668-98 (DRO)

HAYDON St Catherine [Sherborne Hundred; Sherborne Union] [123] Peculiar of the Dean of Sarum until 1847. Rebuilt 1883. United 1972 with FOLKE, NORTH WOOTTON. Redundant 1976. Sold as craft workshop 1980.
OR C 1711-1969 M 1712-51, 1756-1959 B 1711-1976 Banns 1869-1968 (DRO)
     No earlier register noted in 1831.
BT CMB 1595-1602, 1605-06, 1609-39, 1662, 1665, 1666-1840, 1845-80 (W&SRO)
Cop C 1719-1837 M 1708-1841 B 1813-37 (DRO, PRI); CB 1711-1812 M 1708, 1712-1811 (SG, SLC); C 1595-1711, 1813-80 M 1595-1708, 1811-47 from BT (VRI); M 1594-1710, 1756 from BT (DRO); M 1708-51, 1756-1841 (SG); M 1708-1841 from OR. 1594-1756, 1762 from BT (DMI); B 1711-1837 (DBI)
Cop (Mf) CB 1595-1880 M 1595-1847 (Mf of BT, DRO, SLC); C 1711-1812 (Printout, Mf SLC); Extr C 1595-1880 M 1595-1847 (IGI)
MI (S&DFHS); (DFHS); (DRO); Ch cy 1975 (SG)

HAZELBURY BRYAN AND THE HILLSIDE PARISHES. Modern benefice including HAZELBURY BRYAN, STOKE WAKE, BELCHALWELL, FIFEHEAD NEVILLE, IBBERTON, MAPPOWDER, WOOLLAND.

HAZELBURY BRYAN or HASELBURY BRYAN St Mary and St James [Pimperne Hundred; Sturminster Union] [611] Now with HAZLEBURY BRYAN AND THE HILLSIDE PARISHES benefice.
OR C 1562-1967 M 1563-1653, 1661-1964 B 1562-1999 Banns 1754-1813, 1825-1923 (DRO)
BT CMB 1731-1880 (W&SRO)
Cop C 1562-1699, 1777-1837 M 1563-1837 B 1562-1699, 1813-37 (DRO); CMB 1562-87 M 1563-1837 (SG); C 1777-1837 M 1563-1837 B 1813-37 (PRI); C 1731-1880 M 1731-1847 from BT (VRI); M 1563-1837 from OR, 1731-54 from BT (DMI); B 1813-37 (DBI); Extr CMB 1593-1657 (SG)
Cop (Mf) CB 1731-1880 M 1731-1847 (Mf of BT, DRO, SLC); Extr C 1731-1880 M 1731-1847 from BT (IGI)

HAZELBURY BRYAN Mission church room at Kingston [Kelly 1903]

HAZELBURY BRYAN (Presb) Licence to James Rawson, for his house, 1672

HAZELBURY BRYAN (Wes) House owned by Richard Chapman registered 1793 [Biggs]

HAZELBURY BRYAN (Prim Meth) [Harrod 1865] [1882 Return] [Kelly 1903]

HAZELBURY BRYAN (Meth) Partway. North Dorset Circuit

HEATHERLANDS   *see* CANFORD MAGNA

HERMITAGE St Mary the Virgin [Fordington Liberty; Cerne Union] [124] Peculiar of the Dean of Sarum until 1847. Now with YETMINSTER WITH RYME INTRINSECA AND HIGH STOY benefice.
OR   C 1712-47, 1760-1820 M 1713-41, 1763-1837 B 1712-47, 1760-1991
     Banns 1763-1811 (DRO) No earlier registers noted in 1831.
BT   CMB 1605-16, 1619-24, 1631-39, 1668-99, 1700-53, 1755-1880 (W&SRO)
Cop C 1784-1812 M 1713-1849 B 1813-1991 (DRO); CB 1712-1820 M 1712-41,
     1763-1849 (SG, SLC); C 1605-1712, 1820-80 M 1603-1712 from BT (VRI);
     C 1774-1820 M 1717-1849 B 1813-37 (PRI); M 1605-1763 from BT (DRO);
     M 1717-42, 1763-1849 (SG); M 1713-41, 1763-1849 from OR, 1604-1763 from
     BT (DMI); B 1712-1837 (DBI); Extr CB 1712-1820 M 1712-1849 (SG)
Cop (Mf) CB 1605-1880 M 1605-1871 (Mf of BT, DRO, SLC); C 1712-1820
          (Printout, Mf SLC); Extr C 1605-1880 M 1605-1849 (IGI)
MI   (DRO)

HERMITAGE (Presb) Licence for house of George Fox, 1672

HERMITAGE (Wes) An unoccupied Building belonging to John Perris [1882 Return]; chapel [Kelly 1903]

HERRINGSTON   *see* WINTERBORNE HERRINGSTON

HERSTON   *see* SWANAGE

HIGHCLIFFE parish formed from Christchurch and Milton [Hampshire] Transferred to Dorset 1974.
OR   *see* NIPR Vol.8 Part 6 Hampshire

HIGHWOOD hamlet of EAST STOKE

HILFIELD   *see* SYDLING ST NICHOLAS

HILTON All Saints [Whiteway Hundred; Blandford Union] [685]   Now with MILTON ABBAS, CHESELBOURNE, MELCOMBE HORSEY.
OR   C 1603-1849 M 1603-1994 B 1603-1901 Banns 1755-1812, 1823-1954 (DRO)
     Noted in 1831: 'Many Baptisms from 1748 are registered with Melcombe
     Horsey.'
BT   CMB 1731-1880 (W&SRO)
Cop C 1603-1837 M 1603-1837 B 1603-1737, 1813-37 (DRO); C 1731-1880
     M 1731-1838 from BT (VRI); C 1737-1837 MB 1813-37 (PRI); M 1603-49,
     1652-1837 (SG); M 1603-1837 from OR (DMI); B 1813-37 (DBI)
Cop (Mf) CB 1731-1880 M 1731-1838 (Mf of BT, DRO, SLC); Extr C 1731-1880
          M 1731-1838 from BT (IGI)
MI   (S&DFHS); (DFHS); (DRO)

HILTON ('Members of the Church of England') Hilton Reading Room, Ansty [1882 Return]

HILTON (Prim Meth) A building, the property of John Hopkins, Ansty [1882 Return] A building called 'Barn', Ansty [1882 Return]; Reading Room, Ansty [1882 Return]

HILTON (Meth) A room in the Dwelling House of George E.J. Woodhouse, Ansty [1882 Return]

HINTON MARTELL or GREAT HINTON   St John the Evangelist [Badbury Hundred; Wimborne and Cranborne Union] [267] Now with HORTON, CHALBURY, HOLT.
OR   C 1661-1903 M 1663-1992 B 1661-1992 Banns 1754-1809, 1823-28 (DRO)
BT   CMB 1731-1880 (W&SRO)
Cop   C 1566-1837, 1903-92 M 1566-1991 B 1661-1992 (DRO); C 1903-92
      M 1566-1640, 1663, 1671-79, 1684-1991 B 1813-1992 (SG); C 1731-1880
      M 1731-1846 from BT (VRI); C 1774-1837 MB 1813-37 (PRI); M 1566-1837
      from OR, 1812 from BT (DMI); B 1813-1992 (DBI)
Cop (Mf) CB 1731-1880 M 1731-1846 (Mf of BT, DRO, SLC); Extr C 1731-1880
          M 1731-1846 from BT (IGI)
MI   (S&DFHS); (DFHS); (DRO)

HINTON PARVA or LITTLE HINTON or STANBRIDGE   St Kenelm [Badbury Hundred; Wimborne and Cranborne Union] [36] Parish now with WITCHAMPTON, LONG CRICHEL. Redundant 1980. Sold 1981 for use as monument and for occasional services.
OR   C 1621-1980 M 1816-22, 1828, 1831, 1837-1975 B 1813-1977, 1983, 1987
      Banns 1939-75 (DRO) Noted in 1831: C 1621+ M 1727+ B 1623+
BT   CMB 1734-41, 1748, 1752-56, 1779-1801, 1807-80 (W&SRO)
Cop   C 1621-1837, MB 1813-37 (DRO, PRI); C 1734-1880 M 1734-1847 from BT
      (VRI); M 1734-1800 from BT (DRO); M 1816-38 from OR, 1734-1816 from BT
      (DMI); B 1820-37 (DBI)
Cop (Mf) CB 1734-1880 M 1734-1847 (Mf of BT, DRO, SLC); Extr C 1734-1880
          M 1734-1847 from BT (IGI)
MI   (S&DFHS); (DFHS); (DRO)

HINTON ST MARY St Mary [Sturminster Newton Hundred; Sturminster Union] [303] Chapelry in IWERNE MINSTER; separate parish 1863. Rebuilt 1846. Now with STURMINSTER NEWTON.
OR   C 1581-1655/6, ?1675-1887 M 1581-1652, ?1677-1707, 1711-1983
      B 1581-1655/6, ?1675-1972 Banns 1755-1807, 1824-93 (DRO)
BT   CMB 1731-1880 (W&SRO)
Cop   C 1581-1655, 1675-1887 M 1581-1837 B 1581-1655, 1675-1974 (DRO);
      C 1581-1655, 1675-1887 M 1581-1655, 1675-1983 B 1581-1655, 1675-1974
      (I, SG); C 1731-1880 M 1732-1808, 1813-47 from BT (VRI); C 1750-1837
      M 1755-1810 B 1581-1840 with gaps (PRI); M 1753, 1755-1983 (I, DRO);
      M 1584-1614, 1619-52, 1675, 1681-88, 1695-1837 (SG); M 1584-1837 from
      OR, 1750-52, 1811-12 from BT (DMI); B 1813-37 (DBI)
Cop (Mf) CB 1731-1880 M 1731-1847 (Mf of BT, DRO, SLC); Extr C 1731-1880
          M 1731-1847 from BT (IGI)
MI   (S&DFHS); (DFHS); (DRO)

HINTON ST MARY (Prim Meth) [Harrod 1865] [1882 Return] [Kelly 1903]; Meth [Kelly 1939]

HINTON ST MARY (Meth)
OR   *see* Frome Meth Circuit (Somerset) C 1837-81 (SRO)

HOLDENHURST Parish formed from Christchurch Hampshire] Transferred to Dorset 1974.
OR   *see* NIPR Vol.8 Part 6 Hampshire

HOLME, EAST *see* EAST STOKE

HOLNEST St Mary, now church of the Assumption [Sherborne Hundred; Sherborne Union] [159] Chapelry in LONGBURTON. Divided 1929, part joining GLANVILLES WOOTTON, part to separate parish of LONG BURTON. Now with DUNGEON HILL benefice.
OR   C 1602-74, 1696-1802, 1809-1996 M 1590/1-1684, 1695-1738, 1743/4, 1755-1927 B 1589-1668, 1695-1725, 1739-1802, 1809-11, 1813-1995 Banns 1802-12, 1824-1911 (DRO)
BT   CMB 1603-07, 1610, 1613-14, 1618-39, 1666, 1671-99, 1700-59, 1754-1834, 1847-77 (W&SRO)
Cop   CMB C 1602-1812 M 1590-1812 B 1589-1812 (Ptd C.Mayo ed. 1894); CMB 1589-1812 (S&DFHS); CMB 1589-1812 M 1590-1643, 1650, 1662-1835 (SG); C 1602-1994 M 1590-1837 B 1589-1668, 1695-1995 (DRO); C 1626-41, 1813-77 M 1813-34 from BT (VRI); C 1763-1812 M 1590-1837 B 1813-1995 (PRI); M 1603-1802 from BT (DRO); M 1790-1812 (Pallot); M 1591-1835 from OR, 1603-1802 from BT (DMI); B 1589-1995 (DBI)
Cop (Mf)   CMB 1589-1812 (Mf of Mayo, SLC); CB 1603-1877 M 1603-1834 (Mf of BT, DRO, SLC); C 1585-1812 M 1590-1812 (Printout, Mf SLC); Extr C 1602-1877 M 1590-1834 (IGI)

HOLNEST (Wes) House occupied by Mr William Dubbin registered 1793 [Biggs]

HOLT *see* WIMBORNE MINSTER

HOLWELL St Laurence [Horethorne Hundred (Somerset) transferred 1844 to Brownshall Hundred (Dorset); Sherborne Union] Now with THE CAUNDLES WITH FOLKE AND HOLWELL benefice.
OR   C 1653-1888 M 1655-1992 B 1653-1970 Banns 1755-1812, 1823-87 (DRO)
BT   CMB 1731-1880 (W&SRO)
Cop   C 1653-1726/7 M 1655-1837 B 1653-1726/7, 1813-37 (DRO); C 1731-1880 M 1731-1847 from BT (VRI); CB 1813-37 M 1655-1837 (PRI); C 1813-37 (I, DRO); M 1655, 1660-1837 (SG); M 1655-1837 from OR, 1813 from BT (DMI); B 1653-1837 (DBI)
Cop (Mf)   CB 1731-1880 M 1731-1847 (Mf of BT, DRO, SLC); Extr C 1731-1880 M 1731-1847 from BT (IGI)

HOLWELL (Wes) [1882 Return] [Kelly 1903]; Meth [Kelly 1939]

HOLWORTH *see* OWERMOIGNE

HONEY PIDDLE *see* PIDDLEHINTON

HOOKE St Giles [Eggerton Hundred; Beaminster Union] [269] Now with Beaminster Area benefice..
OR   C 1813-1999 M 1814-1989 B 1814-1999 (DRO) Noted in 1831: C 1758+ M 1771+ B 1759+. *see* Phillimore copy below for M 1771+
BT   CMB 1732-62, 1765-1880 (W&SRO)
Cop   M 1771-1812 (Ptd Phil 2: 1907; & on CD-ROM); C 1813-37 M 1814-37 (I, DRO, PRI); C 1732-1880 M 1732-1812 from BT (VRI); M 1734-1837 (SG); M 1732-1813 from BT (DRO); M 1771-1812 (Boyd); M 1790-1812 (Pallot); M 1814-37 from OR, 1732-1813 from BT, 1771-1812 from Phil (DMI); B 1732-1837 (DBI)
Cop (Mf)   M 1771-1812 (Mf of Phil, SLC); CB 1732-1880 M 1732-1837 (Mf of BT, DRO, SLC); Extr C 1732-1880 M 1732-1812 from BT (IGI)

HORTON St Wolfrida [Badbury Hundred; Wimborne and Cranborne Union] [421]
Included chapelry of WOODLANDS; separate parish 1926. Rebuilt 18th cent.
Now with HINTON MARTELL, CHALBURY, HOLT.
OR C 1563-1993 M 1563-1974 B 1563-1962 Banns 1760, 1775-1812, 1823-60
1861-1994 (DRO)
BT CMB 1734, 1739-1880 (W&SRO)
Cop CMB 1563-1870 (DRO, SG); C 1734-1880 M 1734-1846 from BT (VRI);
C 1774-1840 M 1717-1849 B 1813-37 (PRI); M 1563-1837 from OR (DMI);
B 1596-1870 (DBI)
Cop (Mf) CB 1734-1880 M 1734-1846 (Mf of BT, DRO, SLC); Extr C 1734-1880
M 1734-1846 from BT (IGI)
MI (S&DFHS); (DFHS); (DRO)

HORTON The Ascension, Woodlands [Knowlton Hundred; Wimborne and Cranborne
Union] [423] Erected 1892. Chapelry in HORTON, separate parish 1926 from
HORTON, WIMBORNE ST GILES, GUSSAGE ST MICHAEL. Now with CRANBORNE,
BOVERIDGE, EDMONDSHAM, WIMBORNE ST GILES.
OR M 1903-62 (DRO)
BT *see* HORTON
MI (S&DFHS); (DFHS); (DRO)

HORTON Remains of a 16th century chapel at Manor Farm, Woodlands [Kelly
1903]

HORTON Knowlton. 'Must formerly have been of some importance, as it gave
its name to the Hundred'. Remains of a church tower still standing; font
bowl at Woodlands church [Kelly 1903]

HORTON (Cong) Licence for house of Henry Perkins, 1672

HORTON (Wes) f by 1766 [Biggs]

HORTON (Wes) Horton Heath. Erected 1877 [1882 Return] [Kelly 1903]
Wimborne Circuit

HORTON (Wes) Woodlands. Chapel erected 1879 [1882 Return] [Kelly 1939]
Wimborne Circuit
OR *see* POOLE (RG 4/1230, PRO)

HORTON (Prim Meth) Haythorn. Erected 1888 [Kelly 1903]

HOUGHTON WINTERBORNE *see* WINTERBORNE HOUGHTON

HOWE, EAST and WEST *see* CANFORD MAGNA

HUNTINGFORD *see* GILLINGHAM

HURN [Hampshire] Civil parish transferred to Dorset 1974

HYNE PIDDLE *see* PIDDLEHINTON

IBBERTON St Eustace [Whiteway Hundred; Sturminster Union] [225] Now with
HAZLEBURY BRYAN AND THE HILLSIDE PARISHES benefice.
OR C 1761-1988 M 1801-1980 B 1777-78, 1794-97, 1814-1988 Banns 1801-11,
1824-73 (DRO) No earlier register noted in 1831. Early registers
destroyed by fire [Kelly 1903]
BT CMB 1731-1880 (W&SRO)

IBBERTON cont.
Cop C 1731-1880 M 1731-1848 from BT (VRI); C 1761-1837 M 1801-37 B 1813-37
    (PRI); C 1813-37 (I, DRO); M 1731-75 from BT (DRO); M 1801-37 (SG);
    M 1801-37 from OR, 1731-1800, 1812 from BT, 1660, 1680, 17?? from
    Hutchins (DMI); B 1731-1837 M 1801-37 (DRO); B 1731-1837 (DBI)
Cop (Mf) CB 1731-1880 M 1731-1848 (Mf of BT, DRO, SLC); Extr C 1731-1880
        M 1731-1848 from BT (IGI)
MI   (S&DFHS); (DFHS); (DRO)

IBBERTON (Prim Meth) [1882 Return]; 2 Meth chapels [Kelly 1939]

IBBERTON (Meth) Leigh. North Dorset Circuit

ISLE OF PORTLAND *see* PORTLAND

ISLE OF PURBECK *see* PURBECK

IWERNE COURTNEY or SHROTON   St Mary [Redland Hundred; Blandford Union]
[557] United early with Farringdon ancient parish. Now with IWERNE
STEEPLETON, SUTTON WALDRON, FONTMELL MAGNA.
OR   C 1562-1912 M 1563-1988 B 1562-1892 Banns 1754-1811, 1882-1919 (DRO)
BT   CMB 1731, 1736-78, 1761-1836, 1844, 1847-76 (W&SRO)
Cop CB 1562-1900 M 1563-1900 (DRO, SG); C 1708-45 M 1563-1812 (SG);
    C 1719-1837 M 1568-1837 B 1813-37 (PRI); C 1731-1844, 1847-76
    M 1731-1844, 1847-58 from BT (VRI); M 1563-1708 (Boyd); M 1563-1841
    from OR (DMI); B 1562-1900 (DBI); Extr B 1707-49 (SG)
Cop (Mf) CB 1731-1844, 1847-76 M 1731-1858 (Mf of BT, DRO, SLC);
        Extr C 1731-1844, 1847-76 M 1731-1844, 1847-58 from BT (IGI)
MI   (S&DFHS); (DFHS); (DRO)

IWERNE COURTNEY St John the Baptist, Farringdon. Ancient parish united at
an early date with IWERNE COURTNEY, until 1952 when united with EAST
ORCHARD, MARGARET MARSH. Chapel [Kelly 1903] Redundant 1976. Sold for use
as monument 1978.
OR   M 1906-69 (DRO)

IWERNE COURTNEY (Bapt) Licence for house of John Holland of Farringdon,
1672.

IWERNE COURTNEY (Prim Meth) Erected 1886 [1882 Return] [Kelly 1903];
Meth [Kelly 1939]

IWERNE MINSTER St Mary [Sixpenny Handley Hundred; Shaftesdbury
Incorporation/Union] [634] United 1327 with SIXPENNY HADLEY *q.v.* later a
chapelry (separate parish 1844). Also had chapelries of EAST ORCHARD,
MARGARET MARSH (united as separate parish 1863); and chapelry of HINTON ST
MARY (separate parish 1863). Now with IWERNE COURTNEY, IWERNE STEEPLETON,
SUTTON WALDRON, FONTMELL MAGNA.
OR   C 1742-1935 M 1742-1994 B 1742-1885 Banns 1754-1994   (DRO) Noted in
    1831: CMB 1608-62, 1742-1812; 'No account can be given for the
    deficient registers.''The register dates from the year 1742, previous
    records having been destroyed in Blandford great fire' [Kelly 1903]
BT   CMB 1731-81, 1784-1880 (W&SRO)
Cop C 1731-1880 M 1731-1857 from BT (VRI); C 1742-1835 M 1742-1836
    B 1813-37 (PRI); C 1813-35 B 1813-37 (I, DRO); M 1742-1836 (DRO, SG);
    M 1731-41 from BT (DRO); M 1742-1836 from OR, 1731-41 from BT (DMI);
    B 1813-37 (DBI)

IWERNE MINSTER cont.
Cop (Mf) CB 1731-1880 M 1731-1857 (Mf of BT, DRO, SLC); Extr C 1731-1880
        M 1731-1857 from BT (IGI)
MI (S&DFHS); (DFHS); (DRO)

IWERNE MINSTER (Part Bapt) 'Iwerne' f 1831 [*Bapt. Handbook* 1861] Ebenezer.
Erected 1831 [1882 Return] [Kelly 1939]

IWERNE MINSTER (Wes) Erected 1879 [1882 Return] [Kelly 1903]; Meth [Kelly
1939] North Dorset Circuit

IWERNE, STEEPLETON or STEEPLETON PRESTON St Mary   [Pimperne Hundred;
Blandford Union] [36] Noted as extra-parochial in 1831. Now with IWERNE
COURTNEY, SUTTON WALDRON, FONTMELL MAGNA. Redundant 1995.
OR C 1766-1812, 1815-1987 M 1755-1812, 1845-1948, 1963, 1971 B 1776-1811,
    1821-1980 Banns 1755-1812, 1882-1970 (DRO) No earlier register noted
    in 1831
BT CMB 1760-63, 1785, 1792-1880 (W&SRO)
Cop C 1766-1944 M 1753-1942 B 1776-1811, 1821-1931 (DRO, SG); C 1765-1880
    M 1780-1845 from BT (VRI); C 1766-1850 B 1776-1880 (PRI); M 1755-1812
    from OR, 1813-37 from BT (DMI); B 1776-1980 (DBI)
Cop (Mf) CB 1760-1880 M 1760-1846 (Mf of BT, DRO, SLC); Extr C 1765-1880
        M 1760-1845 from BT (IGI)

KIMMERIDGE St Nicholas of Myra [Hasilor Hundred; Wareham and Purbeck Union]
[124] Now with CORFE CASTLE, CHURCH KNOWLE, STEEPLE, TYNEHAM.
OR C 1684/5, 1698/9, 1700-1808 M 1702, 1716, 1720, 1726-28, 1735/6,
    1738/9, 1749, 1755, 1758-71, 1776-1977 B 1701-1812 (DRO) Noted in 1831
    C 1700+ M 1702+ B 1704+
BT CMB 1802-03, 1813-24, 1833, 1851-80 (W&SRO)
Cop C 1684/5, 1698/9, 1700-1808, 1813-37 M 1702, 1716, 1720, 1726-1728,
    1735/6, 1738/9, 1749, 1755, 1758-1837 B 1689-1990 Banns 1824-1977
    (DRO); C 1684-1837 M 1702-1837 B 1689-1837 (PRI); C 1805-33 MB 1802-33
    from BT (DRO); C 1805-80 M 1813-33 from BT (VRI); M 1702-16, 1720,
    1726-28, 1736-38, 1749, 1755-1837 (SG); M 1702-1837 from OR (DMI);
    B 1813-1990 (DBI)
Cop (Mf) CB 1802-80 M 1802-33 (Mf of BT, DRO, SLC); Extr C 1805-80
        M 1813-33 from BT (IGI)
MI (S&DFHS); (DFHS); (DRO)

KING('S) STAG   *see* LYDLINCH

KINGSCOMBE, OVER AND NETHER tithing of TOLLER PORCORUM

KINGSTON   *see* CORFE CASTLE

KINGSTON   *see* HAZELBURY BRYAN

KINGSTON   *see* KINSON (Canford Magna)

KINGSTON LACY   *see* WIMBORNE MINSTER

KINGSTON RUSSELL   hamlet of LITTLEBREDY

KINGSTON WINTERBORNE *see* WINTERBORNE KINGSTON

KINGTON MAGNA or GREAT KINGTON   All Saints [Redland Hundred; Wincanton Union 1835-94; Shaftesbury Union 1894-1930] [539]   Now with GILLINGHAM benefice.
OR   C 1670-1966 M 1671/2-1966, 1968-85 B 1670-1978 Banns 1754-99,1889-1961 (DRO)
BT   CMB 1731-79, 1781-1836, 1839-77 (W&SRO)
Cop   C 1670-1766 M 1671-1837 B 1670-1767 (DRO); C 1731-1877 M 1731-1847 from BT (VRI); C 1768-1837 B 1813-37 (I, DRO); CB 1813-37 M 1671-1837 (PRI); M 1671-1837 (SG); M 1731-54 from BT (DRO); M 1671-1837 from OR, 1731-49 from BT (DMI); B 1813-1900 (DBI)
Cop (Mf)   CB 1731-1877 M 1731-1847 (Mf of BT, DRO, SLC); Extr C 1731-1877 M 1731-1847 from BT (IGI)
MI   (DFHS); (DRO)

KINGTON MAGNA (Prim Meth) [1882 Return] [Kelly 1903]; Meth erected 1851 [Kelly 1939]

KINSON   see CANFOPD MAGNA

KNIGHTON   Ancient parish united 1381 to DURWESTON

KNIGHTON, WEST St Peter [Culliford Tree Hundred; Dorchester Union] [308] United 1563 with FRIERMAYNE ancient parish. Now with BROADMAYNE, OWERMOIGNE, WARMWELL.
OR   C 1693-1728, 1746-1908 M 1693-1728, 1746-1985 B 1693-1728, 1746-1993 Banns 1755-1812, 1864-1974 (DRO)
BT   CMB 1732-1880 (W&SRO)
Cop   CB 1813-37 M 1693-1837 (PRI); CB 1813-37 (I, DRO); C 1731-1880 M 1732-1846 from BT (VRI); M 1693-97, 1708-1837 (DRO, SG); M 1735-54 from BT (DRO); M 1693-1837 from OR, 1732-54 from BT (DMI); B 1813-37 (DBI)
Cop (Mf)   CB 1732-1880 M 1732-1846 (Mf of BT, DRO, SLC); Extr C 1732-1880 M 1732-1846 from BT (IGI)
MI   (S&DFHS); (DFHS); (DRO); (SG)

KNOWLE   see CHURCH KNOWLE

KNOWLE   see Brockhampton and Knowle, tithing of BUCKLAND NEWTON

KNOWLTON   see WOODLANDS

LANGTON HERRING St Peter [Uggscombe Hundred; Weymouth Union] [205] Now with ABBOTSBURY, PORTESHAM.
OR   C 1682-1916 M 1681-1842 B 1682-1813 Banns 1758-1808, 1823-36 (DRO)
BT   CMB 1731-1803, 1809-12, 1814-80 (W&SRO)
Cop   M 1681-1812 (Ptd Phil 6: 1912; & on CD-ROM); C 1682-1801, 1813-37 M 1681-1835 B 1682-1801 (DRO, SG); C 1682-1809 M 1718-1811 B 1682-1801 (S&DFHS); C 1731-1880 M 1731-1839 from BT (VRI); C 1813-37 M 1681-1835 (PRI); M 1753-58 from BT (DRO); M 1681-1812 (Boyd); M 1790-1812 (Pallot); M 1681-1753, 1758-1835 from OR, 1731-58, 1836-37 from BT (DMI); B 1682-1993 (DBI)
Cop (Mf)   M 1681-1812 (Mf of Phil, SLC); CB 1731-1880 M 1731-1839 (Mf of BT, DRO, SLC); Extr C 1731-1880 M 1731-1839 from BT (IGI)
MI   (S&DFHS); (DFHS); (DRO); (SG)

LANGTON HERRING (Meth) Erected 1909 [Kelly 1939]

LANGTON LONG BLANDFORD All Saints [Pimperne Hundred; Blandford Union] [187]
Rebuilt 1861-62. Now with BLANDFORD FORUM.
OR   C 1591/2-1687, 1694-1937 M 1593-1687, 1695-1995 B 1591/2-1687,
     1694-1812 Banns 1754-1800 (DRO); C 1938-99 M 1996-99 B 1813-c.1999
     stolen from church. Noted in 1831: CB 1725+ M 1754+
BT   CMB 1739-56, 1769-79, 1782-86, 1793-1845, 1847-80 (W&SRO)
Cop C 1591/72-1727, 1813-38 M 1593-1837 B 1591/72-1728 (DRO);
     CMB 1591-1728 (SG); CB 1591-1728 (S&DFHS); C 1739-1880 M 1739-1855 from
     BT (VRI); C 1813-37 M 1593-1837 (PRI); M 1593-1687, 1695-1728, 1733-56,
     1761-1837 (SG); M 1593-1837 from OR, 1739-54 from BT (DMI); B 1591-1728
     (DBI)
Cop (Mf) CB 1739-1880 M 1739-1855 (Mf of BT, DRO, SLC); Extr C 1739-1880
          M 1739-1855 from BT (IGI)
MI   (S&DFHS); (DFHS); (DRO); Ch, cy, war memorial (SG)

LANGTON MATRAVERS or EAST LANGTON   St George [Rowberrow Hundred; Wareham
and Purbeck Union] [676] Including Langton Wallis or West Langton. Now with
KINGSTON, WORTH MATRAVERS.
OR   C 1670-83, 1695, 1709-1931 M 1670-83, 1709-1985 B 1670-72, 1678-98/9,
     1710-1946 Banns 1790-1810, 1823-1972 (DRO) Noted in 1831: 'M 1754-89:
     no Register of Marr. can be found after that date'.
BT   CMB 1732-1880 (W&SRO)
Cop CMB 1670-1734 (Ptd R.Saville ed.1973); M 1754-65 from OR and BT
     (Ptd R.Saville ed.1973); CMB 1670-1837 (DRO, SG, SLC); C 1670-1807
     M 1726-1812 B 1765-1840 (DCM); CMB 1670-1812 (W&SRO); CB 1670-1734
     M 1734, 1754-65; CMB 1742-47 from BT (S&DFHS); C 1742-1837 M 1670-1837
     B 1744-1837 (PRI); CB 1763-1812 (I, SG); C 1838-80 M 1812-37 from BT
     (VRI); M 1670-1837 from OR, 1732-54 from BT, 1659 from Hutchins (DMI);
     B 1670-1813 (DBI)
Cop (Mf) CMB 1670-1837 (Mf of Ms, SLC); CB 1732-1880 M 1732-1837 (Mf of BT,
          DRO, SLC); ZCM 1670-1812 (Printout, Mf SLC); Extr C 1670-83, 1709-
          1880 M 1670-82, 1709-1837 (IGI)
MI   (S&DFHS); (DFHS); (DRO); (SG); (Ptd R.Saville *Some Langton tombstones*:
     3 vols: Langton. Mat. Local Hist. & Preservation Soc.: 1973-74)

LANGTON MATRAVERS (Bapt)
OR   Z 1833-37 (RG 4/461, PRO)
Cop (Mf) Z 1833-37 (Mf of OR, SLC); Extr C 1833-37 (IGI)

LANGTON MATRAVERS (Cong) Erected 1896 [Kelly 1903]

LANGTON MATRAVERS (Wes) [Harrod 1865] Erected 1875 [1882 Return]
[Kelly 1903]
OR   For early period *see* POOLE (RG 4/1230, PRO)

LANGTON MATRAVERS Cemetery (Langton Matravers Parish Council)

LANGTON WALLIS   *see* LANGTON MATRAVERS

LARKINGTON   *see* PIDDLETRENTHIDE

LAZERTON   Ancient parish united 1431 to STOURPAINE.

LEIGH   *see* YETMINSTER

LEIGH   (NEW BOROUGH AND LEIGH) *see* WIMBORNE MINSTER

LEWCOMBE   *see* CHELBOROUGH, EAST

LEWESTON Holy Trinity Chapel [Sherborne Hundred; Sherborne Union] [18] Extra-parochial place. Part of parish of LILLINGTON [Kelly 1903] Private chapel rebuilt 1616 by Sir John Fitzjames. In occasional use (St Antony's School). School chapel erected 1968-70.

LEWESTON (Presb) Licence for house of Margaret Fitzcame (Fitzjames ?), 1672

LILLINGTON St Martin [Sherborne Hundred; Sherborne Union] [205] Peculiar of the Dean of Sarum until 1847. Now with SHERBORNE, CASTLETON.
OR   C 1712-1810 M 1712-1975 B 1712-1810 Banns 1754-1812 (DRO) No earlier register noted in 1831.
BT   CMB 1581-88, 1592-1600, 1604-18, 1622-41, 1670-72, 1677-84, 1688-98, 1700-57, 1763-85, 1788-1812, 1814-36, 1847-80 (W&SRO)
Cop   C 1581-1880 M 1581-1836 from BT (VRI); M 1712-1843 B 1813-65 (DRO, PRI); M 1585-1754 from BT (DRO); M 1712-1843 (SG); M 1712-1843 from OR, 1581-1753 from BT (DMI); B 1813-64 (DBI)
Cop (Mf)   CB 1581-1880 M 1581-1836 (Mf of BT, DRO, SLC); Extr C 1581-1880 M 1581-1836 from BT (IGI)

LILLIPUT   *see* PARKSTONE

LITTLE BREDY   *see* LITTLEBREDY

LITTLE FROME   *see* FROME ST QUINTIN

LITTLE HINTON   *see* HINTON PARVA

LITTLE TOLLER   *see* TOLLER FRATRUM

LITTLE WINSOR   *see* DROADWINDSOR

LITTLEBREDY St Michael and All Angels [Uggscombe Hundred; Dorchester Union] [241 including hamlet of Kingston Russell 76] Chapelry in LONG BREDY. Inhabitants of Kingston Russell attended Long Bredy church [Kelly 1939] Now with BRIDE VALLEY benefice.
OR   C 1717-1812, 1858-63 M 1717-1808, 1813-1976 B 1717-1812, 1859-63 Banns 1824-98 (DRO) No earlier register noted in 1831.
BT   CMB 1732-1812, 1814-80 (W&SRO)
Cop   C 1717-1812 M 1717-1836 B 1717-1812 (DRO); C 1717-1812 M 1717-1836 (PRI); C 1732-1880 M 1732-1836 from BT (VRI); M 1717-1836 (SG); M 1717-1837 from OR, 1732-58, 1808-13 from BT (DMI); B 1717-1837 (DBI)
Cop (Mf)   CB 1732-1880 M 1732-1836 (Mf of BT, DRO, SLC); Extr C 1732-1880 M 1732-1836 from BT (IGI)
MI   (S&DFHS); (DFHS); (DRO); Cy (SG)

LITTLEMORE *see* PRESTON

LITTLETON   Ancient parish united 1430 with BLANDFORD ST MARY.

LITTON CHENEY St Mary [Uggscombe Hundred; Bridport Union] [206] Now with BRIDE VALLEY benefice.
OR   C 1614-1999 M 1614-1707, 1714-1993 B 1614-1938 Banns 1755-92, 1802, 1824-1998 (DRO)
BT   CMB 1728-1812, 1814-80 (W&SRO)
Cop   M 1614-1812 (Ptd Phil 4: 1909; & on CD-ROM); C 1614-17 M 1614-1812 B 1614-1820 (S&DFHS); CM 1614-1837 (DRO, SG); CB 1813-37 M 1614-1837 (PRI); M 1614-1812 (Boyd); M 1790-1812 (Pallot); M 1614-1837 from OR, 1728-54 from BT (DMI); B 1614-1770, 1813-37 (I, DRO, SG); B 1614-1837 (DBI); CMB 1728-1880 from BT (Pine: CD 1)

LITTON CHENEY cont.
Cop (Mf) M 1614-1812 (Mf of Phil, SLC); CB 1728-1880 M 1729-1843 (Mf of BT,
            DRO, SLC); Extr C 1728-1880 M 1729-1843 from BT (IGI)
MI (S&DFHS); (DFHS); (DRO); (SG)

LITTON CHENEY (Prim Meth) [1882 Return]

LODERS or **LOTHERS**   St Mary Magdalene [Loders and Bothenhampton Liberty;
Bridport Union] [812] Now with ASKERSWELL, POWERSTOCK, WEST MILTON,
WITHERSTONE, NORTH POORTON
OR C 1636-1991 M 1636-1985 B 1636-1993 Banns 1691-1733, 1754-77, 1904-63
     (DRO) Included BOTHENHAMPTON marriages to 1714.
BT CMB 1732-1833, 1844, 1847-80 (W&SRO)
Cop M 1636-1812 (Ptd Phil 4: 1909; & on CD-ROM); C 1636-1911 M 1636-1837
     B 1813-1990 (DRO); CB 1813-37 M 1636-1837 (PRI); M 1636-1837 (SG);
     M 1636-1812 (Boyd); M 1790-1812 (Pallot); M 1636-1837 from OR, 1731-54,
     1812 from BT (DMI); B 1813-1920 (DBI); CMB 1732-1880 from BT (Pine:
     CD 1)
Cop (Mf) M 1636-1812 (Mf of Phil, SLC); CB 1732-1880 M 1732-1833 (Mf of BT,
           DRO, SLC); Extr C 1752-1880 M 1752-1833 from BT (IGI)
MI (S&DFHS); (DFHS); (DRO)

LODERS St Saviour, Dottery. Hamlet of Dottery in BRIDPORT. Iron mission
church n.d. [Kelly 1903, 1939] Now with LODERS.

LODERS (Wes) Up Loders. Erected 1827 [1882 Return] [Kelly 1939]

LONG BREDY   *see* BREDY, LONG

LONG CRICHEL *see* CRICHEL, LONG

LONG HAM   or **LONGHAM** *see* HAMPRESTON

LONGBREDY   *see* BREDY, LONG

LONGBURTON or **LONG BURTON**   St James [Sherborne Hundred; Sherborne Union]
[361] Peculiar of the Dean of Sarum until 1847. Included chapelry of
HOLNEST until 1929 when latter joined GLANVILLES WOOTTON. Now with DUNGEON
HILL benefice.
OR C 1590-1885 M 1589-1996 B 1589-1999 Banns 1824-45, 1869-1939 (DRO)
BT CMB 1580-82, 1597-1600, 1603-26, 1630-40, 1669-80, 1687-1833, 1847-77
     (W&SRO)
Cop CMB 1580-1812 (Ptd ed C.Mayo: 1894); C 1580-1837 M 1589-1837
     B 1580-1865 (DRO); CM 1813-37 B 1813-65 (PRI); M 1580-1755 from BT
     (DRO); M 1790-1812 (Pallot); M 1589-1842 from OR, 1580-1755 from BT
     (DMI); B 1813-65 (DBI); C 1580?-1877 from BT (Pine: CDs 1 & 2)
Cop (Mf) CMB 1580-1812 (Mf of Mayo, SLC); M 1589-1812 (Mf of Ms, SLC;
           CMB 1580-1813 CB 1814-77 M 1814-33 (Mf of BT, DRO, SLC);
           Extr C 1580-1877 M 1580-1833 (IGI)

LONGBURTON (Wes) [1882 Return]; (Meth) [Kelly 1939] Sherborne and Yeovil
Circuit

LONGFLEET   *see* CANFORD MAGNA

LONGHAM   or **LONG HAM** *see* HAMPRESTON

LOSCOMBE   *see* POWERSTOCK

LOTHERS   *see* LODERS

LOWER FIFEHEAD   tithing of BELCHALWELL

LOWER LYTCHETT   *see* LYTCHETT MINSTER

LUCCOMBE   *see* CHELBOROUGH, EAST

LULWORTH, EAST St Andrew [Winfrith Hundred; Wareham and Purbeck Union]
[345] Now with WEST LULWORTH, WINFRITH NEWBURGH, CHALDON HERRING.
OR   C 1635-1993 M 1561-1748, 1754-1990 B 1561-1991 Banns 1756-1799 (DRO)
       No earlier C register noted in 1831.
BT   CMB 1731-1875 (W&SRO)
Cop C 1635-1837 M 1561-1846 B 1561-1837 (DRO); C 1680-1837 M 1561-1836
       B 1813-37 (PRI); M 1561-1846 (SG); M 1731-53 from BT (DRO); M 1561-1846
       from OR, 1744-53 from BT (DMI); B 1561-1837 (DBI); CMB 1731-1875 from
       BT (Pine: CD 4)
Cop (Mf) CB 1731-1875 M 1731-1856 (Mf of BT, DRO, SLC); Extr C 1731-1875
       M 1731-1856 from BT (IGI)
MI   (S&DFHS); (DFHS)

LULWORTH, EAST (RC) St Mary, Lulworth Castle. Domestic chapel of Weld
family. Mission f 1641. Served by Jesuit priests and later (1794-1817) by
Cistercian monks. Present chapel erected 1786-87. Catholic cemetery 1860.
OR   ZCB 1755-1840 (RG 4/303, PRO); C 1755-80, 1815-44 M 1840-44 B 1841-45
       Confirmations 1827 (DRO); C 1845+ M 1846+ D 1845+ Confirmations 1848+
       (Inc); Confirmations 1857, 1868, 1873, 1878, 1881, 1882, 1885, 1887
       1892-1931 (PDA)
Cop C 1755-1840 (Ptd CRS 6: 1909); ZMB 1755-1840 (Ms, SLC); CM 1840-44
       B 1841-45 Confirmations 1827, 1836, 1844 (DRO, SG, Cath FHS);
       C 1755-80, 1838-45 M 1840-44 B 1841-45 Confirmations 1827, 1836, 1844
       (S&DFHS)
Cop (Mf) ZCB 1755-1840 (Mf of OR, SLC); ZMB 1755-1840 (Mf of Ms, SLC);
       C 1755-1840 (Printout, Mf SLC); Extr C 1755-1840 (IGI)

LULWORTH, WEST Holy Trinity [Bindon Liberty; Wareham and Purbeck Union]
[360] Chapelry in WINFRITH NEWBURGH; separate parish 1863. Rebuilt 1869-70.
Now with EAST LULWORTH, WINFRITH NEWBURGH, CHALDON HERRING.
OR   C 1745-1977 M 1745-53, 1780-1994 B 1745-1992 Banns 1780-1812,
       1887-1945 (DRO) Noted in 1831: CMB 1754+. 'The earlier registers were
       destroyed by fire A.D. 1780'.
BT   CMB 1731-1880 (W&SRO)
Cop C 1746-1837 M 1731-1837 B 1746-1837 (DRO); C 1731-45 M 1731/32-76
       B 1731-1756/46 from BT (DRO); CMB 1731-1837 (PRI); M 1731-45, 1780-1837
       (SG); M 1745-53, 1780-1837 from OR, 1731-79 from BT (DMI); B 1731-1837
       (DBI); CMB 1731-1880 from BT (Pine: CD 4)
Cop (Mf) CB 1731-1880 M 1731-1847 (Mf of BT, DRO, SLC); Extr C 1731-1880
       M 1731-1847 from BT (IGI)
MI   (S&DFHS); (DFHS); (DRO)

LULWORTH, WEST (RC) St Mary f 1886. Served from EAST LULWORTH

LULWORTH, WEST (Cong) Erected 1845 [*Cong. Yearbook* 1871] [Kelly 1939]
OR   C 1869-1924, 1960-95 B 1927-28, 1960-93 (DRO)

LULWORTH, WEST (Wes) House occupied by Mr James Willis registered 1799
[Biggs]

LYDLINCH St Thomas à Becket [Sherborne Hundred; Sturminster Union] [365] Now with STOCK GAYLARD.
OR   C 1559-1873 M 1560-1751, 1757-1966 B 1560-1946 Banns 1754-81, 1824-89 (DRO)
BT   CMB 1731-1812, 1814-75 (W&SRO)
Cop   CMB 1559-1812 (Ptd PRS 1899); C 1559-1837 M 1560-1837 B 1560-1837 (DRO); CMB 1813-37 (PRI); M 1731-55 from BT (DRO); M 1790-1812 (Pallot); M 1560-1836 from OR, 1731-56 from BT (DMI); B 1580-1837 (DBI)
Cop (Mf) CMB 1559-1812 (Mf of PRS, SLC, SG); CB 1731-1875 M 1731-1836 (Mf of BT, DRO, SLC); C 1559-1812 M 1560-1812 (Printout, Mf SLC); Extr C 1570-99, 1618-1885 M 1560-1836 from BT (IGI)

LYDLINCH King's Stag. Memorial chapel to Lady Barbara Yeatman-Biggs. Erected 1814. Now with LYDLINCH, STOCK GAYLARD.

LYDLINCH (Prim Meth) King's Stag [1882 Return] Meth. North Dorset Circuit

LYME REGIS St Michael the Archangel [Whitchurch Canonicorum Hundred; Axminster Union] [2621] Peculiar of Prebend of Lyme Regis and Halstock, Sarum Cathedral until 1847. Now with GOLDEN CAP Team Benefice.
OR   C 1543-72, 1649, 1653-1996 M 1653-58, 1664/5-1972 B 1653-1958 Banns 1754-1823, 1931-84 (DRO) No earlier marriages or burials noted in 1831.
BT   CMB 1579-82, 1594-97, 1606-10, 1613-35, 1666-73, 1676-80, 1684-94, 1697-1727, 1731-34, 1737-42, 1773-1812, 1814-35, 1847-80 (W&SRO)
Cop   M 1653-58, 1661-1812 (Ptd Phil 3: 1908; & on CD-ROM); C 1543-1952 M 1579-1946 B 1579-1635, 1653-1952 (DRO); CB 1813-37 M 1653-1837 (PRI); M 1579-1753, 1658-64 from BT (DRO); M 1653-58, 1664-1837 (SG); M 1653-1775 (Boyd); M 1790-1812 (Pallot); M 1653-1837 from OR, 1579-1653, 1658-64, 1666-1754 from BT (DMI); B 1813-38 (DBI); B 1813-37 (Booklet and mfc from S&DFHS)
Cop (Mf) M 1654-1812 (Mf of Phil, SLC); CMB 1579-1835 CB 1847-80 (Mf of BT, DRO, SLC); Extr CM 1579-1835 from BT (IGI)

LYME REGIS Peek Memorial Chapel, Poulett House, Pound Street. Chapel-of-ease to St Michael. Erected 1884

LYME REGIS (RC) St Michael and St George. Erected 1835-37 [1882 Return] Served from Axminster [Devon]
OR   C 1835+ M 1836+ D 1842+ Confirmations 1836+ (Inc, Axminster) Earlier entries in AXMINSTER. Confirmations 1860, 1872, 1876, 1883, 1890, 1892-1935, 1945 (PDA)

LYME REGIS (Bapt) Silver Street f 1665. Western Association [*Bapt. Handbook 1861*] [Kelly 1939]
OR   B 1823-57 (RG 4/463, PRO)
Cop (Mf) B 1823-57 (Mf of OR, SLC)

LYME REGIS (Ind/Cong) Coombe Street. f 1662. Erected 1750-55 [*Cong. Yearbook* 1871] [Kelly 1939]
OR   C 1775-1836 (RG 4/2269, 462, PRO)
Cop (Mf) C 1775-1836 (Mf of OR, SLC); C 1775-1836 (Printout, Mf SLC); Extr C 1775-1836 (IGI)

LYME REGIS (Presb) General preaching licences to John Kerridge and John Short of Lyme; licence to Amos Short for his house, 1672

LYME REGIS (Wes) Church Street. Erected 1839 [1882 Return] [Kelly 1903];
Meth [Kelly 1939]
OR   *see* AXMINSTER [Devon] and BRIDPORT Circuits

LYME REGIS (Brethren) Subscription Reading Room, Broad Street
[1882 Return]; Coombe Street [Kelly 1903, 1939]

LYME REGIS Cemetery, Charmouth Road 1856

LYSCOMBE Detached part of MILTON ABBAS. Joined CHESELBORNE 1882
[Kelly 1939] A derelict flint cottage was once a church...*c*.1200 [Pevsner]

LYTCHETT MATRAVERS St Mary [Cogdean Hundred; Poole Union] [680]
OR   C 1656/7-1971 M 1656-1988 B 1656/7-1959 Banns 1823-1991 (DRO)
BT   CMB 1731-1812, 1814-80 (W&SRO)
Cop C 1657-1904 M 1656-1904 B 1657-1904 (DRO); CB 1656-1808 M 1657-1837
     (SG); CB 1813-37 M 1657-1837 (PRI); M 1731-55 from BT (DRO);
     M 1657-1837 from OR, 1731-55 from BT (DMI); B 1813-1938 (DBI)
Cop (Mf) Banns 1823-1916 (Mf, PLHC); CB 1731-1880 M 1731-1848 (Mf of BT,
     DRO, SLC); Extr C 1731-1880 M 1731-1848 from BT (IGI)
MI   (S&DFHS); (DFHS)

LYTCHETT MATRAVERS (Wes) Dwelling house of William Lodge at Lytchett
[Matravers ?] registered 1779 [Biggs]; chapel [Harrod 1865] [1882 Return]
[Kelly 1939]

LYTCHETT MATRAVERS (Prim Meth) [Harrod 1865]; [1882 Return as 'Higher
Lytchett']; [Kelly 1903]

LYTCHETT MINSTER or SOUTH or LOWER LYTCHETT Minster. Dedication unknown.
[Cogdean Hundred; Poole Union] [505] Chapelry in STURMINSTER MARSHALL.
Erected 1833-34. Separate parish 1858.
OR   C 1555-1645, 1651-1975 M 1554-1692, 1699-1706, 1711/12, 1721-22,
     1738/9-1994 B 1556-1982 Banns 1805-1924, 1936-85 (DRO) *and see*
     STURMINSTER MARSHALL.
BT   CMB 1814-80 (W&SRO)
Cop C 1555-1837 M 1554-1837 B 1556-1698, 1808-43 (DRO); CMB 1813-37 (PRI);
     M 1554-78, 1587-1623, 1632-44, 1751-92, 1599-1706, 1711-1837 (SG);
     M 1554-1837 from OR (DMI); B 1556-1921 (DBI)
Cop (Mf) C 1555-1975 M 1554-1692, 1699-1953 B 1556-1694, 1698-1932
         Banns 1805-1910, 1936-66 (Mf, PLHC); CB 1814-80 M 1814-47
         (Mf of BT, DRO, SLC); Extr C 1814-80 M 1814-47 from BT (IGI)
MI   (S&DFHS); (DFHS); (DRO)

LYTCHETT MINSTER St Aldhelm, Lytchett Heath. Erected 1898 for Lord Eustace
Cecil of Lytchett Heath House. Now private chapel of Lord Rockley. Public
services held occasionally.
MI   (DFHS)

LYTCHETT MINSTER St Dunstan, Dorchester Road, Upton. District chapel
erected 1900 as school [Kelly 1939]

LYTCHETT MINSTER (Ind/Cong and Bapt now URC) United Independent and Baptist
Chapel f 1770 [*Cong. Yearbook* 1871] [1882 Return] [Kelly 1939]

LYTCHETT MINSTER (Wes) [Harrod 1865] [1882 Return] [Kelly 1903]

LYTCHETT MINSTER Upton Community Cemetery, Blandford Road West, 1957.
(Lytchett Minster and Upton Town Council)

MAIDEN NEWTON St Mary [Tollerford Hundred; Dorchester Union] [538]
United 1925 with FROME VAUCHURCH. Now with MELBURY benefice.
OR C 1555-1645, 1654-1975 M 1556-1645, 1654-1975 B 1553-1645/6, 1654-1905
    Banns 1777-1942 (DRO) Noted in 1831: C 1680+ M 1679+ B 1670+
BT CMB 1731-1880 (W&SRO)
Cop M 1556-1812 (Ptd Phil 4: 1909; & on CD-ROM); C 1555-1837 M 1556-1837
    B 1553-1837 (DRO); C 1555-1648, 1654-1812 M 1556-1812 B 1553-1646,
    1654-1812 (SG); CMB 1813-37 (PRI); M 1556-71, 1578, 1582-1645, 1654-59,
    1695-1739, 1746-1837 (SG); M 1556-71, 1578, 1587-1645, 1654-89,
    1695-1739, 1746-1837 (I, SG); M 1813-15 from BT (DRO); M 1555-1812
    (Boyd); M 1790-1812 (Pallot); M 1556-1837 from OR, 1731-54, 1813-15
    from BT (DMI); B 1553-1837 (DBI)
Cop (Mf) M 1556-1812 (Mf of Phil, SLC); CB 1731-1880 M 1731-1847 (Mf of BT,
        DRO, SLC); Extr C 1731-1880 M 1731-1847 from BT (IGI)

MAIDEN NEWTON (Presb) Licence to William King for house of Joan Toop, 1672

MAIDEN NEWTON (Ind/Cong) f 1790 [*Cong. Yearbook* 1871] [Kelly 1903]
OR ZC 1833-35 (RG 4/2410, PRO); C 1847-57 (DRO)
Cop (Mf) ZC 1833-35 (Mf of OR, SLC); Extr C 1833-35 (IGI)

MAIDEN NEWTON (Wes) Barn occupied by John Jacob registered 1798 [Biggs];
Chapel [1882 Return] [Kelly 1903]; Meth [Kelly 1939] Dorchester Circuit

MAINE MARTEL *see* BROADMAYNE

MANSTON St Nicholas [Redland Hundred; Sturminster Union] [149] United 1971
with CHILD OKEFORD, HAMMOON. Now with THE OKEFORD BENEFICE.
OR C 1626-36, 1649-50, 1657-94, 1702-1812 M 1620-37, 1661, 1665, 1669,
    1681-1837 B 1626-39, 1661, 1666-1992 Banns 1755-91, 1825-1945 (DRO)
BT CMB 1732-1837, 1841-43, 1846-80 (W&SRO)
Cop M 1620-1837 B 1813-37 (PRI); M 1620-37, 1661-69, 1681-95, 1702-1837
    (DRO, SG); M 1735-53 from BT (DRO); M 1620-1837 from OR, 1812 from BT
    (DMI); B 1813-37 (I, DRO); B 1771-1812 (DBI); CMB 1732-1880 from BT
    (Pine: CD 3)
Cop (Mf) CB 1732-1880 M 1732-1846 (Mf of BT, DRO, SLC); Extr C 1732-1880
        M 1732-1846 from BT (IGI)
MI (S&DFHS); (DFHS); (DRO)

MANSTON (Wes) n.d. [Kelly 1903]; Meth [Kelly 1939]

MAPPERTON or SOUTH MAPPERTON All Saints Beaminster Forum and Redhone
Hundred; Beaminster Union] [112] Peculiar of the Dean of Sarum until 1847.
United 1971 with MELPLASH. Now with Beaminster Area benefice. Redundant
1977. Sold as private chapel.
OR C 1669-1975 M 1669-1977 B 1669-1740, [1793-1955 4 entries]
    Banns 1824-1965 (DRO) For B *see also* NETHERBURY.
BT CMB 1585-88, 1591-93, 1596-99, 1603-09, 1613-23, 1626-40, 1672,
    1678-83, 1688-90, 1695-1734, 1746, 1751-60, 1767-1800, 1805-11, 1813-46
    C 1847-80 (W&SRO)
Cop M 1669-1811 (Ptd Phil 1: 1906; & on CD-ROM); C 1813-37 M 1751-1837
    B 1821-1955 (PRI); C 1813-37 (I, DRO); M 1669-1837 (DRO); M 1669-1738,
    1746-77, 1784-91, 1796-1819, 1826-37 (SG); M 1585-1669 from BT (DRO);
    M 1689-1812 (Boyd); M 1790-1812 (Pallot); M 1669-1837 from OR,
    1585-1813 from BT (DMI); B 1735-1955 (DBI)
Cop (Mf) M 1669-1811 (Mf of Phil, SLC); CB 1585-1880 M 1585-1837 (Mf of BT,
        DRO, SLC); Extr C 1585-1880 M 1585-1837 from BT (IGI)

MAPPERTON *see* ALMER

MAPPOWDER St Peter and St Paul [Buckland Newton Hundred; Cerne Union] [308]
Gained PLUSH 1937 from BUCKLAND NEWTON; PLUSH joined PIDDLETRENTHIDE 1954.
Now with HAZLEBURY BRYAN AND THE HILLSIDE PARISHES benefice.
OR C 1650-1700, 1712-1948 M 1655-1997 B 1653/4-1999 Banns 1754-1812,
1823-33, 1840-1999 (DRO)
BT CMB 1731-98, 1802-40, 1847-80 (W&SRO)
Cop C 1813-37 M 1654-1837 (PRI); C 1733-1837 (I, DRO); M 1654-1837 (DRO,
SG); M 1733-85 from BT (DRO); M 1655-1837 from OR, 1618-54 from
Hutchins (DMI); B 1653-1999 (DBI)
Cop (Mf) CB 1731-1880 M 1733-1834 (Mf of BT, DRO, SLC); Extr C 1731-1880
M 1733-1834 from BT (IGI)
MI (S&DFHS); (DFHS); (DRO); Ch cy 1971 (SG)

MAPPOWDER (Cong) Out-station of CERNE ABBAS [*Cong. Yearbook* 1871]

MAPPOWDER (Prim Meth) [1882 Return]

MARGARET MARSH St Margaret [Sturminster Newton Hundred; Shaftesbury
Incorporation/Union] [86] Chapelry in IWERNE MINSTER united 1863 with
chapelry of EAST ORCHARD, as EAST ORCHARD WITH MARGARET MARSH. Now with
SHASTON benefice.
OR C 1692-1776, 1785-1812 M 1694-1730, 1745-46/7 [1815-34 4 entries]
B 1682-1777, 1785-92, 1808-10 (DRO) *see* IWERNE COURTNEY for
M 1756-1812. Noted in 1831: CMB 1682-90, 1692+
BT CMB 1731-32, 1774-77, 1787-92, 1795-1880 (W&SRO)
Cop C 1785-1812 M 1694, 1716-46, 1815-34 (DRO); M 1694-96, 1716-30,
1745-46, 1815, 1826, 1834 (SG); M 1694-1834 (PRI); M 1694-1834 from OR,
1748-1815 from BT (DMI); B 1689-1812 (DBI); CMB 1731-1880 from BT
(Pine: CD 3)
Cop (Mf) CB 1731-32, 1773-1880 M 1812-34 (Mf of BT, DRO, SLC);
Extr C 1731-32, 1773-1880 M 1812-34 from BT (IGI)
MI (S&DFHS); (DFHS); (DRO)

MARNHULL St Gregory [Sturminster Newton Hundred; Sturminster Union] [1309]
OR C 1559-1992 M 1560/1-1656, 1662-1727, 1754-1984 B 1560-1992
Banns 1754-1969 (DRO)
BT CMB 1731-1880 (W&SRO)
Cop C 1559-1661, 1808-37 M 1561-1841 B 1560-1660, 1818-37 (DRO);
CB 1813-37 M 1561-1841 (PRI); M 1561-63, 1570-1656, 1662-1727,
1754-1841 (SG); M 1731-54 from BT (DRO); M 1561-1727, 1754-1841 from
OR, 1731-54 from BT (DMI); B 1560-1837 (DBI); CMB 1731-1880 from BT
(Pine: CD 3); Extr C 1560-1717 M 1561-1726 B 1560-1742 (SG);
Cop (Mf) C 1559-1660, 1662-1883 M 1561-1656, 1662-1727, 1754-1984
B 1560-1660, 1662-1886 Banns 1754-1970 (Mf of OR, SG);
CB 1731-1880 M 1731-1847 (Mf of BT, DRO, SLC); Extr C 1731-1880
M 1731-1847 from BT (IGI)
MI (S&DFHS); (DFHS); (DRO)

MARNHULL (RC) f 1651. Domestic chapel of Hussey family (previously at STOUR
PROVOST) Nash Court, 1725-72. Benedictine monks 1772-86. Benedictine nuns
from Paris 1795-1807. Cistercian Nuns, Priory of St Joseph, left 1920.
St Mary, Old Mill Lane. Erected 1832 [1882 Return] Canons Regular of
St Augustine from 1884.
OR C 1772+ MD 1854+ Confirmations 1781+ (Inc); Confirmations 1869, 1875,
1886, 1891, 1892-1930 (PDA)
Cop C 1772-1826 Confirmations 1753-1809 with recusancy papers of Meynell
family (Ptd CRS 56: 1964)
Cop (Mf) M 1772-1826 (Mf of CRS, SLC; M 1772-1826 (Printout, Mf SLC);
Extr C 1772-1826 (IGI)

MARNHULL (Ind/Cong) f 1790. Village chapel [*Cong. Yearbook* 1871]
[1882 Return] [Kelly 1939]

MARNHULL (Wes) House occupied by William Bartlett registered 1794 [Biggs]
chapel [Harrod 1865] [Kelly 1903]
OR   M 1913-28 (DRO)

MARNHULL (Prim Meth) Chapel [1882 Return] [Kelly 1903]

MARNHULL (Prim Meth) Chapel, Moorside [1882 Return]

MARNHULL (Meth) Burton Street. North Dorset Circuit

MARNHULL (S of F) Meeting House [1882 Return] Hall and reading room erected
1890 on site of old meeting house [Kelly 1903]

MARSH CAUNDLE   *see* CAUNDLE MARSH

MARSHALSEA   *see* MARSHWOOD

MARSHWOOD St Mary [Whitchurch Canonicorum Hundred; Beaminster Union] [538]
Chapelry in WHITCHURCH CANONICORUM, with which united 1700-1840.
Transferred 1953 to BETTISCOMBE. Rebuilt 1841, 1884. Now with GOLDEN CAP
Team Benefice.
OR   C 1614-48, 1652/3-71, 1682, 1696-1700, 1841-1936 M 1614-42, 1654-59,
     1673, 1696/97, 1841-1991 B 1620-24, 1643, 1654-59, 1700, 1721,
     1842-1992 Banns 1842-57 (DRO)
BT   CMB 1841-46, 1849-80; for earlier transcripts *see* WHITCHURCH
     CANONICORUM (W&SRO)
Cop M 1614-73 (Ptd Phil 5, with corrections in 7: 1910, 1914; & on CD-
     ROM); C 1614-1700 M 1614-42, 1654-59, 1673, 1696 B 1620-1721 (SG);
     M 1614-96 (DRO); M 1614-96 from OR (DMI); M 1614-75 (Boyd); CMB 1841-80
     from BT (Pine: CD 2)
Cop (Mf) M 1614-73 (Mf of Phil, SLC); CB 1841-80 (Mf of BT, DRO, SLC);
        Extr C 1841-80 from BT (IGI)
MI   (S&DFHS); (DFHS)

MARSHWOOD (Presb) Licence to John Pinney for house of John Price, 1672

MARSHWOOD (Wes) House occupied by Samuel Mills registered 1799 [Biggs]

mARSHWOOD (Ind) Marshalsea. Out-station of MORCOMBELAKE (Whitchurch
Canonicorum) [*Cong. Yearbook* 1871]; Congregational Home Missionary Chapel.
Erected 1832 [1882 Return] [Kelly 1903]

MARTINSTOWN   *see* WINTERBORNE ST MARTIN

MARWOOD   *see* WINTERBORNE ZELSTONE

MAYNE MARTELL *see* BROADMAYNE

MELBURY   Modern benefice including CATTISTOCK, EAST CHELBOROUGH, WEST
CHELBOROUGH, CHILFROME, CORSCOMBE, EVERSHOT, FROME ST QUINTON, FROME
VAUCHURCH, HALSTOCK, MAIDEN NEWTON, MELBURY BUBB, MELBURY OSMOND with
MELBURY SAMPFORD, RAMPISHAM, TOLLER FRATRUM, TOLLER WHELME, WRAXALL.

MELBURY ABBAS St Thomas [Sixpenny Handley Hundred; Shaftesbury Incorporation/Union] [354] Rebuilt 1851-52. Now with SHASTON benefice.
OR   C 1716/7-1912 M 1717-1968 B 1763-1812 Banns 1754-1809, 1824-1900
     (DRO) No earlier registers noted in 1831.
BT   CMB 1732-1880 (W&SRO)
Cop C 1763-1837 B 1813-1983 (I, DRO); C 1809-37 M 1717-1837 (PRI);
     M 1717-1837 (DRO, SG); M 1717-1837 from OR (DMI); B 1813-1985 (S&DFHS);
     B 1813-38 (DBI); CMB 1732-1880 from BT (Pine: CD 3)
Cop (Mf) CB 1732-1880 M 1732-1835 (Mf of BT, DRO, SLC); Extr C 1732-1880
          M 1732-1835 from BT (IGI)
MI   (DFHS); (DRO); Cy 1905 (*Ye Olde Mortality* 9: Ms, SG)

MELBURY ABBAS (Prim Meth) [1882 Return]

MELBURY BUBB St Mary the Virgin [Yetminster Hundred; Cerne Union] [121]
Included hamlet of Woolcombe (Matravers). Now with MELBURY benefice.
OR   C 1679-1813 M 1681-1836 B 1679-1813 Banns 1754-75, 1824-1925 (DRO)
BT   CMB 1731-1836, 1847-80; including Woolcombe Matravers 1831-36 (W&SRO)
Cop C 1758-1812 B 1678-1758 (I, DRO); M 1681-1836 (DRO); M 1681-97, 1705,
     1717-1836 (SG); M 1681-1830 (PRI); M 1732-76 from BT (DRO);
     M 1681-1837 from OR, 1731-1814 from BT (DMI); B 1678-1758 (DBI);
     CMB 1731-1880 from BT (Pine: CD 1)
Cop (Mf) CMB 1731-1812 CB 1813-80 M 1813-36 (Mf of BT, DRO, SLC);
          Extr C 1731-1880 M 1836 from BT (IGI)
MI   (S&DFHS); (DFHS)

MELBURY OSMOND St Osmund [Yetminster Hundred; Beaminster Union] [380]
United 1972 with MELBURY SAMPFORD. Now with MELBURY benefice.
OR   C 1580-1880 M 1580-1970 B 1581-1929 Banns 1755-1818, 1824-54, 1910-36
     (DRO)
BT   CMB 1751-1836, 1848-80 including MELBURY SAMPFORD (W&SRO)
Cop C 1716-1837 M 1580-1837 B 1581-1716, 1813-37 (I, DRO); CMB 1813-37
     (PRI); M 1580-1642, 1649-1709, 1717-83, 1790-1837 (SG); M 1580-1837
     from OR (DMI); B 1581-1837 (DBI); CMB 1751-1880 from BT (Pine: CD 1)
Cop (Mf) CB 1731-1880 M 1731-1836 (Mf of BT, DRO, SLC); Extr C 1731-1880
          M 1731-1836 from BT (IGI)
MI   (S&DFHS); (DFHS)

MELBURY OSMOND (Plymouth Brethren) 'The Room' in the occupation of Henry
George Childs [1882 Return]

MELBURY SAMPFORD or UPPER MELBURY (dedication unknown) [Tollerford Hundred;
Beaminster Union] [53] United 1972 with MELBURY OSMUND. Now with MELBURY
benefice. Redundant 1972. Sold for use in connection with Melbury House.
OR   C 1606-1978 M 1606-1837, 1843-1969 B 1614-1812, 1819-1970
     Banns 1755-1818, 1824-54, 1909-36 (DRO)
BT   *see* MELBURY OSMOND
Cop C 1716-1978 M 1606-1837 B 1819-1970 (DRO); C 1813-1970 M 1813-37
     B 1819-1970 (PRI); M 1606, 1611-24, 1646-57, 1665, 1674-79, 1684,
     1696-1728, 1734, 1739-51, 1756-82, 1790-1814, 1819-37 (SG);
     M 1606, 1650-1837 from OR (DMI); B 1819-1970 (DBI)
Cop (Mf) CB 1731-1880 M 1731-1836, BT of MELBURY OSMUND (Mf, DRO, SLC)

MELCOMBE BINGHAM *see* MELCOMBE HORSEY

MELCOMBE HORSEY or MELCOMBE BINGHAM St Andrew [Whiteway Hundred; Cerne Union] [172] Now with MILTON ABBAS, HILTON, CHESELBOURNE.
OR   C 1690-1975 M 1696/7-1992 B 1735-1812 Banns 1754-96 (DRO)
BT   CMB 1731-1880 (W&SRO)
Cop   C 1690-1838 M 1698-1846 B 1735-1838 (DRO); C 1690-1812 M 1690-1846
      B 1735-1838 (SG); C 1813-37 M 1698-1846 B 1808-38 (PRI); M 1698-1846
      from OR, 1731-54 from BT, 1613, 1624, 1681 from Hutchins (DMI);
      B 1803-38 (DBI)
Cop (Mf) CB 1731-1880 M 1731-1844 (Mf of BT, DRO, SLC); Extr C 1731-1880
          M 1731-1844 from BT (IGI)
MI   (S&DFHS); (DFHS); (DRO)

MELCOMBE HORSEY Higher Melcombe (House) Chapel pre-1633 [Pevsner]

MELCOMBE REGIS   *see* WEYMOUTH

MELPLASH   *see* NETHERBURY

MERLEY   *see* WIMBORNE MINSTER

MIDDLE GUSSAGE   *see* GUSSAGE ST MICHAEL

MIDDLEMARSH   *see* MINTERNE MAGNA

MILBORNE ST ANDREW (MILBORNE CHURCHSTONE AND ST ANDREW 1831) St Andrew [part Dewlish Liberty, part Puddletown Hundred; Blandford Union] [240] Included ancient parish of DEWLISH as a chapelry. Joined 1890 by hamlet of MILBORNE STILEHAM from LYME REGIS. Now with DEWLISH.
OR   C 1570-1970 M 1570-1648, 1657-88, 1695-1714, 1719-27, 1743-1993
      B 1570-1721, 1743-1993 Banns 1779-1806, 1824-1980 (DRO)
BT   CMB 1731-1832, 1836-44, 1846-80 (W&SRO)
Cop   CB 1570-1837 M 1570-1838 (DRO); CMB 1570-1812 (I, SG); CB 1614-1720
      M 1570-1812 (S&DFHS); CB 1813-37 M 1570-1838 (PRI); M 1687-1742 (SG);
      M 1731-54 from BT (DRO); M 1570-1838 from OR, 1731-54 from BT (DMI);
      B 1570-1837 (DBI)
Cop (Mf) CB 1731-1880 M 1731-1831 (Mf of BT, DRO, SLC); Extr C 1731-80
          M 1736-1832 from BT (IGI)
MI   (S&DFHS); (DFHS)

MILBORNE ST ANDREW (Wes) Erected 1867 [1882 Return] [Kelly 1903]; Meth [Kelly 1939]

MILBORNE STILEHAM [Bere Regis Hundred; Blandford Union] [313] Hamlet and tithing in BERE REGIS; transferred 1890 to MILBORNE ST ANDREW.
OR   C 1687-1719 M 1687, 1708, 1716/17-1717, 1730-42 B 1687-1742 (DRO)
Cop   M 1687-1754 (DRO); M 1687-1742 (SG); M 1687-1742 from OR, 1731-54
      from BT (DMI)

MILTON ABBAS or ABBEY MILTON St James [Whiteway Hundred; Blandford Union] [846] Peculiar of Milton Abbas, with Woolland. Milton Abbey church used until late 18th cent. St James erected 1786 as parish church. Now with HILTON, CHESELBOURNE, MELCOMBE HORSEY.
OR   C 1651-1981 M 1651-1994 B 1651-1879 Banns 1653-60 1754-66 1824-1968
      (DRO) No earlier register noted in 1831. Phillimore states that Vol.1
      1559-1650 existed in 1729.
BT   CMB 1731-1880 (W&SRO)

MILTON ABBAS cont

Cop M 1569, 1575, 1589, 1603, 1621 (all from Hutchins), 1651-1812
(Ptd Phil 1: 1906; & on CD-ROM); C 1651-1723 M 1569-1837 B 1651-1763
(DRO); C 1813-37 B 1813-37 (I, DRO); CMB 1813-37 (PRI); M 1569, 1575,
1589, 1603, 1621, 1652-1837 Banns 1654-59, 1673 (SG); M 1569-1812
(Boyd); M 1790-1812 (Pallot); M 1569-1650 from Phil, 1651-1837 from OR
(DMI); B 1813-37 (DBI); Extr M 1569-1812 (SG)
Cop (Mf) M 1569-1812 (Mf of Phil, SLC); CB 1731-1880 M 1731-1848 (Mf of BT,
DRO, SLC); Extr C 1731-1880 M 1731-1848 from BT (IGI)
MI (S&DFHS); (DFHS); (DRO)

MILTON ABBAS Milton Abbey Church rebuilt 14th-15th cent. Used as chapel by
Milton Abbey School.
OR M 1907-80 Banns 1907-57 (DRO)

MILTON ABBAS St Catherine's Chapel. Ancient chapel, restored [Kelly 1939]

MILTON ABBAS (Presb) Licence to Thomas Moore for house at Milton Abbas of
Robert Alford of Sturminster Newton, 1672

MILTON ABBAS (Nonconformist: unspecified) Licence for house of Nathaniel
Stevens, 1672

MILTON ABBAS (Wes) [1882 Return]; rebuilt 1895 [Kelly 1903];
Meth [Kelly 1939]

MILTON ABBAS (S of F) Constituent meeting of POOLE MM *q.v.* Closed before
1804.

MILTON ON STOUR *see* GILLINGHAM

MILTON, WEST *see* POWERSTOCK

MINCHINTON tithing of SIXPENNY HANDLEY

MINTERNE MAGNA or GREAT MINTERNE St Andrew [part Fordington Liberty, part
Piddletrenthide Liberty, part Cerne, Totcombe and Modbury Hundred; Cerne
Union] [331 including tithing of Hartly] Now with CERNE ABBAS,
GODMANSTONE.
OR C 1635/6-1704/5, 1718-1927 M 1636-1704, 1718-1912 B 1635/6-1992
Banns 1754-1802, 1824-1905 (DRO)
BT CMB 1731-1880 (W&SRO)
Cop C 1813-37 M 1636-1837 B 1635-1704, 1813-37 (I, DRO); CB 1813-37
M 1636-1837 (PRI); C 1635-1704 (DRO); M 1636-1837 (SG); M 1636-1837
from OR (DMI)
Cop (Mf) CB 1731-1880 M 1731-1867 (Mf of BT, DRO, SLC); Extr C 1731-1880
M 1731-1868 from BT (IGI)
MI Ch (Ptd *Miscellanea Genealogica et Heraldica*, series 5: 8: 1932:
237-39)

MINTERNE PARVA tithing of BUCKLAND NEWTON [101]

MONKTON *see* WINTERBORNE MONKTON

MONKTON UP WIMBORNE tithing of CRANBORNE

MONKTON WYLD *see* WHITCHURCH CANONICORUM

MOOR CRICHEL *see* CRICHEL, MORE

MOORS, WEST   *see* WEST PARLEY

MORCOMBELAKE   *see* WHITCHURCH CANONICORUM

MORDEN St Mary, East Morden [Loosebarrow Hundred; Wareham and Purbeck Union] [813] Consisted of East and West Morden. Rebuilt 1873. Now with RED POST benefice.
OR C 1575-1640, 1653-94/5, 1719-1854 M 1575-1639, 1654-56, 1662-77, 1685-93/4, 1719-95, 1813-1989 B 1575-c 1615, 1653-72, 1678-93/4, 1719-1872 Banns 1823-53 (DRO) Noted in 1831: M 1754-1812 'in bad condition'
BT CMB 1731-1833, 1847-80 (W&SRO)
Cop C 1576-1722, 1770-1854 M 1575-1837 B 1575-1837 (DRO); C 1731-1880 M 1731-1846 from BT (VRI); CB 1813-37 M 1575-1837 (PRI); M 1575-1639, 1654-56, 1662-77, 1685-92, 1719-95, 1813-37 (I, SG); M 1796-1811 from BT (DRO); M 1575-1795, 1813-37 from OR, 1796-1812 from BT (DMI); B 1813-37 (DBI); Extr C 1575-1690 M 1575-1692 B 1576-1685 (SG)
Cop (Mf) CB 1731-1880 M 1731-1846 (Mf of BT, DRO, SLC); Extr C 1731-1880 M 1731-1846 from BT (IGI)
MI (S&DFHS); (DFHS); (DRO); (SG)

MORDEN St Mary, Charborough. Ancient parish of Charborough later a chapelry of MORDEN. Chapel erected 1775 in grounds of Charborough Hall. United 1972 with ALMER. Now with RED POST benefice. Redundant 1987. Sold for use as place of prayer and holding of occasional services.
OR *see* MORDEN

MORDEN (Presb) General preaching licence to John White of Morden; licence to Samuel Ball, for the house of John Collins; licence for house of George Filliter senior of West Morden 1672

MORDEN (Cong)) Licence to Philip Lamb for his house at East Morden, 1672

MORDEN (Wes(f by 1789. House occupied by John Butler registered 1798; house at East Morden occupied by William Clarke registered 1798; house at West Morden occupied by Hannah Keat registered 1799 [Biggs]; chapel Esat Morden [Harrod 1865] [1882 Return] [Kelly 1903]; Meth [Kelly 1939]
OR *see* POOLE (RG 4/1230, PRO)

MORDEN (S of F) Constituent meeting of POOLE MM *q.v.* Closed before 1804.

MORDEN ('Persons who object to be designated') Building occupied by Joseph Knapp, West Morden [1882 Return]

MORE CRICHEL *see* CRICHEL, MORE

MORETON St Nicholas [part Winfrith Hundred, part Bindon Liberty; Wareham and Purbeck Union] [304] Rebuilt 1776. Now with WOODSFORD, TINCLETON.
OR C 1565-1632, 1741-1981 M 1565-1630, 1742-1994 B 1565-1629, 1741-1993 Banns 1754-1812, 1818, 1823-1960 (DRO) Noted in 1831: CMB 1741+
BT CMB 1731-34, 1738-1880 (W&SRO)
Cop C 1565-1631, 1741-1837 M 1565-1838 B 1565-1631, 1741-1837 (DRO); CB 1813-37 M 1565-1838 with gaps (PRI); C 1731-1880 from BT (VRI); M 1565-1838 (SG); M 1731-50 from BT (DRO); M 1565-1630, 1742-1838 from OR, 1731-44 from BT (DMI); B 1814-37 (DBI)
Cop (Mf) CB 1731-1880 M 1731-1846 (Mf of BT, DRO, SLC); Extr C 1731-1880 M 1731-1846 from BT (IGI)
MI (S&DFHS); (DRO); Ch cy *c.*1979 (SG)

MOSTERTON St Mary [Beaminster Forum and Redhone Hundred; Beaminster Union] [303] Chapelry in SOUTH PERROTT. Rebuilt 1833 on new site. Now with Beaminster Area benefice.
OR C 1651-1883 M 1656-59, 1671-93, 1706-07, 1712-1836 B 1655-59, 1666-1977 Banns 1755-1812 (DRO) *and see* SOUTH PERROTT
BT CMB 1741-1880; for 1731-41 *see* SOUTH PERROTT (W&SRO)
Cop M 1656-93, 1700-50, 1755-1812, and jointly with South Perrott 1539-1676 (Ptd Phil 4: 1909; & on CD-ROM); CB 1655-1837 M 1656-1836 (DRO); C 1733-1880 M 1733-1846 from BT (VRI); CMB 1813-37 (PRI); M 1656-59, 1671, 1676-93, 1706-07, 1712-1836 (SG); M 1790-1812 (Pallot); M 1656-1836 from OR (DMI); B 1813-37 (DBI)
Cop (Mf) M 1656-1812 (Mf of Phil, SLC); CB 1733?-1880 M 1733?-1846 (Mf of BT, DRO, SLC); Extr C 1733-1880 M 1733-1846 (IGI)

MOSTERTON (Plymouth Brethran) Erected 1894 [Kelly 1903, 1939]

MOTCOMBE St Mary [Gillingham Liberty; Shaftesbury Incorporation/Union] [1405] Chapelry in GILLINGHAM. Rebuilt 1846. Separate parish 1883 as MOTCOMBE WITH ENMORE GREEN. Now with SHASTON benefice.
OR C 1675-1951 M 1676-1949 B 1676-1924 Banns 1754-1812, 1823-1925 (DRO)
BT CMB 1749-50, 1776-1879 (W&SRO)
Cop M 1676-1837 B 1716-89 (DRO); CB 1813-37 (I, DRO); C 1749-1879 M 1749-1839 from BT (VRI); CB 1813-37 M 1676-1837 (PRI); M 1676-1837 (SG); M 1676-1837 from OR (DMI); B 1813-37 (DBI); Extr C 1676-1787 M 1677-1743 B 1671-1787 (SG)
Cop (Mf) CB 1749-1879 M 1749-1839 (Mf of BT, DRO, SLC); Extr C 1749-1879 M 1749-1839 from BT (IGI)
MI (DFHS); (DRO); war memorial (SG); cy 1905 (*Ye Olde Mortality* 9: Ms, SG)

MOTCOMBE St John the Evangelist, Enmore Green. Erected 1843. Formerly part of MOTCOMBE. Now with SHASTON benefice.
BT CB 1843-45, 1847-79; for earlier transcripts *see* MOTCOMBE
Cop (Mf) CB 1843-79 (Mf of BT, DRO, SLC); Extr C 1843-79 from BT (IGI)
MI Cy (*Ye Olde Mortality* 9: Ms, SG)

MOTCOMBE (Presb) Licence for house of John Hussey, 1672

MOTCOMBE (Wes) Chapel erected by 1764. Registered 1796 [Biggs] [1882 Return]

MOTCOMBE (Wes) Enmore Green [Harrod 1865]

MOTCOMBE (Wes =? Prim Meth ?) *see* SHAFTESBURY AND GILLINGHAM CIRCUIT

MOTCOMBE (Prim Meth) Motcombe Circuit. Chapel [Harrod 1865] [1882 Return]
OR C 1827-1950 (DRO)
Cop (Mf) C 1827-73 kept by Motcombe Prim Meth chapel; 1873-1950 kept by Queen Street chapel, Gillingham (Mf of OR, SLC)

MOTCOMBE (Prim Meth) Enmore Green [Harrod 1865] [1882 Return] [Kelly 1903]

MOTCOMBE (Meth) The Street. North Dorset Circuit

MUCKLEFORD   *see* BRADFORD PEVERELL

NETHER CERNE   *see* CERNE, NETHER

NETHER COMPTON   *see* COMPTON, NETHER

NETHERBURY St Mary [Beaminster Forum and Redhone Hundred; Beaminster Union] [1942] Peculiar of the Prebend of Netherbury and Beaminster, Sarum Cathedral until 1847. Included chapelry of BEAMINSTER (separate parish 1849); and tithings of MELPLASH (parish 1847) and SALWAY ASH. Now with Beaminster Area benefice.

OR   C 1592-1947 M 1592-1690, 1695-1989 B 1592-1678, 1683-1857
      Banns 1761-1811, 1870-1954 (DRO)
BT   CMB 1585-88, 1594-97, 1603-09, 1614-44, 1662-63, 1670-75, 1678, 1681,
      1684-91, 1694-1710, 1713-22, 1725-30, 1734-1843, 1847-80 (W&SRO)
Cop M 1592-1839 (Ptd Phil 7: 1914; & on CD-ROM); C 1592-1871 M 1592-1890
      B 1592-1816, 1821, 1850-51 (DRO); C 1592-1709 M 1754-1837 B 1592-1698,
      1813-16, 1821, 1850-51 (SG); CB 1813-37 M 1592-1837 (PRI); C 1695-1758,
      1830-71 (S&DFHS); M 1584-1740 from BT (DRO); M 1592-1837 (Boyd);
      M 1790-1839 (Pallot); M 1593-1736, 1754-1837 from OR, 1585-92 from BT
      (DMI); B 1694-1851 (DBI)
Cop (Mf) M 1592-1839 (Mf of Phil, SLC); CMB 1585-1880 (Mf of BT, DRO, SLC);
       Extr C 1585-1880 M 1585-1838 from BT (IGI)
MI   (S&DFHS); (DFHS); (DRO); Cy (SG); (Ts and Mf, SLC); Cy 1901 (*Ye Olde
     Mortality* 3: Ms, SG)

NETHERBURY Christchurch, Melplash. Tithing of Melplash in Netherbury. Erected 1845-46. Parish created 1847 from NETHERBURY, POWERSTOCK. United 1971 with MAPPERTON. Now with Beaminster Area benefice.

OR   C 1846-1910 M 1847-1978 B 1846-1994 Banns 1847-1926 (DRO)
BT   CMB 1846-80; for earlier transcripts *see* POWERSTOCK, NETHERBURY
     (W&SRO)
Cop (Mf) CB 1846-80 (Mf of BT, DRO, SLC); Extr C 1846-80 from BT (IGI)
MI   Ts and film (SLC); incomplete (SG)

NETHERBURY Holy Trinity, Salway Ash. Chapel-of-ease erected 1887. Now with Beaminster Area benefice.

OR   C 1838-72 (DRO)
Cop C 1838-72 (DRO, S&DFHS)

NETHERBURY (Presb) Licence for house of Richard Forsey; licence for house of Henry Weay of 'Petherbury' ? 1672

NETHERBURY (Cong) Waytown. f 1689. [*Cong. Yearbook* 1871] Rebuilt 1907 [Kelly 1939]

NETHERBURY (Cong) Netherbury. Erected 1839. Out-station of Waytown, above [*Cong. Yearbook* 1871] [Kelly 1939]

NETHERBURY (Cong) Salway Ash. Erected 1843 Out-station of Waytown, above [*Cong. Yearbook* 1871] [Kelly 1939]

NETHERBURY (Ind) A cottage, North Bowood [1882 Return]

NETHERBURY (Wes) House occupied by John Orchard registered 1796 [Biggs] Meeting Room, Salway Ash [1882 Return] Meth: Salway Ash [Kelly 1939]

OR   *see* AXMINSTER [Devon] and BRIDPORT Circuits

NETHERHAY   *see* BROADWINDSOR

NETTLECOMBE   *see* POWERSTOCK

NEW BOROUGH AND LEIGH   *see* WIMBORNE MINSTER

NEWTON, NEWTOWN   *see* CANFORD MAGNA

NORTH BOWOOD   *see* NETHERBURY

NORTH POORTON   *see* POORTON, NORTH

NORTH WOOTTON   *see* WOOTTON, NORTH

OAKDALE ST GEORGE   Modern benefice including OAKDALE St George, CANFORD HEATH St Paul, CREEKMOOR Christ Church. *see* CANFORD MAGNA.

OBORNE St Cuthbert [Sherborne Hundred; Sherborne Union] [83] Peculiar of the Dean of Sarum until 1847. Included chapelry of CASTLETON (separate parish 1716) Old church, replaced 1862, now with Churches Conservation Trust. Now with QUEEN THORNE benefice.
OR   C 1567/8-1992 M 1568-1837 B 1568/9-1993 Banns 1754-1812 (DRO)
BT   CMB 1579-82, 1585-1603, 1606-18, 1622-30, 1633-40, 1669-75, 1679-1836, 1847-76; including CASTLETON 1606-33 (W&SRO)
Cop   C 1567/8-1788 M 1568-1837 B 1568/9-1723/4 (DRO); C 1813-40 M 1754-1837 B 1813-37 (PRI); CB 1813-37 (I, DRO); M 1568-1647, 1662, 1672, 1680, 1694-1840 (SG); M 1579-1759 from BT (DRO); M 1568-1837 from OR, 1579-1759 from BT (DMI); B 1813-37 (DBI)
Cop (Mf)   CB 1579-1876 M 1579-1836 (Mf of BT, DRO, SLC); Extr C 1579-1878 M 1579-1836 from BT (IGI)
MI   (S&DFHS); (DFHS); (DRO); Old chancel, ch cy 1973 (SG)

OKEFORD BENEFICE, (THE) Modern benefice including CHILD OKEFORD, OKEFORD FITZPAINE, MANSTON, HAMMOON, SHILLINGSTONE.

OKEFORD FITZPAINE St Andrew [Sturminster Newton Hundred; Sturminster Union] [620] Now with THE OKEFORD BENEFICE.
OR   C 1592-1906 M 1594-1983 B 1593-1886 Banns 1754-1867, 1891-1937 (DRO)
BT   CMB 1731-1816, 1821-36, 1847-80 (W&SRO)
Cop   C 1598/9-1679 (DRO); CB 1813-37 (I, DRO); CMB 1813-37 (PRI); M 1593-1837 from OR (DMI); B 1813-37 (DBI)
Cop (Mf)   CB 1731-1880 M 1731-1836 (Mf of BT, DRO, SLC); Extr C 1731-1880 M 1731-1836 from BT (IGI)
MI   (S&DFHS); (DFHS); (DRO); (SG); Extr: Pratt (Ms, SG)

OKEFORD FITZPAINE (Wes) Chapel [Harrod 1865] A Building [1882 Return]; chapel [Kelly 1939]

OKEFORD FITZPAINE (Prim Meth) Chapel [Harrod 1865] [1882 Return] [Kelly 1939]

OKEFORD FITZPAINE (Prim Meth) Fiddleford (hamlet formerly in Child Okeford) [Kelly 1903]; Meth [Kelly 1939]

OKEFORD, CHILD St Nicholas [Redland Hundred; Sturminster Union] [612] United 1971 with MANSTON, HAMMOON. Now with THE OKEFORD BENEFICE.
OR   C 1653-1973 M 1658-1925 B 1653-1952 Banns 1653-53/4, 1755-1812, 1909-70 (DRO)
BT   CMB 1731-1820, 1824-78 (W&SRO)
Cop   C 1761-1837 (I, DRO); M 1658-1837 B 1653-1837 (DRO); C 1761-1837 MB 1813-37 (PRI); M 1731-55 from BT (DRO); M 1658-1837 from OR, 1731-55 from BT (DMI); B 1750-1837 (DBI)
Cop (Mf)   CB 1731-1878 M 1731-1847 (Mf of BT, DRO, SLC); Extr C 1731-1878 M 1731-1847 from BT (IGI)
MI   (DFHS); (DRO)

OKEFORD, CHILD (Bapt) [1882 Return]

OKEFORD, CHILD (Wes) [1882 Return] [Kelly 1903]; Meth [Kelly 1939]

OKEFORD, SHILLING see SHILLINGSTONE

ORCHARD, EAST St Thomas [Sixpenny Handley Hundred; Shaftesbury Incorporation/Union] [201] Rebuilt 1859-61. Chapelry in IWERNE MINSTER, united 1863 with MARGARET MARSH to form parish of EAST ORCHARD WITH MARGARET MARSH. Joined 1952 by FONTMELL MAGNA, chapelry of WEST ORCHARD.. Now with SHASTON benefice.
OR   C 1785-1812 M 1783-1836 Banns 1954 (DRO) Noted in 1831: 'Included in the Registers of Iwerne Minster.'
BT   East and West Orchard CMB 1731, 1754-56, 1772-77, 1786-92, 1796-97, 1800, 1803-45, 1847-80; 1843-45 cover East Orchard only (W&SRO)
Cop C 1731-1880 M 1731-1845 from BT (VRI); C 1731-1812 M 1782-1836 (PRI); M 1782-88, 1808-15, 1826-36 (DRO, SG); M 1731-82 from BT (DRO); M 1782-1836 from OR, 1731-82 from BT (DMI)
Cop (Mf) CB 1731-1880 M 1731-1845 (Mf of BT, DRO, SLC); Extr C 1731-1880 M 1731-1845 from BT (IGI)
MI   (S&DFHS); (DFHS); (DRO)

ORCHARD, EAST (Wes) Erected 1876 [Kelly 1903]; Meth [Kelly 1939]

ORCHARD, EAST (Prim Meth) Erected 1890 [Kelly 1903]; Meth [Kelly 1939]

ORCHARD, WEST St Luke [Sixpenny Handley Hundred; Shaftesbury Incorporation/Union] [183] Chapelry in FONTMELL MAGNA transferred 1952 to EAST ORCHARD WITH MARGARET MARSH. Now with SHASTON benefice.
OR   C 1754-58, 1763, 1815-22 M 1755-1839 (DRO) Noted in 1831: M 1754-1812; 'Bapt.Bur, registered at the Mother Church, Fontmell.'
BT   East and West Orchard CMB 1731, 1754-56, 1772-77, 1786-92, 1796-97, 1800, 1803-45, 1847-80; 1843-45 cover East Orchard only (W&SRO)
Cop C 1851-80 from BT (VRI); M 1754-1839 (DRO, SG, DMI, PRI)
Cop (Mf) Extr C 1851-80 from BT (IGI) and see EAST ORCHARD
MI   (S&DFHS); (DFHS); (DRO)

ORCHARD, WEST (Wes) A building registered 1798 [Biggs]

OSMINGTON St Osmund [Culliford Tree Hundred; Weymouth Union] [421] 'with Ringstead' in 1831. United 1969 with POXWELL. Now with PRESTON with SUTTON POYNTZ.
OR   C 1691-1873 M 1693-1991 B 1678-1953 Banns 1754-1966 (DRO)
BT   CMB 1731-1880 (W&SRO)
Cop C 1695-1807 M 1693-1837 B 1678-1807 (DRO); CB 1813-37 (I, DRO); C 1731-1880 M 1731-1847 from BT (VRI); CB 1813-37 M 1693-1837 (PRI); M 1693-1837 (SG); M 1693-1837 from OR (DMI); B 1813-37 (DBI)
Cop (Mf) CB 1731-1880 M`1731-1847 (Mf of BT, DRO, SLC); Extr M 1731-1847 from BT (IGI)
MI   (S&DFHS); (DFHS); (DRO); war memorial (SG)

OSMINGTON (Wes) Preaching room [1882 Return]; chapel [1882 Return]; Meth [Kelly 1939]

OSMINGTON (Wes) Ringstead [1882 Return]

OVER AND NETHER KINGSCOMBE tithing of TOLLER PORCORUM

OVER COMPTON see COMPTON, OVER

OWERMOIGNE St Michael [Owermoigne Liberty; Weymouth Union] [379]   Rebuilt
1883. Now with BROADMAYNE, WEST KNIGHTON, WARMWELL.
OR C 1569-1646, 1660/1-1973 M 1569-1644, 1660-1993 B 1570-1644/5,
    1661-1960 Banns 1755-1812, 1880-1980 (DRO) Gap CMB 1645-59 noted in
    1831.
BT CMB 1731-1880 (W&SRO)
Cop C 1569-1645, 1660-1756 M 1569-1643, 1660-79 B 1569-1643 (I, SG);
    C 1813-37 M 1569-1837 B 1813-37 (I, DRO); C 1756-1805 M 1569-1644,
    1660-1754, 1774-1837 B 1660-1812 (SG); CMB 1569-81 (Ts, SLC);
    C 1731-1880 M 1731-1835 from BT (VRI); CB 1813-37 M 1569-1837 (PRI);
    M 1569-1837 from OR (DMI); B 1573-1837 (DBI)
Cop (Mf) CMB 1569-81 (Mf of Ts, SLC, SG); CB 1731-1880 M 1731-1835
         (Mf of BT, DRO, SLC); C 1569-81 (Printout, Mf SLC);
         Extr C 1569-81, 1731-1880 M 1731-1835 from BT (IGI)
MI (S&DFHS); (DFHS); (DRO); ch, cy, war memorial (SG)

OWERMOIGNE St Catherine by the Sea, Holworth. Wooden church erected 1926.
Now with BROADMAYNE, WEST KNIGHTON, OWERMOIGNE, WARMWELL.
MI (S&DFHS); (DFHS); (DRO); (SG)

OWERMOIGNE (Cong) Licence for house of John Cade alias Cake,
'Ower parish' (?), 1672

PAMPHILL   see WIMBORNE MINSTER

PARKSTONE   see CANFORD MAGNA

PARLEY, WEST All Saints [Cranborne Hundred; Wimborne and Cranborne Union]
[235] Included hamlet of WEST MOORS (separate parish, with VERWOOD, 1887)
OR C 1715-49, 1754-1977 M 1720-49, 1754-1984 B 1720-1967 Banns 1754-1816,
    1829-1982 (DRO) Noted in 1831: CB 1752+ M 1756+
BT CMB 1731-41, 1744, 1748-1839, 1845, 1847-77 (W&SRO)
Cop CB 1813-37 M 1720-1837 (PRI); CB 1813-37 (I, DRO); M 1720-49,
    1756-1837 (DRO, SG); M 1732-54 from BT (DRO); M 1720-1837 from OR,
    1749-87 from BT (DMI); B 1813-37 (DBI)
Cop (Mf) CB 1731-1877 M 1731-1839 (Mf of BT, DRO, SLC); Extr C 1731-1877
         M 1731-1839 from BT (IGI)
MI (S&DFHS); (DFHS); (DRO); 1669-1968 (SG); memorial hall (S&DFHS)

PARLEY, WEST St Mark. In parish of All Saints. Dual-purpose building
erected 1957, now church hall. New church erected 1976.
OR M 1962+; joint registers with All Saints C 1977+ B 1967+ Banns 1991+
    (Inc)

PARLEY, WEST St Mary the Virgin, West Moors. Former hamlet of West Moors in
West Parley. Erected 1897. Parish created 1922 by division of VERWOOD AND
WEST MOORS
OR C 1910-81 M 1910-67, 1981-93 B 1909-78 Banns 1910-60 (DRO)
MI (S&DFHS); (DFHS); (DRO); cy, war memorial (SG)

PARLEY, WEST St John, West Moors. Removed fom a site near Holt 1925-26
[Pevsner] No further information.

PARLEY, WEST (RC) St Anthony, Pinehurst Road, West Moors f 1928. New
building 1975-76.

PARLEY, WEST (Cong, now URC) St Martin's, Station Road, West Moors.
Erected 1903 [Kelly 1939]

PENTRIDGE St Rumbold [Cranborne Hundred; Wimborne and Cranborne Union]
[241] Rebuilt 1855-57. Now with SIXPENNY HANDLEY, GUSSAGE ST ANDREW.
OR C 1714-1987 M 1713/4-1985 B 1714-1983 Banns 1755-1811, 1823-1922 (DRO)
No earlier register noted in 1831.
BT CMB 1731-1880 (W&SRO)
Cop C 1714-1837 M 1713/14-1835 B 1714-1810 (DRO); CB 1718-1810 M 1713-1835
(SG); C 1731-1880 M 1731-1848 from BT (VRI); CB 1813-37 M 1713-1835
(PRI); M 1713-1835 from OR, 1836-37 from BT (DMI); B 1813-37 (DBI)
Cop (Mf) CB 1731-1880 M 1731-1840 (Mf of BT, DRO, SLC); Extr C 1731-1880
M 1731-1846 from BT (IGI)
MI (S&DFHS); (DFHS); (DRO)

PERROTT, NORTH *see* NIPR Vol.8 Part 3 Somerset

PERROTT, SOUTH St Mary [Beaminster Forum and Redhone Hundred; Beaminster
Union] [381] Included chapelry of MOSTERTON. United 1971 with CHEDINGTON.
Now with Beaminster Area benefice.
OR C 1538-1695, 1718-1877 M 1539-1645, 1654-76, 1713-1981 B 1539-1655,
1660-78, 1716-1953 Banns 1755-1812, 1824-99 (DRO)
BT CMB 1731-1880; including MOSTERTON 1731-41 (W&SRO)
Cop M 1539-1812 including Mosterton *q.v.* (Ptd Phil 4: 1909; & on CD-ROM);
C 1538-1837 MB 1539-1837; C 1731-1880 M 1731-1838 from BT (VRI);
CB 1813-37 M 1539-1837 (PRI); M 1539-1645, 1654-56, 1661-65, 1671-76,
1713-1837 (SG); M 1538-1812 (Boyd); M 1790-1812 (Pallot); M 1539-1837
from OR (DMI); B 1813-37 (DBI)
Cop (Mf) M 1539-1812 (Mf of Phil, SLC); CB 1731-1880 M 1731-1838
(Mf of BT, DRO, SLC); Extr C 1731-1880 M 1731-1838 from BT (IGI)
MI (S&DFHS); (DFHS); (DRO)

PERROTT, SOUTH (Bapt) Licences to Jeremiah Day and to William Ireland for
house of Robert Cartisse, 1672

PHILLYHOLME *see* HAWKCHURCH

PIDDLEHINTON formerly HYNE PIDDLE. HONEY PIDDLE   St Mary the Virgin
[Piddlehinton Liberty; Dorchester Union] [403]   Now with PIDDLETRENTHIDE,
PLUSH, ALTON PANCRAS.
OR C 1580-1645, 1651-1992 M 1539-1644, 1654-1993 B 1539-1644, 1654-1923
Banns 1755-1812 (DRO) No earlier baptisms noted in 1831.
BT CMB 1731-1880 (W&SRO)
Cop C 1580-1698, 1813-37 M 1539-1837 B 1539-1698 (DRO); CMB 1539-1652
(I, SG); CMB 1539-1652 (Photocopy of Ts, SLC); C 1731-1880 M 1731-1846
from BT (VRI); CB 1813-37 M 1539-1837 (PRI); M 1539-1837 (SG);
M 1539-1768 (Boyd); M 1539-1837 from OR (DMI); B 1813-37 (DBI);
Extr MB 1659-1768 (SG)
Cop (Mf) CMB 1539-1652 (Mf of Cop, SLC); CB 1731-1880 M 1731-1846
(Mf of BT, DRO, SLC); ZC 1539-1652 M 1539-1652, 1659-1700, 1754,
1768 (Printout, Mf SLC); Extr C 1539-1652, 1731-1880 M 1539-1652,
1659-1700, 1731-1846 from BT (IGI)
MI (S&DFHS); (DFHS); (DRO)

PIDDLEHINTON (Cong) Village chapel [*Cong. Yearbook* 1871]

PIDDLEHINTON (Prim Meth) A Building belonging to Sydney Andrews
[1882 Return]; Meth erected 1894 [Kelly 1939]

PIDDLETOWN *see* PUDDLETOWN

PIDDLETRENTHIDE All Saints [Piddletrenthide Liberty; Cerne Union] [680]
United 1954 with PLUSH (part of MAPPOWDER) Now with PLUSH, ALTON PANCRAS,
PIDDLEHINTON.
OR C 1646-1901 M 1654-1969 B 1654-1923 Banns 1776-95, 1823-1997 (DRO)
BT CMB 1731-1880 (W&SRO)
Cop C 1813-37 M 1654-1837 B 1653-1837 (I, DRO); C 1731-1880 M 1731-1837
    from BT (VRI); CM 1813-37 B 1653-1837 (PRI); M 1654-1808, 1813-37
    (SG); M 1654-1837 from OR (DMI); B 1678-1837 (DBI)
Cop (Mf) CB 1731-1880 M 1731-1837 (Mf of BT, DRO, SLC); Extr C 1731-1880
         M 1731-1837 from BT (IGI)
MI (S&DFHS); (DFHS); (DRO)

PIDDLETRENTHIDE (Bapt) Larkington. Erected 1876 [Kelly 1903]

PIDDLETRENTHIDE (Wes) Erected 1894 [Kelly 1903]

PILSDON or **PILLESDON** St Mary [Whitchurch Canonicorum Hundred; Beaminster
Union] [99] Now with GOLDEN CAP Team Benefice. Redundant 1983. Leased to
Pilsdon Community as place of prayer and for occasional services.
OR C 1757-1994 M 1754-1925, 1939-83 B 1852-1965 Banns 1754-1806,
    1852-1916, 1959-90 (DRO) Noted in 1831: 'No Burial Ground; burials at
    Burstock'. *see* also BURSTOCK
BT CMB 1733-34, 1738, 1757-69, 1773-81, 1786-1880 (W&SRO)
Cop M 1754-1809 (Ptd Phil 5: 1910; & on CD-ROM); C 1779-1837 M 1754-1837
    B 1852-1965 (DRO); C 1733-1880 M 1733-1834 from BT (VRI); M 1754-1837
    (SG, PRI); M 1757, 1814 from BT (DRO); M 1754-1809 (Boyd); M 1790-1809
    (Pallot); M 1754-1837 from OR, 1753-55, 1809-14 from BT (DMI);
    B 1852-1965 (DBI)
Cop (Mf) M 1754-1809 (Mf of Phil, SLC); CB 1733-1880 M 1733-1834 (Mf of BT,
         DRO, SLC); Extr C 1733-1880 M 1733-1834 from BT (IGI)

PIMPERNE St Peter [Pimperne Hundred; Blandford Union] [489] Now with
STOURPAINE, DURWESTON, BRYANSTON.
OR C 1559-1958 M 1559-1646, 1662-1701, 1708/9-1976 B 1561-1646, 1661-1905
    Banns 1754-1800, 1824-1959 (DRO)
BT CMB 1732-1880 (W&SRO)
Cop C 1559-1900 M 1559-1901 B 1561-1900 (DRO, DCM, SG); C 1732-1880
    M 1732-1847 from BT (VRI); C 1813-37 M 1813-36 B 1813-69 (PRI);
    M 1559-1837 from OR (DMI); B 1561-1869 (DBI); Extr C 1559-1774
    M 1562-1765 B 1581-1803 (SG)
Cop (Mf) CB 1732-1880 M 1732-1847 (Mf of BT, DRO, SLC); Extr C 1732-1880
         M 1732-1847 from BT (IGI)
MI (S&DFHS); (DFHS); (DRO)

PIMPERNE (Wes) n.d. [Harrod 1865] [Kelly 1903]

PLUSH *see* BUCKLAND NEWTON

POKESDOWN
OR *see* under BOURNEMOUTH in NIPR Vol.8 Part 6 Hampshire

POKESWELL *see* POXWELL

POOLE Civil parish created 1905 from the civil parishes of POOLE ST JAMES, BRANKSOME, HAMWORTHY LONGFLEET, PARKSTONE. Became a unitary authority in 1997. For ecclesiastical parishes *see also* those under CANFORD MAGNA

POOLE St James [Hasilor Hundred; Poole Union 1835-1905] [6459] Chapelry in CANFORD MAGNA. Separate parish 1538. Royal Peculiar 1538-1847. Rebuilt 1820. *see also* POOLE St Paul, with which united 1957.
OR   C 1550-1975 M 1538/9-1646, 1653-1994 B 1538-1643, 1650-1931 Banns
     1754-94, 1804-1997 (DRO)
BT   CMB 1802-03, 1810-46; St James and St Paul 1847-80 (W&SRO)
Cop C 1722-1837 M 1538-1644, 1813-37 B 1813-37 (I, DRO); C 1802-30
     M 1802-46 from BT (VRI); CMB 1813-37 (PRI); M 1538-1837 from OR (DMI);
     B 1800-37 (DBI)
Cop (Mf) C 1549-1644, 1649-1873 M 1539-1644, 1653-1892 B 1538-1642,
     1653-1873 Banns 1753-1895 (Mf, SG); CB 1550-1873 M 1538-1898
     Banns 1754-1950 (Mf, PLHC); CMB 1802-48 CB 1851-52, 1855-60,
     1862-68, 1871-77, 1880 (Mf of BT, DRO, SLC); Extr C 1802-71
     M 1802-46 from BT (IGI)
MI   (S&DFHS); (DFHS); (DRO)

POOLE St Paul. Erected 1833. Parish created 1861 from POOLE St James. Redundant 1962. Demolished 1963.
OR   C 1833-1956 M 1862-1956 B 1861-1912 Banns 1949-56 (DRO)
BT   CB 1847-80 with POOLE St James (W&SRO)
Cop C 1872-80 from BT (VRI)
Cop (Mf) C 1833-93 M 1862-1901 B 1861-93 Banns 1949-56 (PLHC);
          Extr C 1872-80 from BT (IGI)

POOLE (RC) St Mary and St Philomena, West Quay Road. Erected 1839. Demolished 1973 and new church erected, Wimborne Road.
OR   Early registers lost. C 1865+ M 1934+ B 1912+ Confirmations 1968+
     (Inc); Confirmations 1864, 1876, 1886, 1888, 1892-1934 (PDA)

POOLE (Part Bapt) Hill Street. f 1804. Erected 1815. Southern Association [*Bapt. Handbook* 1861] [1882 Return] [Kelly 1939] SBA
OR   Z 1797-1837 (RG 4/2411, PRO)
Cop (Mf) Z 1797-1837 (Mf of OR, SLC); Extr Z 1687-1837 (IGI)

POOLE (Bapt) Mission chapel, Wimborne Road. Erected 1910 [Kelly 1939]

POOLE (Ind/Cong, now URC) Skinner Street. f 1662. Rebuilt 1777 [*Cong. Yearbook* 1871] [Kelly 1939]
OR   C 1704-52 M 1970 -76 (DRO); ZC 1741-1837 B 1787-94, 1802-37
     (RG 4/2270, 2271, 1229, 121, PRO)
Cop C 1741-47, 1768-1837 B 1787-94, 1802-37 (DRO, PRI); B 1787-1837 (DBI)
Cop (Mf) ZCB 1741-1837 (Mf of OR, SLC); C 1741-47, 1768-1837 (Printout,
          Mf SLC); Extr C 1741-47, 1768-1837 (IGI)
MI   Skinner Street: disused burial ground: removal of remains, Ashburne
     family, d.1804, 1836 (Mf, SLC, of RG 37/197, PRO)

POOLE (Presb/Unit) Old Meeting, Hill Street f 1664. Erected 1705; rebuilt 1868 [1882 Return] Closed 1968. Demolished.
OR   ZC 1750-1837 B 1766-1836 (RG 4/121, 464, PRO); C 1760-83 (DRO)
Cop (Mf) ZC 1760-1837 B 1766-1836 (Mf of OR, SLC); C 1760-1837 (Printout,
          Mf SLC); Extr C 1760-1837 (IGI)
MI   Burial ground 1766-1852 (Mf, SLC, of RG 37/124, PRO)

POOLE (Ind) Licence to William Minty for malthouse of Mr Aire, 1672

POOLE (Presb) Licence for house of Edward Taylor, 1672

POOLE (Wes) Poole Circuit. Formed from WEYMOUTH Circuit 1809. Included
c.1819-37 CORFE CASTLE, CRANBORNE, GUSSAGE, KINGSTON, LANGTON MATRAVERS,
MORDEN, STUDLAND, SWANAGE, WAREHAM, WIMBORNE, WITCHAMPTON, WOODLANDS,
WORTH MATRAVERS and other locations.
OR   ZC 1819-37 (RG 4/1230, PRO); C 1796-1809, 1841-1935 (DRO)
Cop (Mf) ZC 1819-37 C 1841-1935 (Mf of OR, SLC); Extr C 1819-37 (IGI)

POOLE (Wes) The Theatre f by 1793 [Biggs] Chapel Lane, High Street
[Harrod 1865] [1882 Return]; High Street erected 1879 [Kelly 1903]
Poole and Swanage Circuit
OR   ZC 1809-40 (RG 4/2412, 1231, PRO)
Cop C 1809-40 (DRO, SG); Extr from Meth register C 1820-37 (DRO);
     ZC n.d. (S&DFHS)
Cop (Mf) ZC 1809-40 (Mf of OR, SLC); C 1809-40 (Printout, Mf, SLC);
          Extr C 1809-40 (IGI)

POOLE (Wes) Constitution Hill [1882 Return]

POOLE (Prim Meth) Poole Circuit. Formed from MOTCOMBE Circuit 1838.
OR   C 1827-38, 1843-1945 (DRO)
Cop (Mf) C 1843-1906 (Mf of OR, SLC)

POOLE (Prim Meth) North Street. Erected 1842 [1882 Return] Rebuilt 1896
[Kelly 1939]

POOLE (S of F) Poole Monthly Meeting f c.1690 from Dorchester MM, part of
Dorset QM. Meetings at BERE, BLANDFORD, MILTON ABBAS, MORDEN, POOLE,
PURBECK, TARRANT MONKTON. Dorset and Hampshire QM 1804-55. United with
Ringwood MM [Hampshire], and later known as Poole and Southampton MM. From
1855 part of Sussex, Surrey and Hampshire QM.
OR   Z 1659-1837 M 1668-1836 B 1674-1837 (RG 6/198, 278, 350, 398-99, 429,
     1236, 1340, 1344, PRO) No MM registers at HRO. No registers at East
     Sussex RO, Lewes; but some other Hampshire/Dorset records 1855-1958
     including Minutes 1860-1929.
Cop B 1674-1929 (DBI)
Cop (Mf) M 1776-1800 (Mf of OR, SLC)

POOLE (S of F) Lagland Street. Erected 1795-96 [1882 Return] Later part of
a boys' club.
Cop Friends' Burial Ground B 1767-1910 (I, DRO)

POOLE (Latter Day Saints) Mount Road

POOLE (Evangelical) Lagland Street
OR   M 1986-90 (DRO)

POOLE (Gospel Hall) Emmanuel, Welland Road
OR   M 1983-85 (DRO)

POOLE (Gospel Hall) Poole Full Gospel Church, Cranbrock Road
OR   M 1940-77 (DRO)

POOLE (Christian Mission) Temperance Hall, Hill Street [1882 Return]

POOLE (Christian Mission) Friends Meeting House, Layland Street
[1882 Return]

POOLE (Salvation Army) Saw Mill, Fish Street [1882 Return]

POOLE Poole Cemetery, Dorchester Road (1855) (Poole Borough Council)

POOLE Poor Law Union Workhouse, West Street. Erected 1739. New building 1838-39 St Mary's Road, Longfleet, later St Mary's Hospital, demolished 1979

POORSTOCK *see* POWERSTOCK

POORTON, NORTH St Mary Magdalene Beaminster Forum and Redhone Hundred; Beaminster Union] [89] Rebuilt 1861-62 on new site. United 1971 with POWERSTOCK, WEST MILTON, WITHERSTONE Now also with ASKERSWELL, LODERS.
OR   C 1694-1710, 1717-22, 1735, 1744-1995 M 1695-1703, 1717-18, 1747, 1761-1919, 1958, 1964 B 1695-1703, 1754, 1863-1935, 1943-72, 1978-95 Banns 1769-70, 1779, 1826-1970 (DRO) Noted in 1831: 'The Burials for many years past have been at Powerstock'.
BT   CMB 1749-1880 (W&SRO)
Cop   M 1698-1747, 1761-1812 (Ptd Phil 2 and 1: 1907, 1906; & on CD-ROM); C 1695-1765 M 1698-1837 B 1696-1702, 1754 1863-1995 (DRO); M 1696-1703, 1718, 1747, 1761-1837 (SG); M 1755-1812 from BT (DRO); C 1749-1880 M 1755-1836 from BT (VRI); M 1698-1812 (Boyd); M 1790-1812 (Pallot); M 1698-1837 from OR, 1749-68, 1775-1812 from BT (DMI); B 1696-1995 (DBI)
Cop (Mf) M 1698-1812 (Mf of Phil, SLC); C 1749-1880 M 1755-1836 B 1759-1880 (Mf of BT, DRO, SLC); Extr C 1749-1880 M 1755-1836 from BT (IGI)
MI   (S&DFHS); (SG)

POORTON, SOUTH tithing of POWERSTOCK

PORTESHAM St Peter [Uggscombe Hundred; Weymouth Union] [663]   Now with ABBOTSBURY, LANGTON HERRING.
OR   C 1573-1656, 1662-1887 M 1568-1646, 1663-79, 1695-1983 B 1568-1645, 1662-68, 1695-1983 Banns 1754-1812, 1824-67 (DRO)
BT   CMB 1731-1880 (W&SRO)
Cop   C 1662-1835 M 1568-1837 B 1813-37 (DRO, PRI); C 1573-1733 M 1568-1837 B 1568-1730 (SG); C 1731-1880 M 1731-1836 from BT (VRI); M 1568-1812 (Phil Ms at SG); M 1568-1812 (Boyd); M 1568-1837 from OR (DMI); B 1813-37 (DBI)
Cop (Mf) M 1568-1812 (Mf of Phil Ms, SLC); CB 1731-1880 M 1731-1836 (Mf of BT, DRO, SLC); Extr C 1731-1880 M 1731-1836 (IGI)

PORTESHAM St Bartholomew, Corton. 13th cent. Chapel-of-ease consecrated 1897 [Kelly 1939] Now with ABBOTSBURY, PORTESHAM, LANGTON HERRING.

PORTESHAM (Cong) Coryates'. Out-station of UPWEY [*Cong. Yearbook* 1871]

PORTESHAM (Prim Meth) Erected 1867. Weymouth Circuit [1882 Return] [Kelly 1903]; Meth [Kelly 1939] Weymouth Circuit
OR   C 1868-72 (DRO)

PORTLAND, ISLE OF [Isle of Portland Liberty; Weymouth Union] [2670]

PORTLAND St Andrew, Church Ope Cove. Original parish church of Portland. Replaced by St George, Reforne, 1753. Ruined.
OR   transferred to St George
MI   (S&DFHS); (DFHS); (DRO); (SG); Cy (Ptd *Miscellanea Genealogica et Heraldica.* series 5: 5: 1932: 105)

PORTLAND St George, Reforne. Erected 1754-66, replacing St Andrew. Replaced 1914 by All Saints, Easton. Redundant 1970. Churches Conservation Trust.
OR   transferred to All Saints
MI   (S&DFHS); (DFHS); (DRO); (SG)

PORTLAND All Saints, Easton. Erected 1916 to replace St George's as parish church. see also PORTLAND St John, St Peter. United 1966 with PORTLAND St Peter.
OR   C 1630-50, 1660-70, 1694-1979 M 1591-1612, 1694-1991 B 1564-70, 1630-32, 1638-1954 Banns 1755, 1803-1973 (DRO)
BT   CMB 1731-1860, 1862-80 (W&SRO)
Cop M 1591-1837 Banns 1807-62 B 1813-25 (DRO); C 1813-37 (I, DRO); M 1591-93, 1604-1803 (SG); C 1731-1880 M 1731-1852 from BT (VRI); CB 1813-37 M 1803-37 (PRI); M 1731-55 from BT (DRO); M 1591-1837 from OR, 1731-55 from BT (DMI); B 1564-1837 (DBI)
Cop (Mf) CB 1731-1880 M 1731-1852 (Mf of BT, DRO, SLC); Extr C 1731-1880 M 1731-1852 from BT (IGI)

PORTLAND St John the Baptist, Fortuneswell. Erected 1839. Parish created 1841.
OR   C 1840-1953 M 1841-1994 B 1841-1991 Banns 1845-1951 (DRO)
MI   (DRO)

PORTLAND St Peter, Grove. Erected 1870-72. Parish created 1873 from PORTLAND All Saints, with which united 1966. Redundant 1973. Sold for use by Portland Borstal Institution.
OR   C 1870-1932 Banns 1927-44 (DRO)

PORTLAND St Andrew, Southwell. Chapel-of-ease to All Saints. Erected 1878 in memory of crew of wrecked ship 'Avalanche'. Now with PORTLAND All Saints and St Peter.
OR   M 1972-95 (DRO)
MI   (DRO) ?

PORTLAND (RC) Our Lady and St Andrew, Grove. Erected 1868 [1882 Return]
OR   C 1866+ M 1876+ B 1930+ Confirmations 1879+ (Inc). For earlier entries see WEYMOUTH. Confirmations 1872, 1879-1932 (PDA)
Cop C 1866-70 M 1884 (SG, PDA, Cath FHS collection at Catholic Central Library, Lancing Street, London NW1 1ND)

PORTLAND (RC) Convict Prison
OR   Confirmations 1879 (PDA)

PORTLAND (RC) R.N. Chapel, Our Lady Star of the Sea, Victoria Square f 1939

PORTLAND (Ind/Cong, now `URC) Chiswell. f 1825 in converted barn. Chapel 1827. Rebuilt 1858 [Cong. Yearbook 1871] [1882 Return]
OR   ZC 1829-37 (RG 4/2272, 465, PRO)
Cop (Mf) ZC 1829-37 (Mf of OR, SLC); C 1829-37 (Printout, Mf SLC); Extr C 1829-37 from BT (IGI)

PORTLAND (Wes) Portland Circuit
OR   C 1796-1940 M 1838, 1864-65 B 1818-61 (DRO); and see WEYMOUTH (RG 4/469, PRO); C 1940-71 (Retained by Portland Meth Circuit)
Cop C 1796-1971 (DRO, SG); B 1818-61 (DBI)
Cop (Mf) C 1796-1837, 1859-87 M 1838, 1864-65; Fortuneswell C 1838-1911; Easton and others C 1876-94, 1911-25; Easton and others C 1899-1940 (Mf of OR, SLC)

PORTLAND (Wes) f by 1746; revived 1791; house of Matthew Fancey registered 1792 [Biggs]

PORTLAND (Wes) Fortuneswell. Meeting house of R.Brackenbury registered 1793 [Biggs] [1882 Return] Brackenbury Memorial Church 1903 replacing Fortuneswell Meth Chapel, later Underhill Meth.
OR   ZC 1796-1837 B 1818-37 (RG 4/1228, 347, PRO); M 1941-67 (DRO)
Cop (Mf) ZC 1796-1837 B 1818-37 (Mf of OR, SLC); C 1796-1837 (Printout, Mf, SLC); Extr C 1798-1837 (IGI)
MI   (S&DFHS); Brackenbury School (S&DFHS); (SG); Underhill Meth (S&DFHS); (SG)

PORTLAND (Wes) Southwell. House owned by Edward Whittel registered 1792 [Biggs] [1882 Return] [Kelly 1903]

PORTLAND (Wes) Wakeham. House owned by Mary Mitchell registered 1792; house occupied by John Thorner registered 1794 [Biggs] [1882 Return]

PORTLAND (Wes) Easton. House owned by Mary Skinner registered 1793 [Biggs] Chapel [Harrod 1865] [1882 Return] [Kelly 1903]

PORTLAND (Wes) Weston. A Building [1882 Return]

PORTLAND (Prim Meth) Circuit
OR   C 1859-87 (DRO); C 1888-1971 (retained by Portland Meth Circuit)
Cop C 1859-1971 (DRO, SG)

PORTLAND (Prim Meth) Fortuneswell [1882 Return] [1903] Later Royal Manor Theatre.
MI   (SG)

PORTLAND (Prim Meth) Weston [1882 Return] [Kelly 1903]
MI   (SG)

PORTLAND (Prim Meth) Chiswell [Harrod 1865] Ranters' Chapel, opposite Conjuror's Lodge, Chiswell [1882 Return]

PORTLAND (Bible Christian, later U Meth) Zion, Wakeham [Harrod 1865] [1882 Return] [Kelly 1903]
OR   C 1858-1935 M 1931-32 (DRO)
Cop C 1858-1933 (DRO, SG)
Cop (Mf) C 1858-1915 (Mf of OR, SLC)

PORTLAND (Bible Christian, later U Meth) Maidenwell, High Street [1882 Return] [Kelly 1903]
OR   C 1920-71 (Retained by Portland Meth Circuit)
Cop C 1957-79 (DRO); C 1920-71 (SG)
MI   (SG)

PORTLAND (Meth) Easton Methodist Church. Erected 1906-07.

PORTLAND (Protestants) A Room, forming the upper floor of the easternmost building in the village of Castletown [1882 Return]

PORTLAND Cemetery, Weston Road, 1954 (Weymouth and Portland Town Council)

PORTLAND Naval and Military Cemetery. Consecrated 1861
MI   (S&DFHS); (DRO); (SG)

PORTLAND Strangers' Cemetery, parish of St John. Burials mostly of military personnel and their families, including persons who died at sea and were washed ashore. Presumably non-denominational.
MI   (S&DFHS); (SG)

POWERSTOCK or POORSTOCK St Mary [part Powerstock Liberty, part Eggerton Hundred; Beaminster Union] [1024 including tithings of West Milton, Nettlecombe, South Poorton, Witherstone] *see also* MELPLAISH. United 1971 with WEST MILTON, WITHERSTONE, NORTH POORTON Now also with ASKERSWELL, LODERS.
OR   C 1568-1970 M 1568-1995 B 1568-1645/6, 1651-1895 Banns 1754-1812, 1819-56 (DRO)
BT   CMB 1732-1880 (W&SRO)
Cop M 1568-1812 with with West Milton (Ptd Phil 1: 1906; & on CD-ROM);
         C 1568-1837 M 1568-1837 B 1568-1837 (DRO); C 1568-1798 B 1568-1661
         (SG); C 1568-1718 B 1568-1771 (Ts, SLC); C 1732-1880 M 1732-1837
         from BT (VRI); CB 1813-37 M 1568-1837 (PRI); M 1568-1812 (I, SG);
         M 1568-1644, 1647, 1651-1837 (SG); M 1568-1812 (Boyd); M 1568-1837
         from OR (DMI); B 1717-77 (DBI); Extr C 1719-56 M 1717-50 B 1722-84 (SG)
Cop (Mf) C 1568-1718 B 1568-1771 (Mf of Ts, SLC); M 1568-1812 (Mf of Phil,
         SLC); CB 1732-1880 M 1732-1837 (Mf of BT, DRO, SLC); C 1568-1718
         (Pintout, Mf SLC); Extr C 1568-1718, 1732-1880 M 1732-1837 (IGI)

POWERSTOCK St Mary Magdalene, West Milton. Old church ruined; tower redundant 1975; sold for use as monument. New church on new site 1869-74. Redundant 1974. Demolished. Now with ASKERSWELL, LODERS, POWERSTOCK, WITHERSTONE, NORTH POORTON.
OR   M 1837-1962, 1969 (DRO)
BT   *see* POWERSTOCK
MI   (S&DFHS); (DFHS); (DRO); (SG)

POWERSTOCK (Wes) Building occupied by Richard Hine, grocer, of Beaminster, 1797 [Biggs]
OR   *see* AXMINSTER [Devon] and BRIDPORT Circuits

POWERSTOCK (Wes) Nettlecombe erected 1838 [1882 Return] [Kelly 1903];
Meth [Kelly 1939]

POWERSTOCK (Wes) West Milton. Erected 1891 [Kelly 1903]; Meth [Kelly 1939]

POWERSTOCK Beaminster Union Workhouse. Erected 1626; rebuilt 1737.
New building at BEAMINSTER *q.v.* 1838

POXWELL or POKESWELL St John the Evangelist [Winfrith Hundred; Weymouth Union] [99] Rebuilt 1868. United 1969 with OSMINGTON. Now also with PRESTON with SUTTON POYNTZ. Redundant 1968. Demolished 1969/70.
OR   C 1674/5-1968 M 1675-1960 B 1678/9-1965 Banns 1758-1811 (DRO)
BT   CMB 1731-1835, 1841-43, 1846-80 (W&SRO)
Cop CB 1813-37 (I, DRO, PRI); C 1731-1876 M 1731-1812 from BT (VRI);
         M 1675-1837 (DRO, SG); M 1675-1837 from OR (DMI); B 1813-37 (DBI)
Cop (Mf) CB 1731-1880 M 1731-1835 (Mf of BT, DRO, SLC); Extr C 1731-1876
         M 1731-1835 from BT (IGI)
MI   (S&DFHS); (DFHS); (DRO); cy, tithe barn (SG)

POYNTINGTON All Saints [Horsethorne Hundred (Somerset); Sherborne Union] Transferred 1895 to Dorset. Now with QUEEN THORNE benefice.
OR   *see* NIPR Vol.8 Part 3 Somerset.
MI   (S&DFHS); (DFHS)

PRESTON with SUTTON POYNTZ   St Andrew [Sutton Poyntz Liberty; Weymouth Union] [555 including Sutton Poyntz 340] Peculiar of the Prebend of Preston and Sutton Poyntz, Sarum Cathedral until 1847. Now with OSMINGTON with POXWELL
OR   C 1693-1974 M 1695-1994 B 1693/4-1985 Banns 1754-1813, 1847-1993 (DRO)
BT   CMB 1592-97, 1603-10, 1614-15, 1618-21, 1624-30, 1633-39, 1664, 1672-75, 1678-99, 1701-06, 1709-31, 1734-50, 1752-1880 (W&SRO)
Cop   M 1695-1837 (Ptd Phil 6: 1912; & on CD-ROM); C 1693-1772 B 1693-1767 (I, SG); CB 1813-37 M 1695-1837 (PRI); CB 1813-37 (I, DRO); C 1773-98 (SG); M 1695-1837 (DRO, SG); M 1591-1754 from BT (DRO); M 1693-1812 (Boyd); M 1790-1837 (Pallot); M 1695-1837 from OR, 1591-1754 from BT (DMI); B 1791-1870 (DBI)
Cop (Mf)   M 1695-1837 (Mf of Phil, SLC); CB 1592-1880 M 1592-1837 (Mf of BT, DRO, SLC); Extr C 1592-1880 M 1592-1837 from BT (IGI)
MI   (S&DFHS)

PRESTON St Francis of Assisi, Littlemore. District church erected 1986, in parish of PRESTON.
OR   CM 1986+ (Inc) No burials

PRESTON (RC) Our Lady, Sutton Road [*Cath.Dir.* 1965] Seven Acres Road 1967 [*Cath.Dir.* 1968]

PRESTON (Wes) [Harrod 1865] [1882 Return] [Kelly 1903]

PRESTON ('Who object to be designated') Jordan Barn [1882 Return]

PRESTON Gospel Hall [Kelly 1939]

PRESTON or PRESTON CRAWFORD   *see* TARRANT CRAWFORD

PUDDLEHINTON   *see* PIDDLEHINTON

PUDDLETOWN or PIDDLETOWN St Mary [Puddletown Hundred; Dorchester Union] [1223] United 1967 with ATHELHAMPTON, BURLESTON. Now also with TOLPUDDLE.
OR   C 1546/7-1641, 1646-1927 M 1538-1615/6, 1646, 1654-1979 B 1538-1614, 1623-44, 1653-1894 Banns 1756-1960 (DRO) No earlier baptisms noted in 1831.
BT   CMB 1738-1880 (W&SRO)
Cop   M 1538-1812 (Ptd Phil 7: 1914; & on CD-ROM); C 1546/7-1837 M 1538-1837 B 1538-1837 (DRO); C 1546-1812 MB 1538-1812 (DCM); C 1546-1641, 1650-1812 M 1538-1615, 1654-1812 B 1538-1614, 1623-43, 1653-1812 (SG); C 1548-1641, 1650-1812 M 1538-1615, 1654-1812 B 1538-1614, 1625-42, 1653-1812 (I, SG); C 1738-1880 M 1738-1847 from BT (VRI); CB 1813-37 M 1538-1837 (PRI); M 1738-55 B 1812-37 from BT (DRO); M 1538-1812 (Boyd); M 1790-1812 (Pallot); M 1538-1837 from OR, 1738-55 from BT (DMI); B 1538-1837 (DBI)
Cop (Mf)   M 1538-1812 (Mf of Phil, SLC);   CB 1738-1880 M 1738-1847 (Mf of BT, DRO, SLC); Extr C 1738-1880 M 1738-1847 from BT (IGI)
MI   (S&DFHS); (DFHS); (DRO)

PUDDLETOWN (Ind/Cong) Ebenezer. Erected 1862 [1882 Return] [Kelly 1939]
OR   C 1973-81 MB 1963-80 (DRO)

PUDDLETOWN (Cong) Licence to Edward Downer for house of Henry Williams, 1672

PULHAM St Thomas à Becket [part Buckland Newton Hundred, part Bindon Liberty; Cerne Union] Consisted of parish of East Pulham and manor of West Pulham [302] Now with DUNGEON HILL benefice.
OR   C 1734-1942 M 1734-1993 B 1734-1812 Banns 1754-1812, 1824-1940 (DRO)
     No earlier register noted in 1831
BT   CMB 1731-1835, 1838-39, 1841-42, 1844-80 (W&SRO)
Cop C 1734-1837 M 1734-1902 B 1734-1904 (DRO, SG); C 1731-1880 M 1731-1844
    from BT (VRI); C 1734-1837 M 1734-1902 B 1734-1904 (PRI); M 1731-34
    from BT (DRO); M 1736-1843 from OR, 1731-34 from BT (DMI); B 1734-1904
    (DBI)
Cop (Mf) CB 1731-1880 M 1731-1844 (Mf of BT, DRO, SLC); Extr C 1731-1880
    M 1731-1844 from BT (IGI)

PULHAM (Presb) Licence to John Devenish for his house, 1672

PULHAM (Cong) Out-station of CERNE ABBAS [*Cong. Yearbook* 1871]

PULHAM (Wes) House occupied and owned by John Warr registered 1799 [Biggs]

PULHAM (Prim Meth) A Cottage [1882 Return]

PUNCKNOWLE St Mary [Uggscombe Hundred; Bridport Union] [424] United 1451 with BEXINGTON ancient parish. Now with BRIDE VALLEY benefice.
OR   C 1630-58, 1665-85/6, 1697/8-1981 M 1632/3-44, 1666-92, 1700-1926
    B 1631-43/4, 1653-57, 1666/7-77, 1697/8-1942 Banns 1825-1989 (DRO)
BT   CMB 1731-1880 (W&SRO)
Cop M 1632/3-1836 B 1631-1784 (DRO); CB 1813-37 (I, DRO); C 1731-1880
    M 1731-1836 from BT (VRI); M 1632-44. 1666-1836 (SG); M 1632-1753
    (Boyd); M 1632-1836 from OR (DMI); B 1631-1942 (DBI)
Cop (Mf) CB 1731-1880 M 1731-1836 (Mf of BT, DRO, SLC); Extr C 1731-1880
    M 1731-1836 from BT (IGI)
MI   (S&DFHS); (DFHS); Ch (Ptd *Gent.Mag.* 1835: 2: 39)

PUNCKNOWLE (Wes) Erected 1849 [1882 Return] [Kelly 1903]; Meth [Kelly 1939]

PURBECK , ISLE OF   Area between Poole Harbour and the English Channel including the parishes of Corfe Castle, Church Knowle, Langton Matravers, Worth Matravers, Steeple, Studland and Swanage [Kelly 1903]
Purbeck Deanery also includes East Burton, Chaldon, Coombe Keynes, Kimmeridge, Kingston, East Lulworth, West Lulworth, East Stoke, Tyneham, Wareham, Winfrith Newburgh and Wool.

PURBECK (S of F) Constituent meeting of POOLE MM *q.v.* Closed before 1804.

PURSE CAUNDLE   *see* CAUNDLE, PURSE

PUTTON   *see* CHICKERELL

QUEEN THORNE   Modern benefice including OBORNE, OVER COMPTON, NETHER COMPTON, POYNTINGTON, SANDFORD ORCAS, TRENT.

RADIPOLE *see* WEYMOUTH

RADIPOLE AND MELCOMBE REGIS Benefice including RADIPOLE St Ann, St Aldhelm, Emmanuel, WEYMOUTH St John, St Mary.

RAMPISHAM or RAMSOM St Michael and All Angels [Tollerford Hundred; Beaminster Union] [416] Now with MELBURY benefice.
OR   C 1575-1759, 1768-1868 M 1574-1645/6, 1653-1704, 1709-1841
     B 1575-1639, 1653/4-1759, 1768-1932 Banns 1756-1811, 1824-86 (DRO)
     Noted in 1831 that the registers of Wraxall *q.v.* were also kept here at
     'Rampisham-cum-Wraxall'.
BT   CMB 1731-1880 (W&SRO)
Cop M 1574-1741 (Ptd Phil 6: 1912; & on CD-ROM); C 1574-1812 M 1742-53
     B 1574-1758, 1769-1812 (I,SG); CB 1813-37 (I, DRO); C 1731-1880
     M 1731-1846 from BT (VRI); CB 1813-37 M 1573-1841 (PRI); M 1574-1841
     (DRO, SG); M 1574-1741 (Boyd); M 1573-1841 from OR (DMI); B 1578-1932
     (DBI); MB 1731-1880 from BT (Pine: CD 1)
Cop (Mf) M 1574-1741 (Mf of Phil, SLC); CB 1731-1880 M 1731-1846 (Mf of
         BT, DRO, SLC); Extr C 1731-1880 M 1731-1846 from BT (IGI)

RAMPISHAM (Cong) n.d. Out-station of MAIDEN NEWTON [*Cong. Yearbook* 1871]
[Kelly 1903]

RAMSOM   *see* RAMPISHAM

RED POST Modern benefice including ALMER, CHARBOROUGH, BLOXWORTH, MORDEN, WINTERBORNE KINGSTON, WINTERBORNE ZELSTON, WINTERBORNE TOMSON, WINTERBORNE ANDERSON.

REFORNE   *see* PORTLAND

REMPSTONE HEATH *see* CORFE CASTLE

RIDGEWAY   *see* UPWEY

RINGSTEAD   Lost village. *see* OSMINGTON

RUSHTON   *see* TARRANT RUSHTON

RYME INTRINSECA St Hippolytus [Ryme Intrinseca Liberty; Sherborne Union] [171] Peculiar of the Dean of Sarum until 1847. Now with YETMINSTER WITH RYME INTRINSECA AND HIGH STOY benefice.
OR   C 1631-1992 M 1631-1704, 1718-46, 1756-1964, 1967-90 B 1630-1992
     Banns 1756-1818, 1824-1964 (DRO)
BT   CMB 1631-41, 1669-95, 1700-02, 1705-39, 1745-1880 (W&SRO)
Cop C 1631-1812 M 1631-1836 B 1630-1812 (DRO); CB 1813-37 (I, DRO);
     C 1631-1880 M 1631-1847 from BT (VRI); CB 1813-37 M 1631-1836 (PRI);
     M 1631-1836 (SG); M 1631-1756 from BT (DRO); M 1631-1836 (Phil Ms at
     SG; Ts, SLC); M 1631-1836 (Boyd); M 1631-1836 from OR, 1631-1756 from
     BT (DMI); B 1653-1837 (DBI)
Cop (Mf) M 1631-1836 (Mf`of Ts, SG, SLC); M 1631-1836 (Mf of Phil Ms, SLC);
         CB 1631-1880 M 1631-1847 (Mf of BT, DRO, SLC); Extr C 1831-80
         M 1831-47 from BT (IGI)
MI   (S&DFHS); (DFHS); (DRO); (SG)

ST LEONARDS AND ST IVES Parish formed from Christchurch, Ringwood and Holdenhurst [Hampshire] Transferred to Dorset 1974.
OR   *see* NIPR Vol.8 Part 6 Hampshire

ST MARTIN [Wareham and Purbeck Union 1894-1930] Civil parish created 1894 from MORDEN

SALISBURY [Wiltshire] (Prim Meth) Circuit. Included parts of Dorset.
OR C 1832-75 and 1869-1941; the latter dealing mostly with the area of
the later Wilton and Woodfalls stations; *see* CRANBORNE, EDMONDSHAM,
SIXPENNY HANDLEY, WEST WOODYATES (W&SRO)
Cop (Mf) C 1832-1942 (Mf of OR, SLC)

SALWAY ASH *see* NETHERBURY

SANDBANKS *see* CANFORD CLIFFS AND SANDBANKS

SANDFORD *see* WAREHAM

SANDFORD ORCAS St Nicholas [Horethorne Hundred (Somerset); Sherborne Union;
transferred 1895 to Dorset] Now with QUEEN THORNE benefice.
OR *see* NIPR Vol.8 Part 3 Somerset

SEABOROUGH St John [Crewkerne Hundred (Somerset); Beaminster Union;'
transferred 1895 to Dorset] Now with Beaminster Area benefice.
OR *see* NIPR Vol.8 Part 3 Somerset

SHAFTESBURY Borough [3061] Included former parishes of All Saints, and
St Edward (united 1423 to St James); St Andrew (united 1534 with St Peter);
St John (united 1446 with St James); St Lawrence (united 1534 with Holy
Trinity); and St Martin (united 1534 with St Peter)

SHAFTESBURY Holy Trinity [Monkton Up Wimborne Hundred; Shaftesbury
Incorporation/Union] [1184] Rebuilt 1841. United 1534 with SHAFTESBURY
ST LAWRENCE, and 1967 with ST PETER, ST RUMBOLD. Redundant 1977. Sold 1980
to Trinity Trust for use as Scout headquarters and for office and community
purposes.
OR C 1695-1837 M 1695-1839 B 1695-1913 Banns 1823-55, 1754-84, 1793-1811
(DRO)
BT CMB 1731-1880 (W&SRO)
Cop M 1731-54 B 1731-1837 from BT (DRO); C 1731-1880 M 1731-1845 from BT
(VRI); MB 1813-37 (PRI); M 1695-1839 (DRO, SG); M 1695-1839 from OR
(DMI); B 1731-1837 (DBI)
Cop (Mf) C 1695-1837 M 1695-1893 B 1695-1913 Banns 1754-78, 1780, 1783-84,
1793-1811, 1823-55, 1866-88, Banns for all Shaftesbury churches
1709-12; notes on the Bowles family (Mf, SG); CB 1731-1880
M 1731-1845 (Mf of BT, DRO, SLC); Extr C 1731-1880 M 1731-1845
from BT (IGI)
MI (S&DFHS); (DFHS); (DRO); Disposal of tombstones in area to be sold.
D 1745-1970 (Mf, SLC, of RG 37/183, PRO); Cy 1901/09 (*Ye Olde Mortality*
9: Ms, SG); Cy (Ptd *Notes and Queries* series 9: 1914: 44-45, 124-25,
284-85, 504-05); Cy *c.*1969 (SG)

SHAFTESBURY St James [Alcester Liberty; Shaftesbury Incorporation/Union]
[763 including Alcester Liberty] United 1423 with SHAFTESBURY ALL SAINTS,
ST EDWARD; 1446 with ST JOHN. Rebuilt 1866-67. Now with SHASTON benefice.
OR C 1559-1971 M 1560/1-1654, 1661/2-1952 B 1559/60-1654, 1660-1860
Banns 1754-1812, 1849-90, 1942-70 (DRO)
BT CMB 1731-1800, 1803-80 (W&SRO)
Cop M 1560-1842 B 1559-1871 (DRO); C 1731-1880 M 1731-1851 from BT (VRI);
C 1813-37 M 1560-1842 B 1628-1871 (PRI); C 1813-37 (I, DRO);
M 1560-1654, 1661-1842 (SG); M 1560-1842 from OR (DMI); B 1733-2000
(DBI)
Cop (Mf) CB 1731-1880 M 1731-1851 (Mf of BT, DRO, SLC); Extr C 1731-1880
M 1731-1851 from BT (IGI)

SHAFTESBURY St James cont.
MI (DFHS); (DRO) Ch, cy and burial ground on hill 1901/09 (*Ye Olde Mortality* 9: Ms, SG)

SHAFTESBURY St Peter [Monkton Up Wimborne Hundred; Shaftesbury Incorporation/Union] [1114] United 1534 with ST ANDREW, ST MARTIN. 'Dilapidated. Little used since 1878' [Kelly 1903] Redundant 1971. Restored to use 1974. Now with SHASTON benefice.
OR C 1623-43, 1648-1867, 1895-96 M 1623-42, 1653-1893 B 1623-43, 1653-1867 Banns 1754-1812, 1824-54, 1866-85, 1904-84 (DRO)
BT CMB 1731-1880 (W&SRO)
Cop C 1813-37 M 1623-1912 B 1623-1727 (DRO); CMB 1623-1704 (C of A); C 1731-1880 M 1731-1842 from BT (VRI); C 1813-37 M 1629-1836 B 1813-24 (PRI); M 1623-42, 1654-83, 1689-90, 1695-96, 1702-1837 (SG); M 1623-1837 from OR, 1751-54, 1797-1837 from BT, 1797-1825 from SG copy (DMI); B 1813-37 (I, DRO); B 1813-37 (DBI)
Cop (Mf) C 1625-29, 1633-43, 1646, 1648-1867, 1886 M 1623-42, 1655-59, 1661-83, 1689, 1694-97, 1701-1840 B 1623-43, 1653-1867, 1886 Banns 1754-99, 1802-10, 1824-54 (Mf, SG); CB 1731-1880 M 1731-1842 (Mf of BT, DRO, SLC); Extr C 1731-1880 M 1731-1842 from BT (IGI)
MI Extr: Pratt (Ms, SG)

SHAFTESBURY ST RUMBOLD or CANN St Rumbold [Sixpenny Handley Hundred; Shaftesbury Incorporation/Union] [435] Rebuilt 1840. United 1967 with HOLY TRINITY, ST PETER. Redundant 1971. Sold to Shaftesbury Grammar School.
OR C 1563-1927 M 1563-1641, 1652-67, 1675-1969 B 1567/68-1646, 1652-1906 Banns 1757-74, 1870-1969 (DRO)
BT CMB 1732-1880 (W&SRO)
Cop C 1563-1866 M 1563-1837 (DRO); C 1732-1880 M 1732-1847 from BT (VRI); C 1742-1837 MB 1813-37 (PRI); M 1563-1641, 1652-67, 1675-1837 (SG); M 1563-1837 from OR (DMI); B 1813-37 (I, DRO); B 1742-1812 (SG); B 1742-1837 (DBI); Extr C 1582-1824 M 1661-1827 B 1582-1775 (SG)
Cop (Mf) CB 1732-1880 M 1732-1847 (Mf of BT, DRO, SLC); Extr C 1732-1880 M 1732-1847 from BT (IGI)
MI Cy 1901 (*Ye Olde Mortality* 9: Ms, SG)

SHAFTESBURY St John *see* Enmore Green, under MOTCOMBE

SHAFTESBURY (RC) Holy Name and St Edward, Salisbury Street. f 1898; erected 1910

SHAFTESBURY (RC) Belmont House, Cann, 'since 1899 a centre for the RC mission of the Sacred Heart, and a home for French Catholics' [Kelly 1903]

SHAFTESBURY (Ind/Cong, now URC) Mustons Lane. f 1662. Rebuilt 1858 [*Cong. Yearbook* 1871] [1882 Return] [Kelly 1939]
OR ZC 1799-1837 (RG 4/348, PRO)
Cop (Mf) ZC 1799-1837 (Mf of OR, SLC); C 1799-1837 (Printout, Mf SLC); Extr C 1799-1837 (IGI)

SHAFTESBURY (Presb) General preaching licence to William Eastman of Shaftesbury; licences for houses of Richard Harris and Joseph Ward, 1672

SHAFTESBURY (Ind) Licence to Giles Paris for his house, 1672

SHAFTESBURY (Wes) Shaftesbury and Gillingham Circuit. Includes parishes of
Alvediston, Cann, Donhead St Mary, Motcombe, Shaftesbury, Tisbury, Tollard
Royal, West Tisbury [Dorset and Wiltshire]
OR   Shaftesbury section C 1843-1906; Gillingham Section C 1850-1967 (DRO)
Cop (Mf) C 1843-1932 (Mf of OR, SLC)

SHAFTESBURY (Wes) Shaftesbury Circuit
OR   ZC 1796-1839 (RG 4/466, 1232, PRO)
Cop (Mf) ZC 1796-1839 (Mf of OR, SLC); C 1796-1839 (Printout, Mf SLC);
          Extr C 1796-1839 (IGI)

SHAFTESBURY (Wes) St James. f by 1748. Chapel registered 1766. House called
Lydfords registered 1795 [Biggs]

SHAFTESBURY (Wes, now URC) Parsons Pool, Bell Street f 1766. Rebuilt 1827,
1907 [1882 Return] [Kelly 1939] North Dorset Circuit

SHAFTESBURY (Prim Meth) Motcombe Circuit, Shaftesbury section. St James
Street chapel [Kelly 1903]
OR   C 1888-1932 (DRO)

SHAFTESBURY (Prim Meth) Cann. Two chapels, erected 1846, 1870 [1882 Return]
[Kelly 1903]; both Meth [Kelly 1939]

SHAFTESBURY (S of F) Shaftesbury, Bridport and Sherborne MM, part of
Dorset QM 1668-1804, Dorset and Hampshire QM 1804-55, then Bristol and
Somerset QM.
OR   CB 1776-94 (DRO); Minutes of Bristol and Somerset QM at SRO, but no
     registers. see also BRIDPORT, SHERBORNE (RG 6/402, 403, 200, PRO)

SHAFTESBURY (S of F) 'Shaston and Cann'. Meeting House, St James Street
[Harrod 1865] [1882 Return] [Kelly 1903]; 'Now disused; meetings at
Institute, Gold Hill' [Kelly 1939]
OR   Z 1742-1837 M 1776-1836 B 1744-1837 (RG 6/200, 402-03, 1453, 1554,
     PRO); Z 1910-47 B 1838-61, 1879-1950 (DRO)
Cop (Mf) ZMB 1742-1837 (Mf of OR, SLC)

SHAFTESBURY (Brethren) Ebenezer Hall, Salisbury Street. Erected 1886
[Kelly 1939]

SHAFTESBURY Shaftesbury Cemetery, Mampitts Road (1927) (Shaftesbury Town
Council)

SHAFTESBURY St John's burial ground or Bury Litton Cemetery (former
churchyard of demolished church of St John. 'Still in use' [Kelly 1903]

SHAFTESBURY Poor Law Union Workhouse, Castle Hill. Opened 1840. Demolished
1947.

SHAPWICK St Bartholomew [Badbury Hundred; Wimborne and Cranborne Union]
[462] Now with STURMINSTER MARSHALL, KINGSTON LACY.
OR   C 1654-59, 1675-1872 M 1654-59, 1676-1837 B 1654-59, 1675-1948
     Banns 1824-1905 (DRO)
BT   CMB 1731-40, 1744-1837, 1847-80 (W&SRO)
Cop C 1654-1723/3 M 1654-1837 (DRO); CB 1813-37 (I, DRO); C 1731-1880
     M 1731-1837 from BT (VRI); CB 1813-37 M 1654-1837 (PRI); M 1654-59,
     1676-1837 (SG); M 1654-1837 from OR (DMI); B 1813-37 (DBI);
     Extr C 1656-1722 M 1656-1732 B 1654-1732 (SG)

SHAPWICK cont.
Cop (Mf) CB 1731-1880 M 1731-1837 (Mf of BT, DRO, SLC); Extr C 1731-1880
M 1731-1837 from BT (IGI)
MI (S&DFHS); (DFHS); (DRO)

SHAPWICK (Prim Meth) n.d. [Kelly 1903]; Meth [Kelly 1939]

SHASTON *see* SHAFTESBURY

SHASTON Modern benefice including COMPTON ABBAS, EAST ORCHARD, MARGARET
MARSH, WEST ORCHARD, MELBURY ABBAS, MOTCOMBE, SHAFTESBURY St James, St John
Enmore Green, St Peter.

SHERBORNE Abbey Church of St Mary [Sherborne Hundred; Sherborne Union]
[4075] Peculiar of the Dean of Sarum until 1847. Included chapelry of NORTH
WOOTTON (separate parish 1812). United 1970 with CASTLETON. Now also with
LILLINGTON.
OR C 1538-1973 M 1538-1969 B 1538-1977 Banns 1772-1983 (DRO)
BT CMB 1585-88, 1591-97, 1600-03, 1606-22, 1625-27, 1630-36, 1639-40,
1667-1720, 1722-1836, 1847-65, 1867-80 (W&SRO)
Cop CB 1538-1653, 1813-37 M 1538-1837 (DRO); CB 1538-1812 (SG);
CMB 1813-37 (PRI); C of infants 1785-89 (S&DFHS); M 1538-1837 from OR,
(DMI); B 1800-37 (DBI); Extr M 1538-1772 (SG)
Cop (Mf) CMB 1585-1836 CB 1847, 1849, 1851-60, 1862-65, 1867-72, 1874-76,
1880 (Mf of BT, DRO, SLC); Extr CM 1585-1880 from BT (IGI)
MI (S&DFHS) and cemetery; (DFHS); Abbey and cemetery (DRO); Ch, cy 1855,
1884, 1975 (SG); Cemetery 1884, 1973 (SG); war memorial (S&DFHS)

SHERBORNE Sherborne School Chapel. School f 1550. Chapel in old abbey
buildings, consecrated 1853
OR C 1971+ (Chaplain) *and see* Abbey registers

SHERBORNE St Paul, Coombe. Mission church [Kelly 1903] Erected 1929
[Kelly 1939] Now with SHERBORNE Abbey, CASTLETON, LILLINGTON.

SHERBORNE Almshouse of St John the Baptist and St John the Evangelist.
Chapel erected 1442.

SHERBORNE (RC) Sacred Heart and St Aldhelm, Westbury. Erected 1893-94

SHERBORNE (Bapt) Horsecastles. Erected 1844 [Kelly 1903]

SHERBORNE (Bapt) North Road. Erected 1931 [Kelly 1939]

SHERBORNE (Ind/Cong, now) URC/Meth) f 1662 Union Chapel and Long Street
Meeting. Long Street erected 1803. 'Union Cong' [*Cong. Yearbook* 1871]
[Kelly 1903] Now at The Methodist Church:local ecumenical project 1994
OR ZC 1785-1837 (RG 4/ 2413, 532, PRO); M 1968-73 (DRO)
Cop (Mf) C 1785-1837 (Mf of OR, SLC); C 1785-1837 (Printout, Mf SLC);
C 1824-37 (Mf, DRO); Extr C 1785-1837 (IGI)
MI Ptd GT 5: 3: Summer 1980: 14-16); Extr 1876 (SG)

SHERBORNE (Ind) Union Chapel Schools, Long Street [1882 Return]

SHERBORNE (Presb) Licence for house of John Capson; licence to Humphrey
Philips for house of Catherine Chafe, and licence for house of Francis Ford
and Katherine Chaffes 1672

SHERBORNE (Nonconformist: unspecified) Licence for house of Elizabeth Cooth, 1672

SHERBORNE (Wes) Sherborne Circuit
OR   ZC 1819-37 (RG 4/1233, PRO); C 1819-37 (DRO)
Cop (Mf) ZC 1819-37 (Mf of OR, SLC); C 1819-37 (Printout, Mf SLC);
        Extr C 1819-37 from BT (IGI)
MI   (S&DFHS); (DRO); chapel and burial ground 1976 (SG); burial ground
      (*Ye Olde Mortality* 9: Ms, SG)

SHERBORNE (Wes) House occupied by Mr Joseph Avard registered 1795; a chapel
in the old Bridewell registered 1796 [Biggs] Cheap Street chapel erected
1841-42 [1882 Return]; 'near the Abbey' [Kelly 1903, 1939] Sherborne and
Yeovil Circuit

SHERBORNE (Prim Meth) Abbey [Harrod 1865]

SHERBORNE (S of F) Part of Shaftesbury, Bridport and Sherborne Monthly
Meeting *q.v.* under SHAFTESBURY
OR   Z 1742-1837 M 1765-93, 1796-1836 B 1744-1837 (RG 6/200, 349, 402, 403,
      432-33, 1453, 1577, PRO)
Cop (Mf) Z 1742-1837 M 1765-93, 1796-1836 B 1744-1837 (Mf of OR, SLC)

SHERBORNE (S of F) Shaftesbury and Sherborne
OR   C 1910-47 B 1838-61, 1870-1950 (DRO)

SHERBORNE (Latter Day Saints) Sherborne Branch.
OR   Records: compiled 1849 (SLC)
Cop (Mf) Records (Mf, SLC)

SHERBORNE (Brethren) Acreman Street [Harrod 1865]; Half Moon Street
[Kelly 1903]; Finger Lane [Kelly 1939]

SHERBORNE Cemetery 'near Horsecastles' f 1856 [Kelly 1903]

SHERBORNE Poor Law Union Workhouse, Horsecastles and Lower Acreman Street.
Erected 1836. Demolished 1938

SHILLING OKEFORD *see* SHILLINGSTONE

SHILLINGSTONE or SHILLING OKEFORD Holy Rood [Cranborne Hundred;
Sturminster Union] [473] Now with THE OKEFORD BENEFICE.
OR   C 1653-1869 M 1654-1973 B 1654-1902 Banns 1755-1896 (DRO)
BT   CMB 1732-39, 1743-79, 1781-86, 1789-1880 (W&SRO)
Cop   C 1831-37 M 1654-1837 B 1654-1719 (DRO); CMB 1654-1812 (SG, SLC);
      M 1654-1837 (SG, DMI, PRI); B 1813-37 (DBI)
Cop (Mf) CB 1732-1880 M 1732-1847 (Mf of BT, DRO, SLC); ZCM 1654-1812
        (Printout, Mf SLC); Extr C 1653-83, 1732-1880 M 1654-1847 from OR
        and BT (IGI)
MI   (S&DFHS); (DFHS); (DRO)

SHILLINGSTONE (Wes) Chapel [Harrod 1865]; a Building [1882 Return];
chapel [Kelly 1903]; Meth erected 1907 [Kelly 1939]

SHIPTON GORGE *see* BURTON BRADSTOCK

SHITTERTON   tithing of BERE REGIS [170]

SHROTON   *see* IWERNE COURTNEY

SILTON St Nicholas [Redland Hundred; Mere Union 1835-94; Shaftesbury Union 1894-1930] [396]
OR   C 1653-1812 M 1653-1837 B 1653-1812 Banns 1754-1806 (DRO)
BT   CMB 1731-1819, 1825-41, 1844, 1847-76 (W&SRO)
Cop M 1653-1837 (DRO, SG, DMI, PRI); B 1653-1812 (DBI); CMB 1731-1876 from
     BT (Pine: CD 3)
Cop (Mf) CB 1731-1876 M 1731-1838 (Mf of BT, DRO, SLC); Extr C 1731-1876
         M 1731-1838 from BT (IGI)
MI   (S&DFHS); (DFHS); (DRO); (SG); Ch, cy (Ptd *Gent.Mag.*1833: 1: 497-98)

SIXPENNY HANDLEY or SIXPENNY HADLEY   St Mary [Sixpenny Handley Hundred; Wimborne and Cranborne Union] [889 including hamlet of GUSSAGE ST ANDREW and tithings of Minchinton and Woodcots] Ancient parish united 1327 with IWERNE MINSTER. Separate parish 1844 as HANDLEY. Now with PENTRIDGE, GUSSAGE ST ANDREW.
OR   C 1767-1925 M 1754-1963 B 1767-1976 Banns 1754-1812, 1823-1976 (DRO)
     No earlier registers noted in 1831.
BT   CMB 1731-35, 1740-1836, 1843-44, 1847-80 (W&SRO)
Cop CMB 1731-79 from BT (DRO, S&DFHS); C 1731-1880 M 1731-1836 from BT
     (VRI); CB 1813-37 M 1754-1837 (PRI); CB 1813-37 (I, DRO); M 1754-1837
     (DRO, SG); M 1754-1837 from OR, 1731-53 from BT (DMI); B 1813-36 (DBI)
Cop (Mf) CB 1731-1880 M 1731-1836 (Mf of BT, DRO, SLC); Extr C 1731-1880
         M 1731-1836 from BT (IGI)
MI   (S&DFHS); (DFHS); (DRO)

SIXPENNY HANDLEY (Wes) Woodcutts [1882 Return] [Kelly 1939]

SIXPENNY HANDLEY (Prim Meth) Ebenezer [1882 Return]; rebuilt 1892 after fire [Kelly 1939]
OR   *see* Wilton Circuit C 1897-1940 (W&SRO)
Cop (Mf) Wilton Circuit C 1897-1940 (Mf of OR, SLC)

SIXPENNY HANDLEY (Prim Meth) Dean [1882 Return] [Kelly 1903, 1939]

SIXPENNY HANDLEY (Prim Meth) Denland [1882 Return] [Kelly 1903, 1939]

SOPLEY [Hampshire] Part transferred to Dorset 1974, added to HURN civil parish.

SOUTH LYTCHETT   *see* LYTCHETT MINSTER

SOUTH MAPPERTON   *see* MAPPERTON

SOUTH PERROTT   *see* PERROTT, SOUTH

SOUTHWELL   *see* PORTLAND

SPETISBURY or SPLETISBURY   St John the Baptist [Loosebarrow Hundred; Blandford Union] [667] Included chapelry of CHARLTON MARSHALL. Now with CHARLTON MARSHALL, BLANDFORD ST MARY.
OR   C 1705-1991 M 1706-1993 B 1705-1904 Banns 1754-1812, 1823-1965 (DRO)
     No earlier register noted in 1831.
BT   CMB 1731-39, 1744-79, 1781-1825, 1828-44, 1847-80 (W&SRO)
Cop CB 1705-1899 M 1706-1899 (DRO, DCM, SG); CMB 1813-37 (PRI); C 1847-80
     from BT (VRI); M 1706-1837 from OR (DMI); B 1813-38 (DBI)
Cop (Mf) CMB 1731-1844 CB 1847-80 (Mf of BT, DRO, SLC); Extr C 1731-1844,
         1847-80 M 1731-1841 from BT (IGI)
MI   (S&DFHS); (DFHS); (DRO); Ch, cy 1971 (SG)

SPETISBURY (RC) Sion House. Convent of Augustinian nuns 1799-1861. Mission moved to BLANDFORD FORUM. Then Bridgettine nuns [Harrod 1865] Canons Regular of the Lateran, 'Chapel of St Mary' [1882 Return] Ursuline nuns. St Monica's Priory 1886; closed 1926; chapel demolished 1967.
OR C 1837+ M 1844+ Confirmations 1843+ (Inc, Blandford Forum); D 1857-61 (Inc, Newton Abbot, Devon); C 1837, 1840-55 D 1840-49 B 1840-54 Confirmations 1843, 1847, 1853, 1854, 1857, 1872, 1876, 1882+ (PDA)
Cop C 1837-66 M 1844-49 B 1840-54 Confirmations 1843-54 (SG, Cath FHS collection at Catholic Central Library, Lancing Street, London NW1 1ND)

SPETISBURY (FIEC) Spetisbury Baptist Church, High Street

SPETISBURY (Ind/Cong) Erected 1845. Out-station of BLANDFORD
[*Cong. Yearbook* 1871] [Kelly 1939]

SPETISBURY (Prim Meth) Erected 1842 [1882 Return] [Kelly 1903];
Meth [Kelly 1939]

STAFFORD, WEST St Andrew [Culliford Tree Hundred; Dorchester Union] [184] United 1470 with FROME BILLET ancient parish.
OR C 1570-1958 M 1558-1657, 1665-75, 1680-1721, 1729-1837 B 1558-1812 Banns 1823-1912 (DRO)
BT CMB 1731-45, 1749, 1780-89, 1807-08, 1812-80 (W&SRO)
Cop C 1573-1743, 1778 M 1558-1815 B 1558-1766 (SG); C 1813-37 M 1559-1837 (PRI); C 1813-37 (I, DRO); C 1731-1880 M 1731-1846 from BT (VRI); M 1559-1837 (DRO, SG); M 1559-1837 from OR (DMI); B 1645-1899 (DBI)
Cop (Mf) CB 1731-1880 M 1731-1846 (Mf of BT, DRO, SLC); Extr C 1731-1880 M 1731-1846 from BT (IGI)

STALBRIDGE St Mary [Brownshall Hundred; Sturminster Union] [1773 including tithings of Gomershay, Thornhill, Weston]
OR C 1690-1979 M 1691-1995 B 1693-1734/5, 1742-1996 Banns 1754-1803, 1886-1967, 1977-95 (DRO)
BT CMB 1737, 1739, 1741, 1744-79, 1780-81, 1784-1801, 1804-22, 1824-80 (W&SRO)
Cop M 1691-1812 (Ptd Phil 4: 1909; & on CD-ROM); M 1691/2-1837 B 1813-61 (DRO); CB 1813-37 M 1691-1837 (PRI); C 1813-37 (I, DRO); M 1691-1837 (SG); M 1690-1812 (Boyd); M 1790-1812 (Pallot); M 1691-1837 from OR (DMI); B 1813-38 (DBI)
Cop (Mf) C 1690-1979 M 1691-1987 B 1695-1735, 1742-1916 Banns 1754-1878, 1886-1976 confirmations 1911-71 (Mf of OR, SG); M 1691-1812 (Mf of Phil, SLC); CB 1737-1880 M 1737-1847 (Mf of BT, DRO, SLC); Extr C 1727-1880 M 1727-1847 from BT (IGI)
MI (S&DFHS); (DFHS); (SG)

STALBRIDGE (Presb) Licence for house of James Hind; licences to John G(r)offe for house of Ruth Rokeclife at Stalbridge, and to Peter Ince for his house at Thornhill, 1672

STALBRIDGE (Ind/Cong) f 1662 [Harrod 1865] [*Cong. Yearbook* 1871] [1882 Return] [Kelly 1939]
OR ZC 1810-37 (RG 4/586, PRO); C 1847-57 (DRO)
Cop (Mf) ZC 1810-37 (Mf of OR, SLC); C 1810-37 (Printout, SLC); Extr C 1810-37 (IGI)

STALBRIDGE (Cong) Weston. Erected 1904 [Kelly 1939]

STALBRIDGE (Wes) f by 1764. House of John Hawke registered 1786 [Biggs]; Chapel [Harrod 1865] [1882 Return] [Kelly 1903]; Meth [Kelly 1939] Sherborne and Yeovil Circuit

STANBRIDGE   see HINTON PARVA

STANTON ST GABRIEL see WHITCHURCH CANONICORUM

STAPEHILL   see HAMPRESTON

STEEPLE St Michael and All Angels [Hasilor Hundred; Wareham and Purbeck Union] [237] Part united with TYNEHAM 1952, part joined WAREHAM. Now with CORFE CASTLE, CHURCH KNOWLE, KIMMERIDGE, TYNEHAM.
OR   C 1548-1812 M 1548-1836 B 1548-1812 Banns 1754-1812 (DRO)
BT   CMB 1731-38, 1741-1880 (W&SRO)
Cop   C 1548-1660 M 1546-1836 B 1548-1658 (DRO); CB 1548-1660 (S&DFHS);
      M 1546-1836 (SG, DMI, PRI); B 1815-37 (DBI); CMB 1731-1880 from BT
      (Pine: CD 4)
Cop (Mf) CB 1731-1880 M 1731-1847 (Mf of BT, DRO, SLC); Extr C 1731-1880
          M 1731-1847 from BT (IGI)
MI   (S&DFHS); (DFHS); (DRO)

STEEPLE Chapel of St John the Evangelist, Creech Grange. Chapel-of-ease erected 1746. Said to be unused until 1840, and consecrated in 1859 [Kelly 1939] Redundant 1983. Sold 1986 for use as monument.

STEEPLE (Wes) Creech
OR   see POOLE (RG 4/1230, PRO)

STEEPLETON   see WINTERBORNE STEEPLETON

STEEPLETON IWERNE   see IWERNE, STEEPLETON

STEEPLETON PRESTON   see IWERNE, STEEPLETON

STICKLAND   see WINTERBORNE STICKLAND

STINSFORD St Michael [George Hundred; Dorchester Union] [382]   Now with CHARMINSTER.
OR   C 1632-38, 1644, 1656-1863 M 1579-1641, 1662-1988 B 1577-1638,
      1658-96, 1713-1936 Banns 1824-1902 (DRO) Noted in 1831: 'Registers
      1579-1644, 1661-92' etc.
BT   CMB 1732-71, 1774-1815, 1818-80 (W&SRO)
Cop   C 1631/2-1812, 1863-1995 M 1579-1840 B 1577-1812 (DRO); CB 1813-37
      (I, DRO); C 1631-1812 M 1579-1641, 1662-1840 B 1577-1812 (SG);
      CB 1813-37 M 1813-30 (PRI); M 1579-1840 from OR (DMI); B 1813-37 (DBI)
Cop (Mf) CB 1732-1880 M 1732-1847 (Mf of BT, DRO, SLC); Extr C 1732-1880
          M 1732-1847 from BT (IGI)
MI   (S&DFHS); (DFHS); (DRO); Cy 1975 (SG)

STOBOROUGH Former borough and liberty within WAREHAM HOLY TRINITY [347]

STOCK GAYLARD St Barnabas [Brownshall Hundred; Sturminster Union 1835-84] [66] Rebuilt 1884. Now with LYDLINCH
OR   C 1582-1685, 1722-1812 M 1567-1672, 1722-1838 B 1568-1685, 1722-1812
      Banns 1754-?1788 (DRO) Gap to 1722 noted in 1831.
BT   CMB 1731-96, 1799-1802, 1807-45, 1847-80 (W&SRO)

STOCK GAYLARD cont.
Cop C 1582-1685, 1722-1812 M 1567-1672, 1722-1840 B 1568-1685, 1722-1812
    (DRO); C 1582-1811 M 1567-1838 B 1568-1685, 1722-1812 (SG);
    C 1731-1880 M 1731-1840 from BT (VRI); M 1813-38 (PRI); M 1567-1838
    from OR (DMI); B 1568-1812 (DBI)
Cop (Mf) CB 1731-1880 M 1731-1845 (Mf of BT, DRO, SLC); Extr C 1731-1880
    M 1731-1845 from BT (IGI)

STOCKLAND St Michael and All Angels [part Whitchurch Canonicorum Hundred,
part Fordington Liberty (DALWOOD chapelry) until 1830s when transferred to
Devon, and Exeter Diocese; Axminster Union] [1640] Now with Dalwood,
Kilmington, Shute (Devon)
OR C 1640-1976 M 1640-1963 B 1640-1916 (Devon RO)
BT CMB 1731-78, 1780-1823, 1826-36 (W&SRO); CB 1837-38 M 1837 (Devon RO)
Cop C 1789-1804 M 1746-1812 (DRO); C 1731-1836 M 1731-1836 from BT (VRI);
    M 1746-1812 (I, SG); M 1746-1812 from DRO copy (DMI)
Cop (Mf) C 1640-1970 M 1640-1837 B 1640-1858 (Mfc of OR, SG); CMB 1731-1836
    (Mf of BT, DRO, SLC); Extr CM 1731-1836 from BT (IGI)

STOCKLAND (Wes) Millhayes [1882 Return]

STOCKWOOD or STOKE St Edwold [Sutton Poyntz Liberty; Sherborne Union] [33]
Peculiar of the Dean of Sarum until 1847. Joined MELBURY OSMOND 1959.
Redundant 1972. Churches Conservation Trust.
OR C 1813-1937 M 1815-1901 B 1815-95 (DRO) and see YETMINSTER. Noted in
    1831: CB 1779+ M 1754+
BT CMB 1585-88, 1592-99, 1604, 1616-23, 1631-35, 1670, 1673-74, 1680,
    1693, 1707, 1712, 1717-21, 1724-26, 1730-31, 1758, 1762-91, 1794-95,
    1798-1830, 1847-80 (W&SRO)
Cop CMB 1585-1851 from BT (DRO, W&SRO, SG, PRI); C 1618-1880 M 1618-1830
    from BT (VRI); M 1815-38 from OR, 1585-1814 from BT (DMI); B 1586-1851
    (DBI)
Cop (Mf) CB 1585-1880 M 1585-1830 (Mf of BT, DRO, SLC); C 1678 one entry
    (Printout, Mf SLC); Extr C 1618-1880 M 1618-1830 from BT (IGI)
MI (DFHS)

STOKE see STOCKWOOD

STOKE ABBOTT or ABBAS St Mary [Beaminster Forum and Redhone Hundred;
Beaminster Union] [587] Now with Beaminster Area benefice.
OR C 1559/60-1923 M 1560-1953 B 1561-1721, 1738-1983 Banns 1754-1812,
    1824-96 (DRO)
BT CMB 1731-81, 1785-88, 1790-1880 (W&SRO)
Cop M 1560-1837 (Ptd Phil 6: 1912; & on CD-ROM); C 1559/60-1853
    M 1560-1837 B 1561-1738, 1783-1884 (DRO); C 1731-1880 M 1731-1837 from
    BT (VRI); C 1813-53 B 1813-84 (S&DFHS); CB 1813-37 M 1560-1837 (PRI);
    M 1560-1837 (SG); M 1562-1812 (Boyd); M 1780-1837 (Pallot); M 1560-1837
    from OR (DMI); B 1720-1959 (SG); B 1783-1812 (DBI)
Cop (Mf) M 1560-1837 (Mf of Phil, SLC); CB 1731-1880 M 1731-1837 (Mf of BT,
    DRO, SLC); Extr C 1731-1880 from BT, M 1560-1837 from OR (IGI)
MI (DFHS); (DRO); Cy 1720-1959 (SG); (Mf, SG)

STOKE ABBOTT (Presb) Licence to Henry Parsons for the house of Robert
Dalliver, called Swillcots, 'Abbotstoke', 1672

STOKE ABBOTT (Cong) n.d. Out-station of BROADWINDSOR [Cong. Yearbook 1871]
[Kelly 1903, 1939]

STOKE WAKE All Saints [Whiteway Hundred; Sturminster Union] [147]
Rebuilt 1872. Now with HAZLEBURY BRYAN AND THE HILLSIDE PARISHES benefice.
Redundant 1977. Sold for use as private chapel.
OR   C 1565-1967 M 1546-1706/7, 1720/1, 1741-46/7, 1753, 1763-1972
      B 1551-1982 Banns 1757-96, 1823-78, 1889-1975 (DRO)
BT   CMB 1732-39, 1742, 1744, 1746-65, 1768-78, 1781-1805, 1808-30,
      1838-44, 1847-80 (W&SRO)
Cop   C 1565-1707 M 1546-1838 B 1551-1682 (DRO); C 1565-1707 B 1551-1682
      (S&DFHS); CB 1813-37 M 1546-1838 (PRI); C 1813-37 (I, DRO);
      M 1546-1838 (SG); M 1732-42 from BT (DRO); C 1732-1880 M 1736-1844 from
      BT (VRI); M 1546-1838 from OR, 1732-62 from BT (DMI); B 1814-37 (DBI)
Cop (Mf) CB 1732-1880 M 1736-1844 (Mf of BT, DRO, SLC); Extr C 1732-1880
      M 1736-1844 from BT (IGI)
MI   (S&DFHS); part (DFHS)

STOKE, EAST St Mary [Winfrith Hundred; Wareham and Purbeck Union] [561]
Included tithing of Wopgret. Rebuilt 1828. Redundant 1985; sold for
residential use 1992. WOOL AND EAST STOKE BENEFICE.
OR   C 1743-1983 M 1744/5-1969 B 1742-1909 Banns 1754-95, 1909-84 (DRO)
BT   CMB 1732-1803, 1806-41, 1844-80 (W&SRO)
Cop   C 1743-1837 M 1744/5-1838 B 1744-1837 (DRO); C 1731-45 M 1731-43
      B 1732-43 from BT (DRO); C 1732-1880 M 1732-1847 from BT (VRI);
      C 1743-1837 M 1744-1838 B 1813-37 (PRI); M 1746-1838 (SG); M 1744-1838
      from OR, 1732-1848 from BT, 1608, 1614, 1672 from Hutchins (DMI);
      B 1732-1837 (DBI)
Cop (Mf) CB 1732-1880 M 1732-1847 (Mf of BT, DRO, SLC); Extr C 1732-1880
      M 1732-1847 from BT (IGI)
MI   (S&DFHS); (DFHS); (DRO); (SG)

STOKE, EAST St John the Evangelist, East Holme [Hasilor Hundred; Wareham
and Purbeck Union] [55] Formerly part of EAST STOKE. Noted in 1831: 'no
Church at East Holme'. Erected 1865-66. Now with WAREHAM benefice.
OR   C 1866-1995 M 1867-1994 Available on MIC/R/1193 B 1868-1990 (DRO)
BT   CMB 1866-80 (W&SRO)
Cop   B 1868-1990 (DRO); C 1866-80 from BT (VRI); B 1868-1990 (DBI)
Cop (Mf) CB 1866-80 (Mf of BT, DRO, SLC); Extr C 1866-80 from BT (IGI)
MI   (DFHS)

STOKE, EAST (Wes) Binnegar [1882 Return]

STOKE, EAST (Wes) Highwood. Preaching room [1882 Return]

STOUR PROVOST or STOWER PROVOST St Michael and All Angels [Stour Provost
Liberty; Shaftesbury Incorporation/Union] [870] Now with GILLINGHAM
benefice.
OR   C 1701-1980 M 1701-1993 B 1701-1950 Banns 1754-1823 (DRO) No earlier
      register noted in 1831.
BT   CMB 1731-1834, 1842-80; including TODBER 1828 (W&SRO)
Cop   CMB 1702-34 (S&DFHS); CMB 1813-37 (PRI); CB 1813-37 (I, DRO);
      C 1732-1879 M 1731-1858 from BT (VRI); M 1701-1837 (DRO, SG);
      M 1701-1837 from OR (DMI)
Cop (Mf) CM 1701-1980 B 1701-1950 (Mf of OR, SG); CB 1731-1880 M 1731-1858
      (Mf of BT, DRO, SLC); Extr C 1731-1880 M 1731-1858 from BT (IGI)
MI   (S&DFHS); (DFHS); (DRO)

STOUR PROVOST All Saints, Stour Row. Chapel-of-ease erected 1868. Now with
GILLINGHAM benefice.
OR   1878+ (Inc)
MI   (S&DFHS); (DFHS)

STOUR PROVOST (RC) Hussey family, removed to MARNHULL 1725

STOUR PROVOST (Presb) Licence for house of William Good, 1672

STOUR PROVOST (Cong) Stour Row. Erected 1839 [Kelly 1939]

STOUR PROVOST (Prim Meth) New Yeate n.d. [Kelly 1903]
OR *see* Coleford (Somerset) Prim Meth Circuit C 1880-1932 (SRO)

STOUR PROVOST (Meth) Woodville n.d. [Kelly 1939]

STOUR, EAST or EAST STOWER Christ Church [Redland Hundred; Shaftesbury Incorporation/Union] [531] Chapelry in GILLINGHAM. Rebuilt 1842. Now with GILLINGHAM benefice.
OR   C 1584-1680, 1710-1866 M 1584-1680, 1710-1998 B 1584-1906 Banns 1754-92, 1824-1967 (DRO) Noted in 1831: CMB 1598-1680, 1710-1812
BT   CMB 1731-63, 1766-96, 1799-1833, 1836-41, 1844-79; for 1765 and 1768 see WEST STOUR (W&SRO)
Cop M 1584-1812 (Ptd Phil 6: 1912; & on CD-ROM); C 1710-1837 M 1584-1646, 1654-1837 B 1685-1837 (DRO); C 1731-1879 M 1731-1844 from BT (VRI); C 1789-1837 MB 1813-37 (PRI); M 1584-1648, 1654-1837 (SG); M 1584-1812 (Boyd); M 1584-1680, 1710-1837 from OR, 1731-38, 1740-54 from BT (DMI); B 1813-37 (DBI)
Cop (Mf) as East Stower M 1584-1812 (Mf of Phil, SLC); CB 1731-1879 M 1731-1844 (Mf of BT, DRO, SLC); Extr C 1731-1879 M 1731-1844 from BT (IGI)
MI   (S&DFHS); (DFHS); (DRO)

STOUR, EAST (Part Bapt) [1882 Return] [Kelly 1903]

STOUR, EAST (Wes) Building occupied by Christopher Clement, Gent. registered 1796; building occupied by William Hiscock, yeoman, registered 1797 [Biggs]; chapel [1882 Return] [Kelly 1903]; Meth erected 1882 [Kelly 1939]

STOUR, WEST or WEST STOWER   St Mary [Redland Hundred; Shaftesbury Incorporation/Union] [219] Chapelry in GILLINGHAM. Now with GILLINGHAM benefice.
OR   C 1813-1981 M 1754-1990 B 1678/9-1730, 1813-1981 Banns 1823-1970 (DRO) Noted in 1831: CMB 1654-1765, 1769-1812
BT   CMB 1731-78, 1780-1812, 1814-41, 1844-79; for 1759-60 *see* EAST STOUR (W&SRO)
Cop C 1813-23 M 1754-1853 B 1813-37 (DRO); CB 1813-37 M 1754-1853 (PRI); M 1732-54 from BT (DRO); M 1754-1853 (SG); M 1754-1853 from OR, 1731-54 from BT (DMI); B 1813-37 (DBI)
Cop (Mf) CB 1732-1879 M 1732-1848 (Mf of BT, DRO, SLC); Extr C 1732-1879 M 1732-1848 from BT (IGI)
MI   (S&DFHS); (DFHS)

STOUR, WEST (Prim Meth) [1882 Return]; Meth erected 1854 [Kelly 1939]

STOURPAINE Holy Trinity [Pimperne Hundred; Blandford Union] [594] United 1431 with LAZERTON ancient parish. Peculiar of the Dean and Chapter of Sarum until 1847. Rebuilt 1858. Now with PIMPERNE, DURWESTON, BRYANSTON.
OR   C 1631-1925 M 1631-1747, 1752, 1784-1978 B 1631-1881 Banns 1789-1812, 1824-1940 (DRO)
BT   CMB 1620-24, 1635, 1659-70, 1672-73, 1675-97, 1813-15, 1818-23, 1825-28, 1830-80 (W&SRO)

STOURPAINE cont.
Cop CB 1631-1799 M 1631-1752 (Ptd E.Fry *The Register of Stourpaine, Dorset*: 1900); M 1631-1837 (DRO, SG); CB 1813-37 (I, DRO); C 1620-1880 M 1620-1872 from BT (VRI); CB 1813-37 M 1631-1837 (PRI); M 1631-1837 from OR, 1620-33 from BT, 1625-31 from M licences (DMI); B 1631-1837 (DBI)
Cop (Mf) CB 1620-1880 M 1620-1872 (Mf of BT, DRO, SLC); Extr C 1620-1880 M 1620-1872 from BT (IGI)
MI (S&DFHS); (DFHS); (DRO); (SG)

STOURPAINE (Wes) n.d. [Kelly 1903]

STOURPAINE (Prim Meth) Building in the occupation of William Haine [1882 Return]; Meth chapel [Kelly 1939]

STOURTON CAUNDLE *see* CAUNDLE, STOURTON

STOWER *see* STOUR

STRATTON St Mary the Virgin [George Hundred; Dorchester Union] [310 including hamlet of Grimstone] Chapelry in CHARMINSTER; separate parish 1742. Now with BRADFORD PEVERELL, FRAMPTON, SYDLING ST NICHOLAS
OR C 1561/2-1920 M 1562-1748, 1754-1962 B 1561-1993 Banns 1754-1803, 1826-1907 (DRO)
BT CMB 1591-97, 1603-35, 1638-39, 1668-69, 1674-84, 1690, 1693-95, 1698-1737, 1745, 1749-55, 1760-1822, 1825-27, 1829-32, 1847-79 (W&SRO)
Cop CMB 1561-1812 (I, SG, SLC); M 1562-1837 B 1813-37 (DRO); C 1813-79 M 1813-70 from BT (VRI); CMB 1813-37 (PRI); C 1813-37 (I, DRO); M 1562-1648, 1654-1836 (SG); M 1562-1837 (Boyd); M 1562-1836 (Phil Ms at SG); M 1562-1836 from OR (DMI); B 1813-37 (DBI)
Cop (Mf) CM 1561-1812 (Printout, Mf SLC); CB 1591-1879 M 1591-1870 (Mf of BT, DRO, SLC); Extr C 1561-1879 M 1561-1870 (IGI)

STRATTON (Meth) Erected 1915 [Kelly 1939]

STUDLAND St Nicholas [Rowberrow Hundred; Wareham and Purbeck Union] [435] *see also* BRANKSEA. Now with SWANAGE.
OR C 1581-85, 1591-1624, 1636-1749, 1783-1953 M 1636-90, 1695-1749, 1755-1971 B 1636-1727, 1783-1937 Banns 1755-91, 1823-1953 (DRO) Noted in 1831: C 1581+ M 1755+ B 1636+
BT CMB 1731, 1734, 1741, 1744-82, 1785-1822, 1825-80 (W&SRO)
Cop C 1581-1837 M 1637-1837 B 1636-1837 (DRO, PRI); C 1731-1880 M 1731-1847 from BT (VRI); M 1637-1837 (SG); M 1749-54 from BT (DRO); M 1637-1837 from OR, 1750-54 from BT (DMI); B 1813-37 (DBI)
Cop (Mf) CB 1731-1880 M 1731-1847 (Mf of BT, DRO, SLC); Extr C 1731-1880 M 1731-1847 from BT (IGI)
MI (S&DFHS); (DFHS); (DRO); (SG)

STUDLAND St Mary, Branksea. Erected 1853-54 on Brownsea or Branksea Island, Poole Harbour. Parish created 1855 from STUDLAND. United 1971 with PARKSTONE St Peter. Now also with PARKSTONE St Osmund.
OR CMB 1854+ (Inc)
BT CMB 1855-79 (W&SRO); for earlier transcripts *see* STUDLAND
Cop C 1855-79 from BT (VRI)
Cop (Mf) CB 1855-79 (Mf of BT, DRO, SLC); Extr C 1855-79 from BT (IGI)
MI (S&DFHS); (DFHS); (DRO); (SG)

STUDLAND (Wes)
OR *see* POOLE (RG 4/1230, PRO)

STUDLAND (Meth) [Kelly 1939] Poole and Swanage Circuit

STURMINSTER MARSHALL St Mary [Cogdean Hundred; Wimborne and Cranborne Union] [803 including tithing of Coombe Almer] Royal Peculiar, Included chapelries of LYTCHETT MINSTER, CORFE MULLEN, HAMWORTHY, all separate parishes 1858. Now with KINGSTON LACY, SHAPWICK.
OR C 1562/3-1646, 1695-1933 M 1562-1643/4, 1695-1963 B 1563-1645, 1678-1933 Banns 1754-71, 1855-72, 1935-72 (DRO) Noted in1831: 'also Marr. for the Chapelries of Mullen, Lytchet Minster and Hamworthy 1727-42.'
BT CMB 1813-80 (W&SRO)
Cop CMB 1562-1812 (Ptd, E.Hobday: 1901); C 1562/3-1837 M 1562-1836 B 1563-1837 (DRO); CB 1813-37 M 1562-1836 (PRI); C 1813-80 M 1813-37 from BT (VRI); M 1562-1643, 1695-1836 (SG); M 1790-1812 (Pallot); M 1562-1836 from OR (DMI); B 1746-1838 (DBI)
Cop (Mf) CMB 1563-1812 (Mf of Hobday, SLC); CB 1813-80 M 1813-37 (Mf of BT, DRO, SLC); C 1562-1812 M 1561-1812 (Printout, Mf SLC); Extr C 1561-1645, 1696-1880 M 1561-1837 (IGI)
MI (S&DFHS); (DFHS); (DRO)

STURMINSTER MARSHALL St Michael, Blandford Road, Hamworthy [Cogdean Hundred; Poole Union 1835-1905] [308] Chapelry in STURMINSTER MARSHALL. Separate parish 1858. Rebuilt 1826 and 1958-59.
OR C 1826-1963 M 1826-1975 B 1811-1981 Banns 1826-1907, 1942-89 (DRO) and see STURMINSTER MARSHALL, LYTCHETT MINSTER. Noted in 1831: 'There are no Registers anterior to 1813. The Church was destroyed by Cromwell, and not rebuilt until 1826'. Early entries in LYTCHETT MINSTER [Kelly 1903]
BT CMB 1813-80 (W&SRO)
Cop CB 1813-37 M 1826-37 (DRO, PRI); C 1813-80 M 1826-47 from BT (VRI); M 1826-37 (SG); M 1826-37 from OR, 1813-25 from BT (DMI); B 1813-37 (DBI)
Cop (Mf) C 1826-1953 M 1826-1975 B 1811-1981 Banns 1826-1911, 1942-89 Confirmations 1840-72 (Mf, PLHC); CB 1813-80 M 1826-47 (Mf of BT, DRO, SLC); Extr C 1813-80 M 1826-47 from BT (IGI)
MI (S&DFHS); (DFHS); (DRO)

STURMINSTER MARSHALL St Gabriel, Keysworth Road, Turlin Moor, Hamworthy. In the parish of St Michael, Hamworthy.
Cop (Mf) Banns 1984-93 (Mf, PLHC)

STURMINSTER MARSHALL (Presb) Licence for house of Henry Light, 1672

STURMINSTER MARSHALL (Ind/Cong) Erected 1820 [Kelly 1903]; erected 1852 [Kelly 1939] Out-station of WIMBORNE [Cong. Yearbook 1871]

STURMINSTER MARSHALL (Ind) Hamworthy
OR ZC 1833-37 (RG 4/54, PRO)
Cop (Mf) ZC 1833-37 (Mf of OR, SLC); ZC 1833-37 (Printout, Mf SLC); Extr C 1833-37 (IGI)

STURMINSTER MARSHALL (Wes) [1882 Return] [Kelly 1903]

STURMINSTER MARSHALL (Wes) Hamworthy [Kelly 1903]

STURMINSTER MARSHALL (Meth) Carters Avenue [Kelly 1939] Poole and Swanage Circuit.

STURMINSTER NEWTON (CASTLE) St Mary [Sturminster Newton Hundred; Sturminster Union] [1831] Now with HINTON ST MARY
OR C 1681-1937 M 1681-1945 B 1681-1958 Banns 1839-1946 (DRO)
BT CMB 1731-82, 1785-1880 (W&SRO)
Cop CB 1813-37 M 1681-1837 (PRI); CB 1813-37 (I, DRO); M 1681-1837 (DRO, SG, DMI); B 1813-37 (DBI)
Cop (Mf) C 1681-1715, 1717, 1744-1937 M 1697-1717, 1744-1945 B 1681-1715, 1717-18, 1744-1958 Banns 1839-1946 (Mf of OR, SG); CB 1731-1880 M 1731-1847 (Mf of BT, DRO, SLC); Extr C 1731-1880 M 1731-1847 from BT (IGI)
MI 1834-95 (S&DFHS); (DFHS); Cy 1976 (SG)

STURMINSTER NEWTON (Wes) n.d. [Harrod 1865] [1882 Return] [Kelly 1903]; (Meth) Church Street [Kelly 1939] North Dorset Circuit

STURMINSTER NEWTON (Prim Meth) The Bridge [Kelly 1939]
OR M 1957-59 (DRO)

STURMINSTER NEWTON (Prim Meth) A building, the property of Charles Hopkins, Bagber [1882 Return] [Kelly 1903]

STURMINSTER NEWTON (Prim Meth) Chapel. Broad Oak [1882 Return] [Kelly 1903] North Dorset Circuit

STURMINSTER NEWTON (Prim Meth) Chapel. Newton Hill [1882 Return]

STURMINSTER NEWTON ('No distinctive appelation') Temperance Lecture Hall, Church Street [1882 Return]

STURMINSTER NEWTON (Open Brethren) The Row [Kelly 1939]

STURMINSTER NEWTON Cemetery, The Bridge (1882) (Sturminster Newton Town Council)

STURMINSTER NEWTON Poor Law Union Workhouse. Erected 1838. Largely demolished c.1980. Chapel later used as a museum.

SUTTON POYNTZ *see* PRESTON

SUTTON WALDRON St Bartholomew [Redland Hundred; Shaftesbury Incorporation/Union] [236] Rebuilt 1847. Now with IWERNE COURTNEY, IWERNE STEEPLETON, FONTMELL MAGNA.
OR C 1678-1992 M 1678, 1689, 1694-1760, 1767-1992 B 1678-1768, 1782-1994 Banns 1754-1817, 1824-1992 (DRO)
BT CMB 1731-88, 1792-1836, 1849-80 (W&SRO)
Cop CB 1813-37 M 1678-1837 (PRI); CB 1813-37 (I, DRO); C 1849-80 from BT (VRI); M 1678-1837 (DRO, SG); M 1754-60, 1767-79 Banns 1759-81 (SG); M 1731-54 from BT (DRO); M 1678-1837 from OR, 1731-54, 1779-82 from BT (DMI); B 1678-1994 (DBI)
Cop (Mf) CB 1731-1836, 1849-80 M 1731-1835 (Mf of BT, DRO, SLC); Extr C 1731-1836, 1849-80 M 1731-1835 from BT (IGI)
MI (S&DFHS); (DFHS); (DRO); Cy 1909 (*Ye Olde Mortality* 9: Ms, SG)

SWANAGE St Mary the Virgin [Rowberrow Hundred; Wareham and Purbeck Union] [1734] Now with STUDLAND
OR C 1563-72, 1591-1684, 1689-1910 M 1564-68, 1574-75, 1588-1684, 1692-1905 B 1568-77, 1588-1684, 1691-1922 (DRO) Noted in 1831: M 1568-1709 'very imperfect'
BT CMB 1731-1880 (W&SRO)

SWANAGE cont.
Cop CMB 1563-1812 (Ptd PRS 69: 1912); C 1563-1837 M 1564-1841 B 1563-1837
    (DRO); CB 1813-37 M 1564-1841 (PRI); C 1731-1880 M 1731-1847 from BT
    (VRI); M 1747-51 from BT (DRO); M 1564-75, 1588-1837, 1841 (SG);
    M 1790-1812 (Pallot); M 1564-1799, 1813-41 from OR, 1800-12 from PRS
    copy (DMI); B 1756-1837 (DBI)
Cop (Mf) CMB 1563-1812 (Mf of PRS, SLC); CB 1731-1880 M 1731-1847 (Mf of
    BT, DRO, SLC); C 1563-1812 M 1564-1812 (Printout, Mf SLC);
    Extr C 1563-1666, 1691-1880 M 1564-1847 (IGI)
MI   (S&DFHS); (DFHS); (DRO); (SG); disused burial ground, Church Hill
    (S&DFHS); war memorial (S&DFHS)

SWANAGE All Saints, Wavell Road. Erected 1956-57. Now with SWANAGE St Mary,
STUDLAND
OR   1970+ (Inc)

SWANAGE St Aldhelm, Park Road. Erected by George Burt. Opened 1892. Leased
to Rector and churchwardens of St Mary's [Kelly 1939] Demolished 1972.

SWANAGE St Paul, Goathorn Mission church fl. 1925 [Kelly 1939] Demolished.

SWANAGE St Mark, Bell Street, Herston. Erected 1869-70. Now with SWANAGE
St Mary, STUDLAND
OR   1914 (Inc)

SWANAGE (RC) Holy Spirit and St Edward, Victoria Avenue. Erected 1904.

SWANAGE (Bapt) Emmanuel, Howard Road f 1918. SBA

SWANAGE (Ind/Cong now URC) High Street. f 1705. Old chapel erected 1837,
became school. [Cong. Yearbook 1871] New chapel 1902 [Kelly 1939]
OR   ZC 1794-1837 (RG 4/467, 4460, PRO); C 1936-43 (DRO)
Cop C 1794-1847 (S&DFHS)
Cop (Mf) ZC 1794-1837 (Mf of OR, SLC); C 1794-1837 (Printout, Mf SLC);
    Extr C 1794-1837 (IGI)

SWANAGE (Wes) Swanage Circuit. Formed from POOLE Circuit 1871.
OR   C 1805-09, 1841-71 (DRO); and see POOLE (RG 4/1230, PRO)
Cop Poole Circuit C 1807-40 (DRO)

SWANAGE (Wes) f by 1774 [Biggs] High Street erected 1886 [Kelly 1903];
Meth [Kelly 1939] Poole and Swanage Circuit

SWANAGE (Wes) Jubilee Square [1882 Return]

SWANAGE (Wes) Herston [Kelly 1903] Poole and Swanage Circuit

SWANAGE (Prim Meth) Ebenezer, Herston [1882 Return]

SWANAGE (Plymouth Brethren) Mill Pond [Kelly 1903]; Church Hill [Kelly
1939]

SWANAGE Northbrook Cemetery, Northbrook Road. 1855 (Swanage Town Council)

SWANAGE Godlingston Cemetery, Godlingston Lane (1932) (Swanage Town
Council)

SWYRE Holy Trinity [Uggscombe Hundred; Bridport Union] [226] Now with BRIDE VALLEY benefice.
OR C 1587/8-1998 M 1588-1926 B 1588-1812 Banns 1754-1818, 1823-1915 (DRO)
   Noted in 1831: CMB 1718+
BT CMB 1732-36, 1741-97, 1800-80 (W&SRO)
Cop M 1588-1837 (Ptd Phil 6: 1912; & on CD-ROM); C 1587/8-1795 M 1588-1836
   B 1588-1792 (DRO); C 1587-1794 M 1588-1644, 1658-1836 B 1588-1803
   (SG); C 1732-1880 M 1732-1836 from BT (VRI); M 1731-48 from BT (DRO);
   M 1588-1837 (Boyd); M 1790-1837 (Pallot); M 1588-1836 from OR (DMI,
   PRI); B 1813-1998 (DBI)
Cop (Mf) M 1588-1837 (Mf of Phil, SLC); CB 1732-1880 M 1732-1836 (Mf of BT,
   DRO, SLC); Extr C 1732-1880 M 1732-1836 from BT (IGI)
MI (S&DFHS); (DFHS); (DRO); (SG)

SWYRE TOLLER *see* TOLLER PORCORUM

SYDLING ST NICHOLAS St Nicholas [Sydling St Nicholas Liberty; Cerne Union] [617] Included chapelry of HILFIELD (separate parish 1850) and tythings of Upper Sydling and Fifehead Sydling. Now with BRADFORD PEVERELL, STRATTON, FRAMPTON.
OR C 1565-1636, 1665-90, 1695-1910 M 1565-1636, 1665-90, 1695-2000
   B 1565-1636, 1665-90, 1695-1992 Banns 1754-1807, 1823-1971 (DRO)
BT CMB 1731-1844, 1847-80 (W&SRO)
Cop CMB 1565-1660, 1690-1812 (SG); CMB 1813-37 (PRI); M 1568-1837
   B 1813-37 (DRO); C 1813-37 (I, DRO); M 1568-1637, 1665-1837 (SG);
   M 1568-1837 (DMI); B 1813-37 (DBI)
Cop (Mf) CB 1731-1880 M 1731-1837 (Mf of BT, DRO, SLC); Extr C 1731-1880
   M 1731-1837 erroneously as 'Sydling St Nicholas Hope Independent'
   (IGI)
MI (S&DFHS); (DFHS); Extr in Ts of B register, *passim*, 1940 (SG)

SYDLING ST NICHOLAS St Nicholas, Hilfield [Cerne, Totbury and Modbury Hundred; Cerne Union] [150] Chapelry in SYDLING ST NICHOLAS. Separate parish 1850. Now with YETMINSTER WITH RYME INTRINSECA AND HIGH STOY benefice.
OR M 1849-1912 B 1851-1991 (DRO) *and see* SYDLING ST NICHOLAS.
BT CMB 1851-80; for earlier transcripts 1789-1806 *see* SYDLING ST NICHOLAS
   (W&SRO)
Cop C 1852-80 M 1857-71 from BT (VRI)
Cop (Mf) C 1852-80 M 1857-71 B 1851-77 (Mf of BT, DRO, SLC); Extr C 1852-80
   M 1857-71 from BT (IGI)

SYDLING ST NICHOLAS (Ind/Cong) f 1775 Hope Chapel [1882 Return] [Kelly 1939]
OR ZC 1811-35 (RG 4/349, PRO); C 1847-57 (DRO)
Cop (Mf) C 1811-35 (Mf of OR, SLC); C 1811-35 (Printout, Mf SLC);
   Extr C 1811-35 (IGI)

SYDLING ST NICHOLAS (Ind) A cottage in the occupation of William Woodland, Up Sydling [1882 Return]

SYDLING ST NICHOLAS (Wes [Harrod 1865] [1882 Return] [Kelly 1903]

SYMONDSBURY with EYPE and BROADOAK St John the Baptist [Whitchurch Canonicorum Hundred; Bridport Union] [1147] Including EYPE and BROADOAK
OR C 1558/9-1954 M 1558-1646, 1653-76, 1684-1998 B 1558/9-1646, 1653-76
   1684-1903 Banns 1754-?1968 (DRO)

SYMONDSBURY cont.
BT CMB 1731-78, 1780-1880 (W&SRO)
Cop M 1558-1812 (Ptd Phil 2: 1907; & on CD-ROM); C 1558/9-1806 M 1558-1756
    B 1558/9-1626 (DRO); C 1558-1739 B 1558-1626 Banns 1754-93 (SG);
    CMB 1813-37 (I, DRO, PRI); C 1831-80 M 1831-37 from BT (VRI);
    M 1558-1812 (Boyd); M 1790-1812 (Pallot); M 1558-1837 from OR (DMI);
    B 1813-37 (DBI)
Cop (Mf) M 1558-1812 (Mf of Phil, SLC); CB 1731-1880 M 1731-1837 (Mf of BT,
    DRO, SLC); Extr C 1731-1880 M 1731-1837 from BT (IGI)
MI (S&DFHS); (DFHS); (DRO); Ch, cy, war meorial (SG)

SYMONDSBURY St Paul, Broadoak. Chapel-of-ease erected 1865-66. Now with
SYMONDSBURY

SYMONDSBURY St Peter, Eype. Chapel-of-ease erected 1865, Now with
SYMONDSBURY.

TALBOT VILLAGE   see CANFORD MAGNA

TARRANT CRAWFORD or PRESTON CRAWFORD St Mary [Badbury Hundred; Blandford
Union] [78 with Preston] United 1937 with TARRANT GUNVILLE, TARRANT
RUSHTON, TARRANT RAWSTON, TARRANT KEYNESTON. Now with TARRANT VALLEY
benefice. Redundant 1988. Churches Conservation Trust.
OR C 1597-1665, 1670-1705, 1719-31, 1752-73, 1776-1936 M 1599-1643,
    1661-70, 1681-1705, 1720-32, 1752, 1760-1811, 1831-35, 1842-1935
    B 1597-1642, 1657-1706, 1719-32, 1751-1811, 1813-1940 Banns 1825-35,
    1895, 1918-22, 1935 (DRO) Noted in 1831: CB 1774+ M 1760+
BT CMB 1732-45, 1749-67, 1770-72, 1775-78, 1780-81, 1784-1800, 1802,
    1804-30, 1834, 1841-75 (W&SRO)
Cop C 1597-1936 M 1599-1835, 1842-1935 B 1597-1732, 1751-1940 (DRO, DCM,
    SG); CB 1813-37 M 1599-1837 (PRI); M 1599-1643, 1661-70, 1681-1705,
    1720-32, 1752, 1760-1837 (SG); M 1732-1830 from BT (DRO); M 1599-1842
    from OR, 1732-1830 from BT (DMI); B 1597-1857 (DBI)
Cop (Mf) CB 1732-1875 M 1732-1847 (Mf of BT, DRO, SLC); Extr C 1732-1875
    M 1732-1847 (IGI)
MI (S&DFHS); (DFHS); (DRO); Ch cy 1971 (SG)

TARRANT GUNVILLE St Mary [Cranborne Hundred; Blandford Union] [502]
United 1928 with TARRANT RUSHTON, TARRANT RAWSTON, and 1932 with TARRANT
KEYNESTON. Now with TARRANT VALLEY benefice.
OR C 1719-1996 M 1719/20-1993 B 1719/20-1850 Banns 1754-1804, 1823-1981
    (DRO) No earlier register noted in 1831.
BT CMB 1732-59, 1762-67, 1769, 1772, 1776-84, 1788, 1791-1812, 1814-80
    (W&SRO)
Cop CMB 1719-1919 Banns 1754-1919 (DRO, DCM, SG); CB 1813-37 M 1719-1840
    (PRI); M 1737-52 from BT (DRO); M 1719-1840 from OR, 1730-47 from BT
    (DMI); B 1792-1898 (DBI)
Cop (Mf) CB 1732-1880 M 1731-1871 (Mf of BT, DRO, SLC); Extr C 1732-1880
    M 1732-1871 (IGI)
MI (S&DFHS); (DFHS); (DRO)

TARRANT HINTON St Mary [Pimperne Hundred; Blandford Union] [341] Now with
TARRANT VALLEY benefice.
OR C 1545-48, 1585-1600, 1622-1718, 1729-1964 M 1546-48/9, 1613-1714,
    1730-1992 B 1546/7, 1585-1617, 1672-87, 1783-1993 Banns 1754-1809,
    1823-1925 (DRO) Noted in 1831: Register in Latin 1545+ very imperfect
    and dates illegible. 1729-98 also imperfect.

TARRANT HINTON cont.
BT   CMB 1731-1812, 1814-33, 1837-80 (W&SRO)
Cop CMB 1545-1812 (Ptd PRS: 1902); C 1545-1837 M 1546-1837 B 1546/7-1837
     (DRO); CMB 1813-37 (PRI); M 1546-48, 1613-1837 (SG); M 1810-12 from BT
     (DRO); M 1790-1812 (Pallot); M 1546-1837 from OR (DMI); B 1813-37
     (DBI)
Cop (Mf) CMB 1545-1812 (Mf of PRS, SLC); CB 1731-1880 M 1731-1847
       (Mf of BT, DRO, SLC); M 1546-1812 (Printout, Mf SLC);
       Extr C 1545-48, 1779-1880 M 1548-1847 from OR and BT (IGI)
MI   (S&DFHS); (DFHS); (DRO)

TARRANT HINTON (Wes) House of Henry Pain registered 1792 [Biggs]

TARRANT KEYNESTON All Saints [Pimperne Hundred; Blandford Union] [277]
United 1932 with TARRANT GUNSTON, TARRANT RUSHTON, TARRANT RAWSTON.
Now with TARRANT VALLEY benefice.
OR   C 1737-1909 M 1813-1992 B 1737-1994 Banns 1823-1945 (DRO) Noted in
     1831 CB 1737+ M 1754+
BT   CMB 1731-42, 1745-1802, 1806, 1814-45, 1847-80 (W&SRO)
Cop CB 1737-1939 M 1813-1939 (DRO, DCM, SG); C 1813-60 MB 1813-37 (PRI); M
     1813-36 from OR, 1731-1812 from BT (DMI); B 1737-1856 (DBI)
Cop (Mf) CB 1731-1880 M 1731-1837 (Mf of BT, DRO, SLC); Extr C 1731-1880
      M 1731-1837 from BT (IGI)
MI   (S&DFHS); (DFHS); (DRO)

TARRANT KEYNESTON (Anabaptist) Licence for house of Thomas Hall, 1672

TARRANT KEYNESTON (Prim Meth) [1882 Return] [Kelly 1903]; Meth [Kelly 1939]

TARRANT LAUNCESTON *see* TARRANT MONKTON

TARRANT MONKTON All Saints [Monkton Up Wimborne Hundred; Blandford Union]
[220] Included chapelry of TARRANT LAUNCESTON (no church) [72]. United 1928
with TARRANT GUNVILLE, TARRANT RUSHTON, TARRANT RAWSTON. Now with TARRANT
VALLEY benefice.
OR   C 1564/5-1610, 1618-23/4, 1630-34/5, 1692-1783, 1813-1926 M 1565-1609,
     1618/9-21/2, 1630-33, 1697-1752, 1784-1836, 1838-1992 B 1566-1610
     1618/9-23/4, 1630-34, 1697-1783, 1813-1992 Banns 1915-50 (DRO)
     Noted in 1831: CB 1697+ M 1716+
BT   CMB 1731-80, 1783-1802, 1806-12, 1814-80 (W&SRO)
Cop M 1565-81, 1589-1609, 1618-21, 1630-33, 1697-1752, 1784-1836 (DRO,
     SG); CB 1813-37 M 1565-1836 (PRI); CB 1813-37 (I, DRO); M 1754-80 from
     BT (DRO); M 1565-1836 from OR, 1765-83 from BT (DMI); B 1785-1837
     (DBI)
Cop (Mf) CB 1731-1880 M 1731-1847 (Mf of BT, DRO, SLC); Extr C 1731-1880
      M 1731-1849 from BT (IGI)
MI   (S&DFHS); (DFHS); (DRO)

TARRANT MONKTON ((Presb) Licence to Henry Martin for his house, 1672

TARRANT MONKTON (Wes) House owned by Lot Carter registered 1792; house
owned by Harry Barnes registered 1793 [Biggs]; chapel [Harrod 1865]
[Kelly 1903]; Meth [Kelly 1939]

TARRANT MONKTON (S of F) Constituent meeting of POOLE MM *q.v.* Closed before
1804.

TARRANT RAWSTON St Mary [Pimperne Hundred; Blandford Union] [48] United 1928 with TARRANT GUNVILLE, TARRANT RUSHTON. Now with TARRANT VALLEY benefice. Redundant 1972. Sold for use as accommodation for Rawston House.
OR C 1814-1957 M 1760-1810, 1815-1921 B 1815-94 Banns 1760-1810 (DRO)
    Noted in 1831: C 1754-1812 defective, M 1754-1812 B 1749-1808
BT CMB 1731-33, 1756, 1759-63, 1768-70, 1776-78, 1781, 1784-99, 1802-09,
    1812, 1814-29, 1833-80 (W&SRO)
Cop C 1814-1931 M 1760-1921 B 1815-94 (DRO, DCM, SG); C 1813-37
    M 1760-1837 (PRI); M 1732-33 from BT (DRO); M 1760-1837 from OR,
    1731-60, 1811-14 from BT (DMI); B 1733-1872 (DBI)
Cop (Mf) CB 1731-1880 M 1731-1840 (Mf of BT, DRO, SLC); Extr C 1731-1880
    M 1731-1840 from BT (IGI)
MI (S&DFHS); (DFHS); (DRO)

TARRANT RUSHTON St Mary [Cranborne Hundred; Blandford Union] [226] United 1928 with TARRANT GUNVILLE, TARRANT RUSHTON. Now with TARRANT VALLEY benefice.
OR C 1696-1993 M 1698-1992 B 1697-1812, 1814-1993 Banns 1754-1812,
    1823-50, 1915-53 (DRO)
BT CMB 1731-1812, 1814-80 (W&SRO)
Cop C 1696-1919 M 1698-1919 B 1697-1919 (DRO, DCM, SG); CB 1813-37
    M 1698-1836 (PRI); C 1847-80 from BT (VRI); M 1698-1836 from OR (DMI);
    B 1814-1900 (DBI)
Cop (Mf) CB 1731-1880 M 1731-1841 (Mf of BT, DRO, SLC); Extr C 1731-1880
    M 1731-1841 from BT (IGI)
MI (S&DFHS); (DFHS); (DRO)

TARRANT VALLEY Benefice including TARRANT GUNVILLE, TARRANT HINTON, TARRANT KEYNSTON, TARRANT LAUNCESTON, TARRANT RUSHTON, TARRANT RAWSTON.

THORNCOMBE St Mary. Formerly a detached part of Devonshire [Axminster Hundred; Diocese of Exeter]. Transferred to Diocese of Sarum 1836, and to Dorset [Whitchurch Canonicorum Hundred] 1844 [Axminster Union 1836-94; Beaminster Union 1894-1930]. Diocese of Bath and Wells from early 1980s; now with Chard and District Team Ministry. Rebuilt 1867-68. This information amends that in NIPR Vol.8 Part 5 Devon. Some printed sources present conflicting information.
OR C 1551/2-1860 M 1552/3-1989 B 1551/2-1952 Banns 1754-1812 1925-66
    (DRO)
BT CMB 1606?, 1624, 1628-30, 1633, 1638-39, 1669-70, 1675, 1678, 1683,
    1685, 1687, 1690, 1696, ?1697-99, 1703-05, 1711, 1713-35, 1737,
    1740-47, 1749-50, 1752, 1754-1812 (Devon RO); CMB 1838-80 (W&SRO)
Cop M 1552-1812 (Ptd Phil 2: 1907; & on CD-ROM); M 1813-37 (Ptd Devon
    FHS); C 1551/2-1690/1 M 1552/3-1850 B 1551/2-1690/1 (DRO);
    CB 1551-1840 M 1552-1850 (SG); C 1813-37 M 1552-1837 B 1813-41 (PRI);
    C 1813-37 B 1813-41 (I, DRO); C 1838-80 from BT (VRI); M 1813-37
    (S&DFHS); M 1624-1753 from BT (DRO); M 1552-1812 (Boyd); M 1790-1812
    (Pallot); M 1552-1837 from OR, 1624-1754 from BT (DMI); B 1813-41 (DBI)
Cop (Mf) M 1552-1812 (Mf of Phil, SLC); CB 1838-80 (Mf of BT, DRO, SLC);
        Extr C 1838-80 from BT (IGI)

THORNCOMBE Forde Abbey. Home of Prideaux, Gwyn, and other families from 16th cent. Domestic chapel, former Norman chapter-house of abbey.

THORNCOMBE Holditch Court, former residence of Brook family. Ruined. 'Chapel desecrated and used as a barn' [Kelly 1903]

THORNCOMBE (Plymouth Brethren) Erected 1881 [Kelly 1939]

THORNFORD St Mary Magdalene [Sherborne Hundred; Sherborne Union] [383] Peculiar of the Dean of Sarum until 1847. Now with BRADFORD ABBAS, BEER HACKETT.
OR   C 1676-1976 M 1677-1998 B 1677-1932 Banns 1754-1811, 1882-1985 (DRO)
BT   CMB 1579-82, 1591-1641, 1671, 1674-1783, 1788-1812, 1814-35, 1840-80
     (W&SRO)
Cop CB 1677-1812 M 1677-1754 (Ptd E.Fry *The Registers of Thornford*: 1903);
     CB 1677-1812 M 1677-1837 (DRO, SG); CB 1677-1812 M 1677-1754 (W&SRO);
     C 1579-1880 M 1579-1835 from BT (VRI); CB 1813-37 M 1677-1837 (PRI);
     CB 1813-37 (I, DRO); M 1579-1677, 1681-1747 from BT (DRO); M 1677-1837
     from OR, 1579-1754 from BT (DMI); B 1677-1837 (DBI)
Cop (Mf) CB 1579-1880 M 1579-1835 (Mf of BT, DRO, SLC); Extr CMB 1780-1862
         (Mf of Ms, SLC); Extr C 1579-1880 M 1579-1835 from BT (IGI)

THORNFORD (Wes) [1882 Return] [Kelly 1903]; Meth [Kelly 1939] Sherborne and Yeovil Circuit

THORNHILL   tithing of STALBRIDGE [257]

THORNICOMBE *see* TURNWORTH, BLANDFORD ST MARY

THREE LEGGED CROSS or THREE CROSS   hamlet in CRANBORNE

TINCLETON St John the Evengelist [Puddletown Hundred; Dorchester Union] [171] Now with MORETON, WOODSFORD.
OR   C 1576-1658, 1663-1996 M 1576-1654, 1669-1752, 1759-1993 B 1576-1658,
     1666-1998 Banns 1806-1997 (DRO)
BT   CMB 1733, 1737-79, 1781-1812, 1814-80 (W&SRO)
Cop C 1576-1814 M 1576-1837 B 1576-1812 (SG); M 1579-1837 B 1813-1913
     (DRO); C 1733-1880 M 1733-1847 from BT (VRI); M 1579-1837 (PRI);
     M 1735-59 from BT (DRO); M 1579-1837 from OR, 1733-59 from BT (DMI);
     B 1813-1913 (DBI)
Cop (Mf) CB 1733-1880 M 1733-1847 (Mf of BT, DRO, SLC); Extr C 1733-1880
         M 1733-1847 from BT (IGI)
MI   (S&DFHS); (DFHS)

TODBER St Andrew [Redland Hundred; Shaftesbury Incorporation/Union] [119] Annexed to STOUR PROVOST. Now with GILLINGHAM benefice.
OR   C 1814-1994 M 1754-1992 Banns 1754-1816, 1915-91 (DRO) Noted in 1831:
     C 1750-1812. 'Burials at Stour Provost. No Marr. Register prior to
     1812'.
BT   CMB 1731-33, 1736-39, 1742-97, 1800-03, 1807-12, 1814-32, 1842-46
     C 1847-76; for 1828 see also STOUR PROVOST (W&SRO)
Cop C 1731-1880 M 1731-1854 from BT (VRI); C 1813-37 M 1754-1836 (PRI);
     C 1811-37 (I, DRO); M 1754-1836 (DRO, SG); M 1731-48 from BT (DRO);
     M 1754-1836 from OR, 1731-54 from BT (DMI)
Cop (Mf) CB 1731-1880? M 1731-1854 (Mf of BT, DRO, SLC); Extr C 1731-1880
         M 1731-1854 from BT (IGI)
MI   (S&DFHS); (DFHS); (DRO); Cy 1905 (*Ye Olde Mortality* 9: Ms, SG)

TOLLARD ROYAL St Peter ad Vincula [part Cranborne Hundred (Dorset), part Chalke Hundred (Wiltshire); entirely Wiltshire from 1860s; Tisbury Union] In Archdeaconry of Dorset from 1951. Now with Dorset parishes of FARNHAM, GUSSAGE ST MICHAEL, GUSSAGE ALL SAINTS, ASHMORE, CHETTLE.
OR   *see* NIPR Vol.8 Part 2 Wiltshire

TOLLER FRATRUM or **LITTLE TOLLER** St Basil [Tollerford Hundred; Dorchester Union] [56] Included chapelry of WYMFORD EAGLE (separate parish 1911). Now with MELBURY benefice.

OR C 1561-1812 M 1560/1-1757, 1781-82, 1787-1802, 1814-36, 1843-1949 B 1558-1812 (DRO)

BT CMB 1731-79, 1782-1803, 1805, 1807-30, 1834, 1841, 1846-80; includes WYNFORD EAGLE 1731-1846 (W&SRO)

Cop M 1616-1836 B 1813-1994 (DRO); C 1731-1880 M 1731-1841 from BT (VRI); M 1616, 1661-1754, 1782-1800, 1814-36 (SG); M 1731-1812 from BT (DRO); M 1616-1836 (Phil Ms at SG, PRI); M 1616-1837 (Boyd); M 1616-1754, 1782-1836 from OR, 1731-1812 from BT (DMI); B 1558-1994 (DBI)

Cop (Mf) M 1616-1836 (Mf of Phil Ms, SG, SLC); CB 1731-1880 M 1731-1841 (Mf of BT, DRO, SLC); Extr C 1731-1880 M 1731-1841 from BT (IGI)

TOLLER PORCORUM or **GREAT TOLLER** or **SWYRE TOLLER** St Andrew [part Tollerford Hundred, part Beaminster Forum and Redhone Hundred; Dorchester Union] [540] Included tithing of Over and Nether Kingscombe. Now with Beaminster Area benefice.

OR C 1758-1941 M 1758-1838 B 1758-1914 Banns 1869-1972 (DRO) Noted in 1831: CB 1671+ M 1654+. Phillimore noted in 1908 'Vol.I: 35 parchment sheets black with age... long lost...finally discovered partly eaten away by mice, at Maiden Newton.' Contained CB 1615-58 M 1615-53. Vol.II 1654-1754. *see* copies below.

BT CMB 1732-79, 1781-1812, 1814-80 (W&SRO)

Cop M 1615-1812 (Ptd Phil 3: 1908; & on CD-ROM) ; CB 1615-58 M 1615-1838 (DRO); C 1615-80 M 1615-39 B 1615-58 (Ms, SLC); CMB 1615-80 (SG); CB 1813-37 (I, DRO); CMB 1813-37 (PRI); M 1615-44, 1654-1703, 1709-11, 1716-34, 1743-1838 (SG); M 1733-57 from BT (DRO); M 1615-1775 (Boyd); M 1790-1812 (Pallot); M 1758-1838 from OR, 1732-57 from BT, 1615-1758 from Phil (DMI); B 1813-37 (DBI)

Cop (Mf) C 1615-80 M 1615-39 B 1615-58 (Mf of Ms, SLC); M 1615-1812 (Mf of Phil, SLC); CB 1732-1880 M 1732-1847 (Mf of BT, DRO, SLC); CB 1615-80 (Printout, Mf SLC); Extr C 1615-44, 1655-80, 1732-1880 M 1615-39, 1732-1847 from OR and BT (IGI)

MI (S&DFHS); (DFHS); (DRO); (SG); Cy plan only *c.*1978 (SG)

TOLLER WHELME *see* CORSCOMBE

TOLLERFORD *see* FROME VAUCHURCH

TOLPUDDLE St John the Evangelist [Puddletown Hundred; Dorchester Union] [349] Now with PUDDLETOWN.

OR C 1718/9-1996 M 1719-1985 B 1718/9-1968 Banns 1754-1812, 1823-1994 (DRO) No earlier registers noted in 1831.

BT CMB 1732-1812, 1814-80 (W&SRO)

Cop CB 1813-37 M 1719-1837 (PRI); CB 1813-37 (I, DRO); M 1719-1837 (DRO, SG); M 1747-49 from BT (DRO); M 1719-1837 from OR, 1632-86 from Hutchins (DMI); B 1813-37 (DBI)

Cop (Mf) CB 1732-1880 M 1732-1849 (Mf of BT, DRO, SLC); Extr C 1732-1880 M 1732-1849 from BT (IGI)

MI (S&DFHS); (DFHS); (DRO)

TOLPUDDLE (Wes) [Harrod 1865] [Kelly 1903]; Meth [Kelly 1939] Dorchester Circuit

TOMSON *see* WINTERBORNE TOMSON

TONERS PUDDLE *see* TURNERSPUDDLE

TRENT St Andrew [Horethorne Hundred (Somerset) transferred 1895 to Dorset; Sherborne Union] Now with QUEEN THORNE benefice.
OR   *see* NIPR Vol.8 Part 3 Somerset

TURNERSPUDDLE or TONERS PUDDLE   Holy Trinity [Hundredsbarrow Hundred; Wareham and Purbeck Union] [82] Peculiar of the Dean of Sarum until 1847. United 1970 with AFFPUDDLE. Now also with BERE REGIS. Redundant 1974. Sold 1981 for use as monument.
OR   C 1640-55, 1661-66, 1678-90, 1745-1956 M 1640-53, 1661-66, 1673-84, 1745-50, 1790-1943 B 1640-55, 1661-79, 1749-1957, 1969 Banns 1790-1811, 1830-1919 (DRO) Noted in 1831: CMB 1632-88 imperfect, and gaps CB 1689-1744 M 1689-1789 between volumes.
BT   CMB 1580-82, 1591-99, 1605-10, 1623, 1627-35, 1638-40, 1664-79, 1686, 1697-1701, 1704-69, 1772-1880; for 1770 *see* WINTERBORNE KINGSTON (W&SRO)
Cop   C 1640-90 M 1640-84, 1745-1837 B 1640-79, 1813-1919 (DRO); CB 1813-37 M 1745-1837 (PRI); C 1813-37 (I, DRO); M 1580-1780 from BT (DRO); M 1745-50, 1790-1837 (SG); M 1640-84, 1745-1837 from OR, 1580-1790 from BT (DMI); B 1640-1919 (DBI)
Cop (Mf) CB 1579-1880 M 1579-1847 (Mf of BT, DRO, SLC); Extr C 1579-1880 M 1579-1847 from BT (IGI)
MI   (S&DFHS); (DFHS); (DRO); Ch cy 1758-1969: 1971 (SG)

TURNWORTH St Mary [Cranborne Hundred; Blandford Union] [78]   Now with WINTERBORNE STICKLAND, WINTERBORNE HOUGHTON, WINTERBORNE WHITECHURCH, WINTERBORNE CLENSTON.
OR   C 1578-1812 M 1577-1808, 1814-35, 1838-1972 B 1578-1812 Banns 1754-78, 1804 (DRO)
BT   CMB 1731-41, 1748-85, 1788-1830, 1832-80; for 1742-47 *see* WINTERBORNE WHITECHURCH (W&SRO)
Cop   CB 1578-1684 M 1577-1837 (DRO); CMB 1577-1684 (I, SG); M 1813-37 (PRI); M 1577-1837 (SG); M 1731-41, 1808-13, 1836-37 from BT (DRO); M 1577-1835 from OR, 1808-13, 1836-37 from BT (DMI)
Cop (Mf) CB 1731-1880 M 1731-1845 (Mf of BT, DRO, SLC); Extr C 1731-1880 M 1731-1845 from BT (IGI)
MI   (S&DFHS); (DFHS); (DRO)

TYNEHAM St Mary [Hasilor Hundred; Wareham and Purbeck Union] [247] In military training area from 1940s. United 1952 with STEEPLE. Now with CORFE CASTLE, CHURCH KNOWLE, KIMMERIDGE, STEEPLE. Redundant 1977; leased to Ministry of Defence for use as rest and exhibitions centre.
OR   C 1694-1942 M 1694-1943 B 1789-1942 Banns 1825-1943   (DRO) Noted in 1831 B 1581+
BT   CMB 1731-36, 1745-1880; *and see* STEEPLE (W&SRO)
Cop   C 1694-1837 M 1694-1836 B 1734-1837 (DRO); C 1694-1837 M 1694-1836 B 1792-1837 (PRI); C 1731-1880 M 1731-1836 from BT (VRI); M 1694-1836 (SG); M 1695-1836 (DMI); B 1734-1837 (DBI)
Cop (Mf) CB 1731-1880 M 1731-1836 (Mf of BT, DRO, SLC); Extr C 1731-1880 M 1731-1836 from BT (IGI)
MI   (S&DFHS); (DFHS); (DRO); Extr: Pratt (Ms, SG); Ch cy 1976 (SG); Ch n.d. (SG)

UPCERNE   see CERNE, UP

UPLODERS   or UP LODERS *see* LODERS

UPPER MELBURY   *see* MELBURY SAMPFORD

UPPER SYDLING   *see* SYDLING ST NICHOLAS

UPTON hamlet in CANFORD MAGNA *q.v.* and CORFE MULLEN; for St Dunstan's, Upton, *see* LYTCHETT MINSTER

UPTON   hamlet in OSMINGTON

UPWEY St Laurence [part Culliford Tree Hundred, part Wabyhouse Liberty; Weymouth Union] [618] Now with BINCOMBE, BROADWEY, BUCKLAND RIPERS.
OR   C 1654-1948 M 1654-1973 B 1654-1948 Banns 1871-1971 (DRO)
BT   CMB 1731-61, 1776-1880; 1799 includes FLEET (W&SRO)
Cop   CB 1813-37 M 1654-1837 (PRI); CB 1813-37 (I, DRO); M 1654-1837 (DRO,
      SG, DMI); B 1654-1948 (DBI)
Cop (Mf) C 1731-1880 M 1731-1846 (Mf of BT, DRO, SLC); Extr C 1731-1880
      M 1731-1845 from BT (IGI)
MI   (S&DFHS); (DFHS); (DRO); Ch, cy, war memorial (SG)

UPWEY (RC) The Holy Family, Chapel Lane f 1954. Served from WEYMOUTH
St Augustine

UPWEY (Ind/Cong) Erected 1809 [*Cong. Yearbook* 1871] Upwey Chapel, near the
Westbrook House [1882 Return]; Congregational chapel, Dorchester Road
[1882 Return] [Kelly 1939]
OR   C 1875-86 M 1877-1957, 1973-74, 1976-92 B 1876-83, 1890-1944 (DRO)
MI   URC (S&DFHS)

UPWEY (Wes) Ridgeway. House of Tregonwell Roper registered 1795 [Biggs];
chapel erected 1870 [1882 Return] [Kelly 1903]; Meth [Kelly 1939]

VENN   *see* BROADWINDSOR

VERWOOD *see* CRANBORNE

WAKEHAM *see* PORTLAND

WALDITCH St Mary [Gooderthorne Hundred; Bridport Union] [164]   Rebuilt
1863. Now with BRIDPORT benefice.
OR   C 1739-1976 M 1738-1988 B 1739-1988 Banns 1780-81, 1826-74 (DRO)
      No earlier registers noted in 1831
BT   CMB 1733-62, 1766-68, 1771-76, 1779-1839, 1843-44, 1847-80 (W&SRO)
Cop   M 1738-1812 (Ptd Phil 1: 1906; & on CD-ROM); C 1813-37 M 1738-1837
      B 1838-1988 (PRI); C 1813-37 (I, DRO); M 1738-1837 B 1813-1988 (DRO);
      M 1738-1837 (SG); M 1738-1812 (Boyd); M 1790-1812 (Pallot); M 1738-1837
      from OR, 1733-54, 1813-15 from BT (DMI); B 1739-1988 (DBI);
      CMB 1733-1880 from BT (Pine: CD 1)
Cop (Mf) M 1738-1812 (Mf of Phil, SLC); CB 1733-1880 M 1733-1837 (Mf of BT,
      DRO, SLC); Extr C 1733-1880 M 1740-1837 from BT (IGI)

WALDITCH Christ Church, East Road, In borough of BRIDPORT but in parish of
WALDITCH. Iron church erected 1880 [Kelly 1903]

WAMBROOK St Mary [Beaminster Forum and Redhone Hundred; Chard Union. Parish
created from CHARDSTOCK. Transferred 1895 to Somerset [217] Peculiar of the
Prebend of Chardstock and Wambrook, Sarum Cathedral until 1847. United with
COMBE ST NICHOLAS, HAM [Diocese of Bath and Wells, Somerset]
OR   C 1653-1909 M 1655-1970 B 1655-1812 Banns 1754-1811, 1824-1900 (SRO)
BT   CMB 1579-82, 1588-96, 1600-07, 1610, 1613-35, 1639-41, 1690-93,
      1698-99, 1734-46, 1752-1880 (W&SRO)

WAMBROOK cont.
Cop C 1653-1812 M 1655-1811 B 1655-1812 (SRO); C 1625-1909 M 1655-1970
     B 1643-1891 (Dr Campbell's Index at SRO); C 1654-1812 M 1655-1811
     B 1655-1733, 1755, 1766-1812 (DCRS at Exeter Library); M 1655-1837
     (DRO, PRI, DMI, Boyd, SG, Phil Ms at SG)
Cop (Mf) C 1653-1904 M 1655-1720, 1730-35, 1750-1900 B 1655-1733, 1776-1812
     Banns 1754-1811, 1824-1902 (Mf of OR, SLC); C 1654-1812
     M 1655-1811 B 1655-1733, 1755, 1766-1812 (Mf of Cop, SLC);
     M 1655-1720, 1730-1836 (Mf of Phil Ms, SLC); CB 1579-1880
     M 1579-1836 (Mf of BT, DRO, SRO, SLC); C 1654-1812 M 1654-1811
     (Printout, Mf SLC); Extr C 1579-1880 M 1579-1836 from OR and BT
     (IGI)

WAMBROOK (Wes) Chard Road. Erected 1908; closed by 1961.

WAREHAM Modern benefice including WAREHAM Lady St Mary, St Martin,
SANDFORD, ARNE, EAST HOLME.

WAREHAM Holy Trinity [Winfrith Hundred; Wareham and Purbeck Union]
[675 including Stoborough Liberty] Included chapelry of ARNE, borough of
Stoborough. From 1678 formed part of parish of WAREHAM. 'Not in use for
public services' [Kelly 1939] Redundant 1970. Leased as Arts Centre.
OR   *see* Lady St Mary
BT   CMB 1731-1812, 1814-24, 1827; includes WAREHAM St Mary 1805-06;
     for 1847-80 *see* WAREHAM St Mary (W&SRO)
Cop C 1591, 1605-12, 1617-34, 1731-1837 M 1594-1602, 1618-27, 1634, 1649,
     1652, 1731-1837 B 1587, 1599-1608, 1615-45, 1650-56, 1661-62, 1678-84,
     1697, 1722-29, 1731-1837 (DRO); CMB 1731-63 from BT (DRO); M 1754-81
     (SG); M 1754-81 from OR, 1731-54 from BT, 1597-1653 from Hutchins
     (DMI); CMB 1731-1824 from BT (Pine: CD 4)
Cop (Mf) CB 1762-1812 M 1763-74 (Mf, SG); CMB 1731-1824 (Mf of BT, DRO,
     SLC); Extr CM 1731-1824 from BT (IGI)
MI   Extr: Pratt (Ms, SG); Ch cy index 1983 (Ms, SG)

WAREHAM Lady St Mary [Winfrith Hundred; Wareham and Purbeck Union] [1120]
United early with WAREHAM ST MICHAEL. From 1678 formed part of parish of
WAREHAM.
OR   Holy Trinity, St Martin and St Mary C 1762-1964 M 1754-1980
     B 1762-1976 Banns 1772-83, 1823-1918 (DRO) Noted in 1831: 'Wareham
     comprises three parishes...for each of which there is one Register of
     Baptisms, Burials and Marriages A.D. 1762-1812. The earlier Registers
     were destroyed by fire, A.D. 1762.'
BT   CMB 1731-78, 1780-99, 1803-12, 1814-80; for 1805-06 *see* Holy Trinity
     (W&SRO)
Cop Wareham CB 1813-37 M 1594-1837 (PRI); M 1754-1841 from OR, 1731-54
     from BT, 1594-1649 from Hutchins (DMI); B 1811-37 (DBI); CMB 1731-1880
     from BT (Pine: CD 4)
Cop (Mf) C 1762-1965 M 1762-1920 B 1762-1976 Banns 1823-66 (Mf, SG);
     CB 1731-1880 M 1731-1846 (Mf of BT, DRO, SLC); Extr C 1731-1880
     M 1731-1846 from BT (IGI)
MI   (S&DFHS); (DFHS); (DRO); (SG)

WAREHAM St Martin [Winfrith Hundred; Wareham and Purbeck Union 1894-1930]
[530] From 1678 formed part of parish of WAREHAM. 'Only used for the
burials of one or two families' [Kelly 1903]
OR   *see* Lady St Mary
BT   CMB 1731-78, 1780-1811, 1814-24; for 1847-80 *see* Lady St Mary (W&SRO)
Cop M 1754-81 (SG); M 1754-81 from OR, 1731-54 from BT, 1601-34 from
     Hutchins (DMI); CMB 1731-1824 from BT (Pine: CD 4)

WAREHAM St Martin cont.
Cop (Mf) CB 1762-1812 (Mf, SG); CMB 1731-1824 (Mf of BT, DRO, SLC);
        Extr C 1731-1824 M 1732-1824 from BT (IGI)

WAREHAM St Michael. United early with WAREHAM LADY ST MARY.

WAREHAM St Martin, North Street, Sandford. 'Disused 200 years'. Restored
1936 [Kelly 1939] Now with WAREHAM benefice

WAREHAM (RC) Community of Passionist Monks f 1888. Church erected 1889.
Community closed 1901. Church dismantled 1907 and rebuilt at DORCHESTER
q.v. Church of St Edward the Martyr, Pinehurst Road, West Moors, Shanters
Hill erected 1933.

WAREHAM (FIEC) Wareham Evangelical Church, Ropers Lane

WAREHAM (Ind/Cong, now URC) Church Street/Chapel Lane. f 1670. Erected 1762
[Harrod 1865] [*Cong. Yearbook* 1871] [Kelly 1939]
MI (DFHS); (DRO); (SG); booklet from M. Blakeston (address p.18)

WAREHAM (Presb) Licence for house of Dorothy Chapman, 1672

WAREHAM (Presb/Unit) South Street f 1828. Erected 1830 [1882 Return]
[Kelly 1939] Closed. Used as a library.
OR   ZC 1788-1837 (RG 4/1727, PRO); C 1828-36 (DRO)
Cop C 1789-1837 (DRO)
Cop (Mf) ZC 1788-1837 (Mf of OR, SLC); C 1788-1837 (Printout, Mf SLC);
        Extr C 1788-1837 (IGI)

WAREHAM (Ind) Old Meeting, Meeting House Lane / West Street [1882 Return]
OR   ZC 1740-1857 B 1821-57 (RG 4/60, 2273, 2274, 468, 533, 1883, 122,
        PRO); C 1740-89; West Street C 1789-1845; Old Meeting C 1789-1849
        B 1824-49; United Church C 1849-1918 M 1857-1918 B 1849-1918 (DRO)
Cop West Street B 1820-30 (DRO); B 1820-30 (DBI); Old Meeting B 1824-48
        (DBI)
Cop (Mf) C 1740-1918 M 1864-1918, B 1825-1902 membership records 1770-1921
        (Mf of OR, SLC); ZCB 1740-1857 (Mf of OR, SLC); ZC 1740-1857
        (Printout, Mf SLC); Extr C 1740-1857 (IGI)

WAREHAM (Wes) f Dollins Lane 1851. Rebuilt 1896 North Street;
Meth [Kelly 1939] Poole and Swanage Circuit
OR   for earlier period *see* POOLE (RG 4/1230, PRO)

WAREHAM (Wes) Ebenezer [1882 Return]

WAREHAM (Prot Diss) Mission church, High Street [1882 Return]

WAREHAM Wareham and Purbeck Union Workhouse. Erected 1836-37. Became
Christmas Close Hospital 1964. Converted into residences in 1990s.

WARMWELL Holy Trinity [Winfrith Hundred; Dorchester Union] [87] Now with
BROADMAYNE, WEST KNIGHTON, OWERMOIGNE.
OR   C 1641-1754 M 1641/2-1642, 1657-1992 B 1641-42, 1656-1752, 1813-1992
        Banns 1754-1811, 1928-72 (DRO)
BT   CMB 1731-79, 1781-1835, 1841-43, 1846-80 (W&SRO)
Cop C 1641-1754 M 1641-1836 B 1641-1758, 1813-37 (DRO, SG); M 1641-1836
        B 1813-37 (PRI); C 1731-1880 from BT (VRI); M 1641-1836 from OR (DMI);
        B 1813-1993 (DBI)

WARMWELL cont.
Cop (Mf) CB 1731-1880 M 1731-1835 (Mf of BT, DRO, SLC); Extr C 1731-1880
          M 1731-1835 from BT (IGI)
MI   (S&DFHS); (DFHS); (DRO); (SG)

WATERCOMBE [Winfrith Hundred from 1858; Dorchester Union] Extra-parochial
place. Civil parish 1858. Ecclesiastically joined WARMWELL 1969.

WATERLOO   *see* CANFORD MAGNA

WAYTOWN   *see* NETHERBURY

WEST BAY   *see* BRIDPORT

WEST CHALDON   *see* CHALDON BOYS

WEST CHELBOROUGH   *see* CHELBOROUGH, WEST

WEST COMPTON   *see* COMPTON ABBAS WEST

WEST FORDINGTON   *see* FORDINGTON

WEST HOWE   *see* CANFORD MAGNA

WEST KNIGHTON   *see* KNIGHTON, WEST

WEST LANGTON   *see* LANGTON MATRAVERS

WEST LULWORTH   *see* LULWORTH, WEST

WEST MILTON   *see* MILTON, WEST

WEST MOORS   *see* WEST PARLEY

WEST MORDEN   *see* MORDEN

WEST ORCHARD   *see* ORCHARD, WEST

WEST PARLEY   *see* PARLEY, WEST

WEST PULHAM   *see* PULHAM

WEST STAFFORD   *see* STAFFORD, WEST

WEST STOUR   *see* STOUR, WEST

WEST WOODYATES   *see* WOODYATES, WEST

WESTHAM   *see* WEYMOUTH St Paul

WESTON   tithing of STALBRIDGE [225]

WESTON   *see* PORTLAND

WEYMOUTH Former chapelry in WYKE REGIS. For the purposes of this volume Weymouth includes the parishes of WYKE REGIS, RADIPOLE and MELCOMBE REGIS

WEYMOUTH All Saints, Wyke Regis [Wyke Regis and Elwell Liberty; Weymouth Union] [1197] Included chapelry and borough of WEYMOUTH (separate parish 1836). *see also* WEYMOUTH St Paul, St Edmund
OR C 1676-1959 M 1676-1715, 1721-1987 B 1676-1719, 1724-1973
    Banns 1691-98, 1765-1809, 1823-1952 1965-90 (DRO) Noted in 1831:
    'Marr. Register from 1752-1765 lost.' Now at DRO.
BT CMB 1731-1880 (W&SRO)
Cop M 1676-1812 (Ptd Phil 5: 1910; & on CD-ROM); C 1802-1911 B 1886-1992
    (I, DRO); C 1731-1880 M 1731-1847 from BT (VRI); CMB 1813-37 (PRI);
    M 1676-1837 (DRO); M 1676-1812 (Boyd); M 1790-1812 (Pallot);
    M 1676-1837 from OR (DMI); B 1800-61 (DBI); Extr B 1703-12 (SG)
Cop (Mf) C 1676-1959 M 1676-1928 B 1676-1923 Banns 1765-1809, 1823-1952,
    1965-80 (Mf of OR, SG); M 1676-1812 (Mf of Phil, SLC);
    CB 1731-1880 M 1731-1847 (Mf of BT, DRO, SLC); Extr C 1731-1880
    M 1731-1847 from BT (IGI)
MI (S&DFHS); (DFHS); (DRO); Ch, cy, war memorials, list of missing
    memorials (SG)

WEYMOUTH St Nicholas Chapel, Chapelhay. Chapel-of-ease to Wyke Regis until the Civil War, when used as a fort. Later demolished.

WEYMOUTH St Paul, Abbotsbury Road, Westham. Erected 1893-96. Parish created 1901 from WYKE REGIS.
OR C 1896-1952 M 1902-78 Banns 1915-18, 1928-37, 1947-82 (DRO)

WEYMOUTH Holy Trinity [Uggscombe Hundred; Weymouth Union] [2529] Erected 1834-36. Formerly part of WYKE REGIS; separate parish 1836. Now with WEYMOUTH St Nicholas.
OR C 1836-1966 M 1841-1975 Banns 1940-91 (DRO)
BT CMB 1836-80; for earlier transcripts *see* WYKE REGIS (W&SRO)
Cop C 1836-80 from BT (VRI); B 1844-54 (DBI)
Cop (Mf) C 1836-1903 M 1841-1901 (Mf, SG); C 1836-80 (Mf of BT, DRO, SLC);
    Extr C 1836-80 from BT (IGI)
MI (S&DFHS); (DFHS); (DRO); Ch 1974 (SG); Bury Street cemetery: removal
    of graves MI 1815-51 (Mf, SLC, of RG 37/163, PRO)

WEYMOUTH St Nicholas, Buxton Road Iron church. Chapel-of-ease to Holy Trinity [Kelly 1939]

WEYMOUTH St Ann, Radipole [Culliford Tree Hundred; Weymouth Union] [382] Included chapelry of MELCOMBE REGIS (separate parish 1606). Now with RADIPOLE AND MELCOMBE REGIS benefice. *see also* WEYMOUTH St Mary, St Edmund.
OR C 1813-1963 M 1797-1989 B 1813-1979 Banns 1824-1994 (DRO) For earlier
    entries see MELCOMBE REGIS
BT CMB 1775?-80, 1795-1880; *and see* MELCOMBE REGIS (W&SRO)
Cop C 1813-95 M 1813-33 B 1813-85 (I, DRO); C 1757?-1880 M 1781-1848 from
    BT (VRI); CB 1813-37 M 1813-33 (PRI); M 1797-1833 from OR, 1757-97
    from BT, 1564-1632 from Hutchins (DMI); B 1813-37 (DBI)
Cop (Mf) CB 1757?-1880 M 1757?-1848 (Mf of BT, DRO, SLC); Extr C 1757-1880
    M 1781-1848 from BT (IGI)
MI (S&DFHS); (DFHS); (DRO); Ch, cy, cremation garden, war memorial (SG)

WEYMOUTH St Aldhelm, Spa Road, Radipole. Erected 1941. Now with RADIPOLE AND MELCOMBE REGIS benefice.
OR M 1950-89 Banns 1951-69, 1979-94 (DRO)
MI (S&DFHS)

WEYMOUTH Emmanuel, Southill, Radipole. Erected 1973. Now with RADIPOLE AND MELCOMBE REGIS benefice.
OR   (Inc)

WEYMOUTH St Mary, Melcombe Regis [Culliford Tree Hundred; Weymouth Union 1836-1920] [5126] Chapelry in RADIPOLE. Separate parish 1606. Rebuilt 1815-17. Now with RADIPOLE AND MELCOMBE REGIS benefice.
OR   C 1595-1955 M 1560-1648, 1664-65, 1671-1962 B 1560-1660/1, 1672-1911
     Banns 1653-63, 1764-1802, 1823-1905 (DRO)
BT   CMB 1731-1880 (W&SRO)
Cop C 1594-1641, 1813-37 M 1560-1699 B 1560-1641 (DRO); C 1776-1955
     M 1764-1934 B 1776-1911 (I, DRO); CMB 1813-37 (PRI); M 1560-1837 from
     OR (DMI); B 1776-1803 (SG); B 1776-1914 (DBI)
Cop (Mf) CB 1731-1880 M 1731-1847 (Mf of BT, DRO, SLC); Extr C 1731-1880
          M 1731-1847 from BT (IGI)
MI   Ch 1974 (SG)

WEYMOUTH Christchurch, King Street, Melcombe Regis. Chapel-of-ease to St Mary, Melcombe Regis. Erected 1874 [Kelly 1939] Demolished 1956
OR   C 1874-1938 M 1874-1938 Banns 1874-1938 (DRO)

WEYMOUTH St John, Dorchester Road and Greenhill Road, Melcombe Regis Erected 1850-54. Parish created 1856 from MELCOMBE REGIS, RADIPOLE. Now with RADIPOLE AND MELCOMBE REGIS benefice.
OR   C 1856-1975 M 1873-1986 Banns 1890-1963, 1978-93 (DRO)
BT   C 1856-80; for earlier transcripts *see* RADIPOLE, MELCOMBE REGIS
     (W&SRO)
Cop C 1856-80 from BT (Pine: CD 4)
Cop (Mf) C 1856-80 (Mf of BT, DRO, SLC); Extr C 1856-80 from BT (IGI)
MI   (S&DFHS); (DRO); Ch 1974 (SG)

WEYMOUTH St Martin, Chickerell Road. Mission church erected 1908 [Kelly 1939] Disused.
OR   C 1908-49 (DRO)

WEYMOUTH St Edmund of Canterbury, Lanehouse Rocks Road. Erected and parish created 1950 from WYKE REGIS, WEYMOUTH St Paul, RADIPOLE, CHICKERELL.
OR   CMB 1950+ (Inc)

WEYMOUTH (RC) Mission in Radipole established *c.*1819. Possible early connections with Dartmouth [Devon] and EAST LULWORTH. St Augustine of Canterbury, Dorchester Road, Radipole, erected 1835 [1882 Return]
OR   C 1819+ M 1836+ D 1837+ Confirmations 1844+ (Inc); Confirmations 1856,
     1871, 1881, 1892-1935, 1944 (PDA)

WEYMOUTH (RC) St Joseph, Stavordale Road. Erected 1934-35

WEYMOUTH (RC) St Charles, Sunnyside Road, Wyke Regis f 1955. Served from WEYMOUTH St Joseph

WEYMOUTH (Part Bapt) Bank Buildings, Melcombe Regis. f 1813. Erected 1814. Western Association [*Bapt. Handbook* 1861] [1882 Return] Rebuilt 1830 [Kelly 1939] SBA
OR   Z 1810-37 (RG 4/350, PRO); Z *c.*1824-91 (DRO)
Cop (Mf) Z 1810-37 (Mf of OR, SLC); Extr C 1810-37 (IGI)

WEYMOUTH (Cong) Licence to George Thorne for house of James Bud, 1672

WEYMOUTH (Presb) Licence for house of Esther Churchey, 1672

WEYMOUTH (Ind/Cong) Gloucester Street, Melcombe Regis. f 1688. Erected 1864
[*Cong. Yearbook* 1871] [1882 Return] [Kelly 1939]
OR   M 1864-81, 1901-63 B 1864-69 membership 1793-1814 (DRO)
Cop (Mf) M 1864-1914 membership 1794-1814 (Mf of OR, SLC)

WEYMOUTH (Ind) St Nicholas Street.
OR   ZC 1734-1837 (RG 4/45, 534, PRO)
Cop (Mf) C 1734-1837 (Mf of OR, SLC); C 1734-1837 (Printout, Mf SLC);
          Extr C 1734-1837 (IGI)

WEYMOUTH (Ind/Cong now URC) Hope Congregational Church, Trinity Street.
f 1821. Erected 1861-62 [*Cong. Yearbook* 1871] Hope Chapel, High Street
[1882 Return] [Kelly 1939]
OR   C 1858-1924 M 1858-86 B 1858-86 membership 1820-1923 (DRO)
Cop (Mf) C 1858-1924 M 1858-86 B 1858-88 membership 1820-1923 (Mf of OR,
          SLC)
MI   (S&DFHS)

WEYMOUTH (Cong, now URC) Roman Road, Radipole f 1905 [Kelly 1939]

WEYMOUTH (Wes) Preaching house by 1776. House of John Lodder registered
1792. House of Benjamin Barlow registered 1793. Room of Edward Bailey
registered 1797 [Biggs] Conygar Lane, later Maiden Street, Melcombe Regis,
erected 1869-70 [1882 Return] [Kelly 1903] Weymouth Circuit
OR   ZC 1796-1837 (RG 4/469, 1234, PRO); C 1796-1932 (DRO)
Cop (Mf) ZC 1796-1837 (Mf of OR, SLC); C 1796-1837 (Printout, Mf SLC);
          Extr C 1796-1837 (IGI)
MI   Maiden Street (S&DFHS)

WEYMOUTH (Wes) Wyke Regis. House owned by John Loader, mariner, registered
1799 [Biggs]; chapel [1882 Return]

WEYMOUTH (Wes) The Park, Melcombe Regis [1882 Return]; rebuilt 1903
[Kelly 1903]

WEYMOUTH (Wes) School room, Queen's Place, Chapelhay [1882 Return]

WEYMOUTH (Wes) Mission chapel, Newstead Road, Westham. Erected 1902
[Kelly 1903]; Meth [Kelly 1939] Weymouth Circuit

WEYMOUTH (Prim Meth) Weymouth Circuit
OR   C 1859-86, 1891-1932 (DRO)

WEYMOUTH (Prim Meth) Hope Square [1882 Return]

WEYMOUTH (Prim Meth) St Leonard's Road. Erected 1876 [Kelly 1939]
OR   M 1939-56 (DRO)

WEYMOUTH (UMFC) Lower Bond Street, Melcombe Regis [1882 Return]

WEYMOUTH (Meth) Derby Street. Erected 1903 [Kelly 1939]

WEYMOUTH (Meth) Portland Road, Wyke Regis. Weymouth Circuit

WEYMOUTH (Meth) Lanehouse Rocks, Lynch Lane. Weymouth Circuit

WEYMOUTH (Ind, Bapt and Meth) Sailors' Bethel, The Quay, Melcombe Regis
[1882 Return]

WEYMOUTH (S of F) Wyke Regis
Cop B 1703-12 (SG)
MI (S&DFHS); (SG)

WEYMOUTH (Latter Day Saints) 396 Chickerell Road.

WEYMOUTH (Ind.Evangelical) Weymouth Independent Evangelical Church, Gallwey Road.

WEYMOUTH (Brethren) Auction Mart, Market Street [1882 Return]

WEYMOUTH (Protestant Churchmen) Building belonging to John Thorn, High Street [1882 Return]

WEYMOUTH (Advent Christians) Ground-floor Room at Mr Chalker's Stores, Melcombe Regis [1882 Return]

WEYMOUTH Poor Law Union Workhouse, Wyke Road. Erected 1805; rebuilt 1836. Became Portway Hospital 1929. Redeveloped for residential use 1992-93 as Union Court.

WEYMOUTH Melcombe Regis Cemetery, Newstead Road, 1856.
Cop B 1856-1980 (I, DRO); B 1822-1985 (DBI)

WEYMOUTH Holy Trinity Cemetery, Abbotsbury Road, 1886.
Cop B 1888-1992 (I, DRO); B 1885-1991 (DBI)

WEYMOUTH Wyke Regis Cemetery, Wyke Road, 1886.
Cop B 1886-1992 (I, DRO); B 1887-1992 (DBI)

WEYMOUTH Weymouth Cemetery, Abbotsbury Road, 1899.
Cop B 1899-1966 (I, DRO, DBI)

WHITCHURCH   see WINTERBORNE WHITECHURCH

WHITCHURCH CANONICORUM St Candida and Holy Cross [Whitchurch Canonicorum Hundred; Bridport Union] [1399] Included chapelries of CHIDEOCK (separate parish 1886), MARSHWOOD and FISHPOND (both joined BETTISCOMBE 1953) and STANTON ST GABRIEL. Now with GOLDEN CAP Team Benefice.
OR   C 1558-1680, 1691-1985 M 1558-1623, 1632-1984 B 1558-1676, 1681-1878
      Banns 1754-1969 (DRO) Noted in 1831: CMB 1632+
BT   CMB 1730-31, 1735-1839, 1847-81; including MARSHWOOD pre-1841 (W&SRO)
Cop   M 1558-1812 (Ptd Phil 5: 1910; & on CD-ROM); CMB 1558-1729 (I, DRO);
      CB 1558-1728 M 1538-1812 (SG); CB 1813-37 M 1754-1837 (PRI);
      CB 1813-37 (I, DRO); C 1813-81 M 1813-36 from BT (VRI); M 1558-1837
      (DRO); M 1558-1812 (Boyd); M 1790-1812 (Pallot); M 1558-1837 from OR
      (DMI); B 1558-1837 (DBI)
Cop (Mf) C 1558-1681, 1691-1985 M 1558-1623, 1632-79, 1681-1731, 1733-1984
      B 1558-1625, 1632-76, 1681-1731, 1735-1878 Banns 1754-92,
      1796-1819, 1822-1969 (Mf of OR, SG); M 1558-1812 (Mf of Phil, SLC);
      CB 1736-1880 M 1736-1836 (Mf of BT, DRO, SLC); Extr C 1730-1881
      M 1730-1836 from BT (IGI)
MI   (S&DFHS); (DFHS); (DRO); (SG); (SLC)

WHITCHURCH CANONICORUM St John the Baptist, Fish Pond Bottom.
Chapel-of-ease erected 1854. Now with GOLDEN CAP Team Benefice.
OR   Banns 1953-75 (DRO)

WHITCHURCH CANONICORUM St Andrew, Monkton Wyld. Erected 1848-49.
Parish created 1850 from WHITCHURCH CANONICORUM, UPLYME (Devon)
Now with GOLDEN CAP Team Benefice.
OR   M 1851-1983 Banns 1852-1981 (DRO)
BT   CMB 1851-80; for earlier transcripts *see* WHITCHURCH CANONICORUM
(W&SRO)
Cop (Mf) CB 1851-80 M 1851-52 (Mf of BT, DRO, SLC); Extr C 1851-80
        M 1851-52 from BT (IGI)
MI   (DFHS); (DRO); (SG)

WHITCHURCH CANONICORUM St Gabriel, Stanton St Gabriel, Morcombelake [101]
Stanton St Gabriel a chapelry in WHITCHURCH CANONICORUM. Rebuilt 1841 on
new site. 'Old church now a ruin, near the sea-coast' [Kelly 1903]. Now
with GOLDEN CAP Team Benefice.
OR   M 1840-1982 Banns 1938-78 (DRO)
BT   CB 1843-80 (W&SRO) *and see* WHITCHURCH CANONICORUM
Cop (Mf) M 1840-1982 Banns 1938-78 (Mf, SG); CB 1843-80 (Mf of BT, DRO,
      SLC)

WHITCHURCH CANONICORUM (Bapt) Harcombe, Monkton Wyld [Kelly 1903]

WHITCHURCH CANONICORUM (Ind/Cong) Morcombelake, Stanton St Gabriel. Erected
1834 [*Cong. Yearbook* 1871] [Kelly 1939]; (Ind Prot Diss) Congregational
Home Missionary Chapel, Morecomblake [1882 Return]
OR   ZC 1831-37 (RG 4/585, PRO)
Cop (Mf) ZC 1831-37 (Mf of OR, SLC); C 1831-37 (Printout, Mf SLC);
      Extr C 1831-37 (IGI)

WHITCHURCH CANONICORUM (Cong) Fishpond. Erected 1857 Out-station of
MORCOMBELAKE [*Cong. Yearbook* 1871] [1882 Return] [Kelly 1903] 'now closed'
[Kelly 1939]

WHITCHURCH CANONICORUM (Ind) Monkton Wyld [Harrod 1865]

WHITCOMBE Dedication unknown [Culliford Tree Hundred; Dorchester Union]
[64] United 1971 with WINTERBORNE CAME. Redundant 1971. Churches
Conservation Trust.
OR   C 1762-1967 M 1780-1819, 1826-1923, 1935-62 B 1774-1968
      Banns 1860-1977 (DRO) Noted in 1831: C 1770+ M 1780+ B 1781+;
      'The earlier registers were destroyed by fire A.D. 1776'.
BT   CMB 1732-50, 1755-78, 1780-1803, 1806-30, 1841-44, 1849-80 (W&SRO)
Cop CB 1813-37 M 1780-1852 (PRI); CB 1813-37 (I, DRO); M 1732-80 from BT
     (DRO); M 1780-1852 (DRO, SG); M 1780-1852 from OR, 1732-80 from BT
     (DMI); B 1813-38 (DBI)
Cop (Mf) CB 1732-1880 M 1732-1841 (Mf of BT, DRO, SLC); Extr C 1732-1880
      M 1732-1841 from BT (IGI)

WHITECHURCH *see* WINTERBORNE WHITECHURCH

WIMBORNE ALL SAINTS or ALL HALLOWS [Wimborne St Giles Hundred] United 1732
to WIMBORNE ST GILES] [384 with St Giles]
OR   C 1687-1731 M 1692-1727/8B 1687-1731 (DRO) Noted in 1831 at WIMBORNE
     ST GILES: M 1600-67, 1687-1731 for Wimborne All Saints; CMB 1732+ for
     the united parishes.
BT   CMB 1731-1880 with Wimborne St Giles (W&SRO)
Cop CMB 1589-1689 (I, SG); M 1600-48, 1656, 1664-67, 1692-1727 (SG);
     M 1589-1648, 1692-1727 from OR, 1589-1689 from incumbent's memoranda
     bundle (DMI)

WIMBORNE MINSTER St Cuthberga [Badbury Hundred; Wimborne and Cranborne Union] [4009 including tithings of Cowgrove alias Kinson, Holt, Leigh] Royal Peculiar until 1847. Included chapelry of HOLT (separate parish 1882). *see also* NEW BOROUGH AND LEIGH, KINGSTON LACY.
OR   C 1635-1935 M 1635-1994 B 1635-1932 Banns 1813-41, 1875-93, 1955-78, 1986-98 (DRO)
BT   CMB 1667-68; 1721-31, 1813-33, 1847-80; including HOLT from 1847 (W&SRO)
Cop   C 1635-37, 1645-92 M 1635-72 B 1637-40 (SG); CMB 1721-96, 1804-12 (SG); C 1645-92 M 1635-1754 (DRO); CMB 1813-37 (PRI); CB 1813-37 (I, DRO); C 1813-62 from BT (VRI); M 1721-1813 (Boyd); M 1635-1837 from OR, 1590-1626 from M licences (DMI); B 1637-1837 (DBI)
Cop (Mf) CB 1813-80 M 1813-33 (Mf of BT, DRO, SLC); CMB 1721-1813 from BT (Mf of Cop, SLC); CM 1721-1813 (Printout, Mf SLC);
          Extr C 1721-1880 M 1721-1833 from BT (IGI)
MI   (S&DFHS); (DFHS); (DRO); (Ptd G.Score *Guide to Wimborne Minster, its monuments and curiosities*: 1923)

WIMBORNE MINSTER St James, Holt [Wimborne and Cranborne Union 1894-1930] [1265] Tithing in WIMBORNE MINSTER; separate parish 1882. Rebuilt 1834-36. Now with HINTON MARTELL, HORTON, CHALBURY.
OR   C 1836-1918 M 1836, 1838-1983 B 1836-1994 Banns 1869-1966 (DRO)
      and see WIMBORNE MINSTER
BT   *see* WIMBORNE MINSTER
Cop   M 1650-53 from WIMBORNE MINSTER registers, 1836 (DRO, DMI); C 1645-56 M 1650-53, 1836 (SG)
MI   (S&DFHS); (DFHS); (DRO)

WIMBORNE MINSTER Mission chapel at Holt Heath. Erected 1897 [Kelly 1903]

WIMBORNE MINSTER St Stephen, Kingston Lacy, Pamphill. Erected 1907 by Bankes family of Kingston Lacy. Parish created 1922 from WIMBORNE MINSTER. Now with STURMINSTER MARSHALL, SHAPWICK.
OR   CM 1907+ (Inc)

WIMBORNE MINSTER St John, New Borough and Leigh, or Wimborne St John [Leigh 532] Erected 1876. Parish created 1877 from WIMBORNE MINSTER. Part joined COLEHILL 1903
OR   C 1877-1958 M 1877-1991 B 1882-1972 Banns 1877-1923, 1955-83 (DRO)

WIMBORNE MINSTER (RC) St Catherine, Lewens Lane. Temporary church 1926. New building 1933
OR   (Inc)

WIMBORNE MINSTER (Anabaptist) Licence to John King for his house, 1672

WIMBORNE MINSTER (Bapt) n.d. [*Bapt. Handbook* 1861] [Harrod 1865]
OR   Z 1778-1834 (RG 4/470, PRO)
Cop (Mf) Z 1778-1834 (Mf of OR, SLC); Extr C 1778-1834 (IGI)

WIMBORNE MINSTER (Bapt) Grove Road. Erected 1882 [Kelly 1903, 1939] SBA

WIMBORNE MINSTER (Ind/Cong now URC) Chapel Lane f 1672; West Boro' f 1670 [*Cong. Yearbook* 1871] [Kelly 1903]
OR   ZC 1768-1837 B 1791-1837 (RG 4/1884, PRO)
Cop (Mf) ZCB 1768-1837 (Mf of OR, SLC); C 1768-1837 (Printout, Mf SLC);
          Extr C 1768-1837 from BT (IGI)
MI   (S&DFHS); (DRO)

WIMBORNE MINSTER (Presb) Licence to   Thomas Rowe (Roe) for his house; licence for house of John Gifford 1672

WIMBORNE MINSTER (Wes) Wimborne Circuit. Formed from POOLE Circuit 1841
OR   C c.1805-09, 1841-1932 (DRO); and see POOLE (RG 4/1230, PRO)
Cop C 1809-41 (DRO)

WIMBORNE MINSTER (Wes) [Harrod 1865] [1882 Return]

WIMBORNE MINSTER (Wes) Holt [Kelly 1903]

WIMBORNE MINSTER (Wes) A Building, Holtwood [1882 Return]; Meth [Kelly 1939]

WIMBORNE MINSTER (Wes) Broomhill [1882 Return]; Meth [Kelly 1939] Wimborne Circuit

WIMBORNE MINSTER (Wes) King Street. Erected 1869 Kelly 1903] Meth [Kelly 1939] Rebuilt 1967

WIMBORNE MINSTER (Plymouth Brethren) East Street [Kelly 1903] Eastbrook Gospel Hall, Park Lane [Kelly 1939]

WIMBORNE MINSTER Cemetery, Cemetery Road, 1856. (Wimborne Cemetery Joint Management Committee)

WIMBORNE MINSTER Cranborne Poor Law Union Workhouse. Erected by 1760. Enlarged 1836. Demolished 1958
OR   C 1839-1914, 1920, 1929 (DRO)

WIMBORNE ST GILES St Giles [Wimborne St Giles Hundred; Wimborne and Cranborne Union] United with WIMBORNE ALL SAINTS 1732 [384 with All Saints] see also WOODLANDS. Now with CRANBORNE, BOVERIDGE, EDMONDSHAM, WOODLANDS.
OR   C 1594/5-1641, 1646-1869 M 1594-1640, 1650-1990 B 1594-1641/2, 1646-1922 Banns 1823-1918 (DRO) Noted in 1831: CB 1589+ M 1594+
BT   CMB 1731-1880 with Wimborne All Saints (W&SRO)
Cop CB 1589-1689 M 1589-1837 (DRO); CMB 1594-1685 M 1594-1640, 1650-1837 (SG); CB 1813-37 M 1800-37 (PRI); C 1813-37 (I, DRO); M 1594-1837 from OR (DMI); B 1813-37 (DBI)
Cop (Mf) CB 1731-1880 M 1731-1836 (Mf of BT, DRO, SLC); Extr C 1731-1880 M 1731-1836 from BT (IGI)
MI   (S&DFHS); (DFHS); (DRO); burial ground (S&DFHS)

WIMBORNE ST GILES Monkton up Wimborne see CRANBORNE

WINFORD EAGLE see WYNFORD EAGLE

WINFRITH NEWBURGH St Christopher [Winfrith Hundred; Wareham and Purbeck Union] [891] Included chapelry of WEST LULWORTH (separate parish 1863) Now with EAST LULWORTH, WEST LULWORTH, CHALDON HERRING.
OR   C 1585-1604, 1616-23, 1634-44/5, 1677-1912 M 1585-1622, 1634-45, 1671/2-1973 B 1585-1623, 1634-44/5, 1676-1992 Banns 1754-1812, 1866-1943 (DRO)
BT   CMB 1731-1800, 1803-80; including WEST LULWORTH 1781 (W&SRO)
Cop CMB 1585-1837 (DRO); CM 1585-37 B 1622-37 with gaps (PRI); CMB 1585-1644, 1671-1742 (I, SG); C 1743-50 M 1585-1622, 1634-45, 1672-1837 (SG); C 1732-1880 M 1732-1847 from BT (VRI); M 1585-1837 from OR, 1662-66 from Hutchins (DMI); B 1743-1837 (DBI)

WINFRITH NEWBURGH cont.

<u>Cop (Mf)</u> CB 1731-1880 M 1731-1847 (Mf of BT, DRO, SLC); Extr C 1732-1880
        M 1732-1847 from BT (IGI)

WINFRITH NEWBURGH East Burton Chapel (dedication unknown) Erected 1836-40.
Now with WOOL AND EAST STOKE BENEFICE. Redundant 1972. Sold as harpsichord
workshop 1978.
<u>BT</u> *see* WINFRITH NEWBURGH
<u>MI</u> (S&DFHS); (DFHS); (DRO)

WINFRITH NEWBURGH (Cong) Licence to William Clarke for house of Rebecca
Hastings, 1672.

WINFRITH NEWBURGH (Wes) Weymouth Circuit. Meth erected 1914 [Kelly 1939]
<u>OR</u> C 1851-1918 (DRO)

WINSOR, LITTLE *see* BROADWINDSOR

WINTERBORNES AND COMPTON VALENCE Modern benefice including WINTERBORNE
ST MARTIN, WINTERBORNE ABBAS, WINTERBORNE STEEPLETON, COMPTON VALENCE.

WINTERBORNE ABBAS St Mary [Eggerton Hundred; Dorchester Union] [133]
Now with THE WINTERBORNES AND COMPTON VALENCE benefice.
<u>OR</u> C 1791-1992 M 1754-1988 B 1791-1992 (DRO) No earlier registers noted
        in 1831
<u>BT</u> CMB 1731-82, 1785-1880; including WINTERBORNE STEEPLETON 1847-80
        (W&SRO)
<u>Cop</u> CB 1813-37 M 1754-1837 (PRI); C 1792-1812 M 1754-1837 (SG);
        C 1731-1880 M 1731-1835 from BT (VRI); C 1813-37 (I, DRO); C 1792-1812
        (SG); M 1732-57 from BT (DRO); M 1754-1837 (SG); M 1754-1837 from OR,
        1731-57, 1810-11 from BT (DMI); B 1813-1901 (DBI)
<u>Cop (Mf)</u> C 1731-1880 M 1731-1835 (Mf of BT, DRO, SLC); Extr C 1731-1880
        M 1731-1835 from BT (IGI)

WINTERBORNE ABBAS (Bapt) Erected 1872 [Kelly 1939]

WINTERBORNE ANDERSON St Michael [Coombs Ditch Hundred; Blandford Union]
[54] Peculiar of the Dean of Sarum until 1847. United 1972 with WINTERBORNE
ZELSTON, WINTERBORNE TOMSON. Rebuilt 1889 'having fallen into decay' [Kelly
1903]. Now with RED POST benefice. Redundant 1972. Sold 1973 for use as
private chapel.
<u>OR</u> C 1771-1974 M 1757-1812, 1817-36, 1841-1960 B 1772-1973 (DRO)
        Noted in 1831: CB 1763+ M 1754+
<u>BT</u> CMB 1604-06, 1609-15, 1622-40, 1662-99, 1702, 1709-58, 1764-74,
        1777-1880 (W&SRO)
<u>Cop</u> CB 1813-37 M 1757-1836 (PRI); C 1813-37 (I, DRO); M 1757-1838 (DRO);
        M 1757-58, 1770-1819, 1836 (SG); M 1813-37 (SG); M 1604-1757 from BT
        (DRO); M 1757-1836 from OR, 1604-1757, 1813-17 from BT (DMI);
        B 1764-1836 (DBI)
<u>Cop (Mf)</u> as ANDERSON: CB 1604-1880 M 1604-1846 (Mf of BT, DRO, SLC);
        Extr C 1604-1880 M 1604-1846 from BT (IGI)
<u>MI</u> (S&DFHS); (DFHS); (DRO); (SG)

WINTERBORNE ASHTON tithing of WINTERBORNE ST MARTIN

WINTERBORNE CAME St Peter [part Culliford Tree Hundred, part Frampton
Liberty; Dorchester Union] [80; including tithing of Cripton 18] United by
1291 with WINTERBORNE FARINGDON. United 1971 with WINTERBORNE CAME,
WHITCOMBE. Redundant 1989. Churches Conservation Trust.

WINTERBORNE STEEPLETON cont.
BT   CMB 1731-1846; for 1847-80 see WINTERBORNE ABBAS (W&SRO)
Cop   CMB 1558-1812 (I, SG); CB 1558-1786 M 1559-1838 (DRO); CB 1813-37
      M 1559-1838 (PRI); C 1813-37 (I, DRO); M 1559-1838 (SG); M 1559-1838
      from OR, 1731-54 from BT (DMI); B 1813-37 (DBI)
Cop (Mf) CB 1731-1846 M 1731-1836 (Mf of BT, DRO, SLC); Extr C 1731-1846
      M 1731-1836 from BT (IGI)
MI   (S&DFHS); (DFHS); (DRO); (SG)

WINTERBORNE STICKLAND St Mary [Pimperne Hundred; Blandford Union] [461]
Included tithing of Winterborne Quarleston. Now with TURNWORTH, WINTERBORNE
HOUGHTON, WINTERBORNE CLENSTON. WINTERBORNE WHITECHURCH.
OR   C 1615-1783, 1797-99, 1813-83 M 1616-1837 B 1615-1783, 1813-1969 Banns
      1754-1810, 1824-93 (DRO) Noted in 1831: 'B 1615-1783, from that date
      missing.'
BT   CMB 1731-1841, 1845-80 (W&SRO)
Cop   CM 1615-1850 B 1613-78 (SG); CB 1813-37 M 1616-1836 (PRI): C 1813-37
      (I, DRO); M 1616-1837 (DRO); M 1616-1750 (Boyd); M 1616-1837 from OR,
      1751-53 from BT (DMI); B 1813-37 (DBI)
Cop (Mf) CB 1731-1880 M 1731-1858 (Mf of BT, DRO, SLC); Extr C 1731-1880
      M 1731-1858 from BT (IGI)
MI   (S&DFHS); (DFHS); (DRO)

WINTERBORNE STICKLAND (Cong) Licence to Edward Dammer for house of John
Bingham, 1672

WINTERBORNE STICKLAND (Wes) Erected 1863 [Kelly 1903]

WINTERBORNE STICKLAND (Prim Meth) Chapel [Harrod 1865] Formerly a Club-room
[1882 Return]; chapel erected 1877 [1882 Return] [Kelly 1903]

WINTERBORNE TOMSON St Andrew [Coombs Ditch Hundred; Blandford Union] [41]
Peculiar of the Dean of Sarum until 1847. United 1972 with WINTERBORNE
ZELSTONE, WINTERBORNE ANDERSON. Now with RED POST benefice. Redundant 1972.
Churches Conservation Trust.
OR   C 1723, 1770-1811, 1816-1970 M 1751-52, 1760-65, 1802-37, 1844-1968
      B 1769-97, 1812-1915 (DRO) Noted in 1831: C 1803-11 M 1802-12 B 1812
BT   CMB 1637, 1639, 1670-71, 1711, 1723-28, 1763-66, 1770, 1781-83,
      1791-1830, 1847-80 (W&SRO)
Cop   C 1770-1893 M 1767-1890 B 1769-97 (SG); C 1813-37 M 1751-1837
      B 1812-1915 (PRI); C 1813-37 (I, DRO); M 1751-1837 (DRO); M 1726-28
      from BT (DRO); M 1793-1802 (Pallot); M 1751-1837 from OR, 1637-1751
      from BT (DMI); B 1813-37 (DBI)
Cop (Mf) CB 1637-1880 M 1637-1830 (Mf of BT, DRO, SLC); Extr C 1637-1880
      M 1637-1830 from BT (IGI)
MI   (S&DFHS); (DFHS); (DRO) Extr: Pratt (Ms, SG)

WINTERBORNE WHITECHURCH St Mary [Coombs Ditch Hundred; Blandford Union]
[513] Now with WINTERBORNE STICKLAND, TURNWORTH, WINTERBORNE HOUGHTON,
WINTERBORNE CLENSTON.
OR   C 1599-1955 M 1599-1659, 1666-1701, 1711-1993 B 1614-1721, 1726-1897
      Banns 1755-74, 1782-83, 1795, 1823-1962 (DRO)
BT   CMB 1731-49, 1752-1880; for 1750-51 see TURNWORTH; for 1818 see
      WINTERBORNE CLENSTON (W&SRO)
Cop   CB 1813-37 M 1599-1837 (PRI); C 1813-37 (I, DRO); M 1599-1837 (DRO,
      SG); M 1731-42 from BT (DRO); M 1599-1836 from OR, 1731-42 from BT
      (DMI); B 1812-37 (DBI)

WINTERBORNE WHITECHURCH cont.
Cop (Mf) CB 1731-1880 M 1731-1847 (Mf of BT, DRO, SLC); Extr C 1731-1880
      M 1731-1847 from BT (IGI)
MI   (S&DFHS); (DFHS); (DRO); war memorial (SG)

WINTERBORNE WHITECHURCH (Presb) Licence to John Price (Brice) for house of
Eleanor Floyer, Whitechurch; licence for house of Henry Pitfield,
Whitechurch, 1672

WINTERBORNE WHITECHURCH (Wes) Erected 1847 [1882 Return] [Kelly 1903];
Meth [Kelly 1939] Wimborne circuit

WINTERBORNE ZELSTON(E) or MARWOOD St Mary [Rushmore Hundred; Blandford
Union] [233] United 1972 with WINTERBORNE TOMPSON, WINTERBORNE ANDERSON.
Now with RED POST benefice.
OR   C 1548-69, 1577-90, 1606-1993 M 1548-80, 1606-33, 1638-45, 1650,
     1695-1711, 1716-1839 B 1548/9-96, 1606-53, 1678-1706, 1712-1992
     Banns 1823-99, 1948-81 (DRO)
BT   CMB 1731-33, 1736-1880 (W&SRO)
Cop CB 1813-37 M 1548-1839 (PRI); C 1813-37 (I, DRO); M 1548-83, 1606-1839
     (DRO, SG); M 1731-56 from BT (DRO); M 1548-1839 from OR, 1731-56 from
     BT, 1583, 1656, 1660, 1662, 1674 from Hutchins (DMI); B 1813-37 (DBI);
     Extr C 1548-1692 M 1565-1697 B 1551-1740 (SG)
Cop (Mf) CB 1731-1880 M 1731-1839 (Mf of BT, DRO, SLC); Extr C 1731-1880
      M 1731-1839 from BT (IGI)
MI   (S&DFHS); (DFHS); (DRO)

WINTERBORNE ZELSTON(E) (Presb) Licence to Timothy Sacheverill for his
house, 1672

WINTERBORNE ZELSTON(E) (Wes) [Harrod 1865]

WINTERBORNE ZELSTON(E) (Prim Meth) Erected 1869 [1882 Return] [Kelly 1903];
Meth [Kelly 1939]

WITCHAMPTON St Mary and St Cuthberga [Cranborne Hundred; Wimborne and
Cranborne Union] [478] Now with STANBRIDGE, LONG CRICHEL.
OR   C 1656-1988 M 1656, 1663-1985 B 1656-1908 Banns 1754-64, 1781-84,
     1792-1812, 1823-1980 (DRO)
BT   CMB 1733-81, 1783-1812, 1814-80 (W&SRO)
Cop C 1886-1988 M 1656-1985 B 1908-92 (DRO, SG); CB 1813-37 M 1656-1838
     (PRI); C 1733-1880 M 1733-1847 from BT (VRI); C 1813-37 (I, DRO);
     M 1731-54 from BT (DRO); M 1656-1838 from OR, 1731-54 from BT (DMI);
     B 1813-1992 (DBI)
Cop (Mf) CB 1733-1880 M 1733-1847 (Mf of BT, DRO, SLC); Extr C 1733-1880
      M 1733-1847 from BT (IGI)
MI   (S&DFHS); (DFHS); (DRO)

WITCHAMPTON (Wes) House occupied by William Bundy registered 1799 [Biggs];
chapel [Harrod 1865]; a building [1882 Return]; chapel erected 1890
[Kelly 1903] Wimborne Circuit
OR   *see* POOLE (RG 4/1230, PRO)
MI   (S&DFHS); (DRO)

WITHERSTONE Ancient parish, later part of POWERSTOCK. Sinecure rectory.
United 1971 with WEST MILTON, NORTH POORTON.
OR   *see* POWERSTOCK

WOGRET   tithing of EAST STOKE